W9-CLW-292

PORTRAITS FROM A LIFE

msey.

June 7/97.

e ; I thoroughly enjoyed
e ; to my surprise much
han I thought I would.
f thoughtful coments — humou
m with gossip tid bits - what
could you ask for !
Many thanks
much love.
Norah

From the desk of:

Norah Ra

Dear Betty,

your

more

Rita

ties

mu

Portraits
from a Life

❧

HEWARD GRAFFTEY

Véhicule Press

ACKNOWLEDGEMENTS

My thanks go to so many people: to John Metcalf, my original editor for whom I developed a great respect and friendship; to Andi McInenly for typing and retyping the manuscript, and for her timely editorial comments and suggestions; to Nancy Marrelli who edited the manuscript in its final stages, and to Simon Dardick who brought it through the publishing process.

This book would never have been realized without the sustaining love of my three children—Arthur Heward, Clement Tai Yong, and Lea Yoon Lee; my sister Ann, my brother Bim and his wife Jayne; my life companion Darren Coleman; and my friends Ian and Marnie Rankin, Jacques and Hopey Tetrault, Lorne and Meredith Webster, Bob Morrow, Luc Fortin, Michael O'Neill, Cynthia Baxter, and Jean Wadds.

Published with the assistance of The Canada Council.

Cover photograph: Thomas Königsthal Jr.
Cover design: J. W. Stewart
Imaging: Simon Garamond
Printing: Imprimerie d'Édition Marquis Ltée

Copyright © Heward Grafftey 1996
All rights reserved.
Dépôt légal, Bibliothèque nationale du Québec and
the National Library of Canada, third quarter 1996.

CATALOGUING IN PUBLICATION DATA

Grafftey, Heward, 1928-
    Portraits from a life

ISBN 1-55065-077-7

    1. Grafftey, Heward, 1928- 2. Politicians–Canada
–Biography. 3. Cabinet ministers–Canada–Biography. I. Title

FC601.G72A3 1966   354.7104'092   C96-900243-2
F1034.3G72A3 1966

Published by Véhicule Press, P.O.B. 125, Place du Parc Station,
Montreal, Quebec H2W 2M9

Distributed by General Distribution Services, 30 Lesmill Road,
Don Mills, Ontario M3B 2T6

Printed in Canada on alkaline paper.

To the memory of Wilder Penfield and Hugh MacLennan
—two dear friends who, by example,
encouraged me in my life's work.

I am a part of all that I have met;
yet all experience is an arch where through
gleams that untravelled world, whose margin fades
for ever and for ever when I move

—"Ulysses," Tennyson

Contents

＄

Temperamentally, I am unsuited to writing traditional autobiography or memoirs. I do, however, like to tell a good story. This is a book of stories—yarns and anecdotes about some of the people who have influenced me through a varied and sometimes tumultuous life. I have set out to introduce the reader to people I would like to honour— some of the people who have played an important role in my life.

＄

CHAPTER ONE

The Early Years

On August 5, 1928, I was born in the City of Montreal on the eve of the Great Depression. My parents had rented a semi-detached red brick house at 2 de Casson Road on what was called the Priest's Farm, in the City of Westmount.

The Montreal of my youth was a cacophony of sights, sounds, and smells. There were the factory whistles at 7:00 a.m. as morning shifts began, together with the long bellowing from ships' funnels in the port. I remember train whistles and the clanging of trains on the tracks in the distance, the screeching of cats fighting in the lane behind our home as I lay in bed in the evening hours, trams making their way along Sherbrooke Street, my dad singing with his mandolin on his knee, the toot, toot, toot of Eddy Cantor horns on old Model T Fords, the *rdrdrdrdrdrdrdrd...* of my mother's sewing machine and her voice calling, *helloooo*, as she came home in the evening—the same kind of long *hellooo* she used to answer the telephone. Then there was Dad's sharp whistle as he arrived home from work, the Montreal Symphony tuning up at His Majesty's Theatre, the sound of bagpipes at the Black Watch Armory Christmas Party. I can remember leaving the Forum at night with my father, hearing the news vendors shouting, "Paper, paper, read all about it."

And then there was the music from the organ grinder. We called him the hurdy-gurdy man. He stood on the sidewalk outside our house and always smiled. He turned the organ with one hand and held his hat in the other, nodding his head in appreciation when anyone dropped in a coin. One evening, hearing him play, I rushed to my bedroom for a coin. He was playing in the lane behind our house. As I rushed across our kitchen floor, I fell flat on my face and remember admonishing God for letting a little boy fall and hurt himself in the middle of such an act of kindness.

Church bells rang out at all times across the city. In the country, I would hear the click-clack of horses' hooves on the asphalt highway and the eerie whining of winter winds. There was the buzzing of bees in summer, the familiar noise of crickets and the rhythmic singing of the cardinals. So often I would hear the steady tapping of woodpeckers on the trees, the crowing of the rooster early on hot July mornings, the frantic clucking of hens about to lay their eggs and the distant cawing of crows as the snow left the ground at the end of winter. I can still hear the sound of ringing sleighbells in winter; the intermittent explosions of popcorn striking against the basket over the fire, and the click-clacking of Elmer Ferguson's typewriter outside my bedroom window in Montreal, as the famous sports writer typed into the early morning hours by an open window opposite my room.

At Fernbank, where my grandmother lived, west of Brockville on the shores of the St. Lawrence by the Thousand Islands, ships would signal each other as they passed, and I would hear the swishing of the water as waves from the ships hit upon the rocks. Côte-des-Neiges Road in Montreal runs from Sherbrooke Street north towards Mount Royal. When I was small, before each winter, a sign was placed at the bottom of the street. It read: "Use your brains. Put on your chains and don't depend on ashes." In those early days, snow tires didn't exist, and drivers normally put chains on the back wheels of their cars. When the chains passed over bare pavement or asphalt, they often broke. Who could ever forget their rhythmic clacking against the inside of the mudguards.

Then there are smells from the past. The sense of smell, it seems to me, is the most powerful of our senses in reinforcing and focussing memories. Sometimes smells and sounds went together, such as the horse-drawn chipwagons with their unique aroma and little whistling steam outlet on the roof. My grandmother called the perfume she wore her "scent," and when I smell it now I can see Granny Heward.

And then there was the comforting pungency of balsam puffing from a steam humidifier in her bedroom, as she lay in her bed with the flu.

At 3467 Peel Street, there was the thick smell of paint and turpentine in my Aunt Prue's third floor art studio. There was the fragrance of pine needles on the rocks at the family summer colony at Fernbank. I remember well the springtime scent of lilacs in our Montreal garden and the pungent smell of geraniums in our city greenhouse; the sweet aroma of steam rising from the sugar house in the early spring, the fragrance of fresh-cut hay in the fields, the dreadful smell of ether as I was put to sleep for countless operations; the hot tar on country highways in mid-summer; the stench outside the stockyards on Mill Street as we passed by on our way to the country; pine and spruce wood at my Dad's lumber yard; and the pipe of our neighbour, Jim Davis, in the evening, as he sat in his big armchair.

I remember attending funerals in Montreal. Joseph C. Wray, on Mountain Street in mid-town Montreal, had the most upscale funeral parlour in the city. It was later transformed into a disco and then a strip club. The moment I would enter Wray's establishment, I was aware of the fragrant smell of flowers mixed with the chapel's oak panelling. This unique smell had a quality all its own, to be associated only with Joseph C. Wray—that is, until I reached Ottawa.

After I was sworn in as a Member of Parliament, it was not long before I, with my other colleagues in the House, was summoned to the Senate for Royal Assent to Bills. Upon entering the Senate chamber, I could see large arrangements of flowers on each side of the entrance hall. The hall and the Senate Chamber itself were both panelled with wood. The sense of smell is very evocative, and at first whiff I was sure I was attending a funeral at Wray's! To add to the macabre scene in the Senate was the spectacle of the aged Senators themselves. Many were having an early afternoon nap, their bodies tilted to one side, their heads slumped over their chests, their eyes shut, their mouths half open; their hands neatly folded, resting on substantial bellies. Some had a cadaverous look about them as if they were passing through Shakespeare's *seventh stage*. It was all very funereal. I say funereal unreservedly because I believe a Senate nomination is akin to a death sentence. All these Senate observations on my part

Grandmother Efa Heward, circa 1925

stem from my sense of smell and its association with things past.

In my youth, church-going on Sundays pointed out sharp differences in my family background. While my name is Grafftey, I was never allowed to forget that I was also a Heward. Heward was my mother's name and the Heward clan was formidable. Granny Heward was widowed at a young age and was the unquestioned clan leader, ably assisted by her oldest son, Chilion, who had inherited her brilliance and authoritarian streak.

My grandmother on my mother's side would often send her limousine and chauffeur to drive us to church, the high Anglican church of St. John the Evangelist in the centre of Montreal. Her husband helped dig the foundation, after work, at the end of the last century. Grandmother, after a relatively hard life, was well fixed in her old age. Her brother, Frank Jones, known as Cement Jones, had given her one million dollars. He had also given one million dollars to each of my grandmother's two sisters, Elsie and Irene. He was my great-uncle and, with Max Aitken (Lord Beaverbrook), put Canada Cement on the map. When the Beaver went overseas, Uncle Frank took over and ran the cement company. He was Prime Minister Borden's Director of Munitions in World War I. He lived in a beautiful mansion called the "Old House" on magnificent grounds on the slopes of Mount Royal. Once he and his wife Helen visited us at our Rockwood cottage in Knowlton. Their Rolls Royce couldn't get through the gates and my dad had to dig up a gatepost to allow passage. The regal Aunt Helen brought her own mattress. Things really didn't work out—my uncle wanted to stay, but they left early the very next day. The attendant at the local gas station in Knowlton was flabbergasted as he filled up the Rolls; never before had he put so much gas into the tank of one car.

Grandmother's limousine would leave us at the side door of the parish hall. Dad had been born into the Baptist faith, but went to the High Church of St. John's primarily to please my mother. Granny Heward led the clan into a pew at the very center of the church. At the point of the Creed where it is said, "and he came down from Heaven," the congregation knelt in unison, except for my family which remained standing conspicuously along the centre pew. Grandmother said she and everybody else had stood in the early years and that she disapproved of the kneeling innovation. So as the entire congregation kneeled, the Heward clan was left defiantly on its feet. As I remained standing, while feeling slightly conspicuous, I must confess to a sense of superiority towards my fellow worshippers below me on their knees.

As a Baptist, my father wasn't really very happy at St. John's. He bellowed out the hymns with a swinging Baptist lilt, sometimes, I'm sure, to the unspoken consternation of the Hewards. Dad told me what it was like to be a Baptist youth. On Sundays, the family never left home except to attend church—sometimes twice. The blinds were pulled down and the piano locked up. In the evenings, Grandfather Grafftey read from the Bible, referred to by the Graffteys as "the good book." Swearing of any kind was taboo in front of my father and when he was young he took the Baptist temperance pledge. In spite of the Biblical citation, "take enough wine for thy stomach's sake and thy many infirmities," there was no booze in the Grafftey household. My dad's sister, my Aunt Alice, told me, "Heward, lips that touch liquor shall never touch mine." My father forgot the oath in World War I and forgot it with a vengeance in the post-war years.

Uncle Chil, my mother's brother, was my devoted godfather. His lovely wife, Aunt May, was a Langhorne from Virginia. They had no children of their own and consequently lavished much affection on their nieces and nephews. In the summer, they lived beside grand-mother at "Crowsland" at the summer family colony, Fernbank. Uncle Chil was head boy at Lower Canada College and an outstanding boxer at McGill University. He went on to win the gold medal in law at McGill and study, with a scholarship, in Dijon, France. He served with my father in the Black Watch during World War I and was wounded. Visiting Dijon, at the end of the war, he was saddened to find that over two-thirds of his college mates from France had been killed during the hostilities. After the war, he went on to become an outstanding corporate and banking lawyer in Montreal.

My other godfather was the Hon. Mr. Justice C. Gordon MacKinnon, who sat on the Quebec Superior Court and was Chancellor of Bishop's University in Lennoxville. His wife, my stately Aunt Miriam, was a Robson from Salem, Massachusetts. She had a lovely smile and spoke with a most cultivated New England accent.

They had no children.

Uncle Gordon ruled on Quebec's famous Roncarelli Case, known in Quebec as the Padlock Law Case involving the Jehovah's Witnesses. Roncarelli was a Jehovah's Witness and owned a fine restaurant in Montreal. Because of his affiliation with the religious group, Premier Maurice Duplessis padlocked his restaurant and confiscated his liquor license. Civil rights' activists, such as F.R. Scott, took up Roncarelli's cause and pleaded his case. Uncle Gordon subpoenaed Duplessis— this was considered courageous in those days. Roncarelli won his case, but the premier appealed. After many years in appeal, the case finally went before the Supreme Court of Canada and Uncle Gordon's initial judgement was upheld. For good or for bad, he had never been overruled in appeal. When he heard about the Supreme Court verdict, he invited me to his summer retreat (Sherrygroom) overlooking Brome Lake, to celebrate and have a drink. By then, he was an old man and a widower. He died soon after my visit.

When I was six, an event took place that surely underlined the cleavage between my Anglican and Baptist backgrounds and the Grafftey-Heward heritage. I was literally dying in the emergency ward of the Children's Memorial Hospital, situated on the southern slopes of Mount Royal. I had collapsed in our bathroom at home, having lost a great quantity of blood from a ruptured vessel situated between my stomach and upper intestines. My mother was not at home, and I was discovered by our cook, who summoned Granny Heward. I was sped to the hospital in the back of her limousine. In the emergency room, my father lay on a stretcher situated well above me. Doctors were rushing about and I knew the situatin was serious, and was terrified. Plasma technology was unknown in those days, and so dad's blood ran through tubes directly down to me. Because my arteries had collapsed, a doctor rapidly made an incision in my ankle, into which the tube was inserted to permit the entry of my father's blood. At this point, Canon Davison, the Rector at St. John's, entered the emergency room. He immediately began to perform the sacrament of the last rites— the anointing of the sick or dying. I sensed that my father never really liked the Canon. When he realized what was going on, dad rose from his stretcher and bellowed at the rector, "Get out of here!" The rector was taken aback, but completed his task before beating a hasty retreat. I cried out for calm and silence, and the doctors lectured my father, whose Baptist sensitivities didn't appreciate the sacramental significance of this high Anglican rite, especially while his son lay dying. Obviously Canon Davison didn't get too far, because before long, he too, was on the stretcher above me since his blood type fitted the bill. A distant cousin, who came by later on, wasn't so lucky. He was a heavy drinker, and my mother wouldn't permit his blood to mix with mine. Standing beside me in the emergency room was the legendary Montreal pediatrician, Alton Goldbloom, in formal wear. He had been called to my bedside from some event and stayed the whole night. In later years, when I met Dr. Goldbloom in public, he would announce to all and sundry that I was his closest call in all his years of practice. I was eventually wheeled out of the emergency room to a nearby recovery room. I will never forget the look on the faces of four strangers in the room—the parents of two little boys who had just died. One had put a hairpin into a wall socket and the other little boy drank lye, which he found under the kitchen sink. How sad they were, and yet they wanted to comfort my parents, since I wasn't expected to survive.

At the Children's Memorial Hospital, the nurse in charge of my case was Jane McCulloch. I truly liked her. When I went home to convalesce, she came to look after me. Two or three weeks later, my mother told me Jane would soon leave. This saddened me, for I had fallen madly in love with Jane and told her so. I suggested we might marry some day and nervously asked her what she thought about it. She smiled and said she would think it over. The next day, Jane produced a small ring and helped me out of bed. When the time came for us to part, I was truly overcome. She left me her telephone number—I remember it to this day; it was MA8532. She lived on Durocher Street near the McGill campus, and invited my sister and me to tea the week after she left and told me to call her any time. For quite a while, I called her each evening, standing on a stool to reach the telephone on the wall. "How are you, Jane?" I would ask tearfully. She would come over in the afternoons from time to time to take me out to buy ice cream.

Apart from church-going on Sundays, the visits to my two grandmothers only served to emphasize the difference between the Graffteys and the Hewards. After church, we invariably drove out before lunch to see my father's mother at 56 Thornhill Avenue in Westmount. An elderly gray-haired lady, obviously not well, she sat silently for the most part, in a straight stuffed Victorian chair in her front living room in the upper duplex of her red brick house. A house-keeper, Miss Donnelly, normally prepared Sunday dinner and I often smelled the aroma of roast beef as we mounted the stairs. My spinster Aunt Alice took care of my elderly grandmother. She routinely took my sister and me on a short tour of the duplex, pointing out individual plates, saucers and bowls, neatly arranged in a glass cabinet made of buffed, dark walnut wood. She would point out the objects intended for each of us when she and Granny Grafftey passed on. Aunt Alice had a limited repertoire for the piano and towards the end of our visit would ask us if we would like to hear her play. Before we could answer, she would adjust the piano stool and proceed to thump out the same old tunes. How many times I had heard them—"There's an old spin-ning wheel in the garden..." and "When I grow too old to dream..."

Granny Heward's limousine was usually parked at the bottom of the stone steps that led to the second floor of the house at 3467 Peel. The first ground floor level housed the staff—Alice Dill, the head cook, Danny O'Connor, the chauffeur, and three maids who per-formed sundry tasks and duties. Granny Heward held court in the third storey living room. Sunday afternoon was the time for high tea, when the clan would dutifully gather around the matriarch. Sunday midday or evening dinners at Granny Heward's were formal affairs with staff discreetly operating in the background. Their continued presence had a stultifying effect on conversation which was perfunctory to say the least. The meals were unbelievably delicious. If Uncle Chil wasn't there, Granny Heward carved the roast beef. The food came up from the kitchen to a room adjacent to the dining room on a dumbwaiter.

Christmas dinners at Granny Heward's were truly magnificent. "And the word was made flesh, and dwelt amongst us..." from John, Chapter 1 Verse 14, had tremendous significance for my grandmother.

For her, the birth of Christ and its subsequent anniversaries meant total celebration. She pulled out all the stops with complete joy and selflessness. Who could forget this annual reunion of most family members with the matriarch in total command, the holly and decorations, the succulent turkey and ham, the fine wines and sparkling champagne, mincemeat pies and the brandy burning over the plum pudding with white hard sauce. Then there were peppermints and nuts in small silver dishes, and red Christmas crackers by each place mat.

These Christmas dinners were black tie events, never to be forgotten. After cocktails in the downstairs living room, we made our way to the dining area where forty to fifty family members would sit down to a five-course banquet. Granny presided and carved at one end of the table and Uncle Chil did the same at the other end. At the appropriate time, my dad would jump to his feet and, with a raised glass, proclaim "The King, God love him!" We all followed suit, dutifully touching glasses with our neighbour on each side. Then there was the toast to "absent friends," followed by the same ritual. At the end of the ritual, coloured paper hats were produced from the Christmas crackers situated at each place setting. Granny was a good sport and put on her hat, but never for more than a couple of minutes. I always sensed she felt her dignity was somewhat compromised. When the grandchildren were young, we played musical chairs after the meal before we all made our way to the upstairs living room. This was the time for long distance calls to family and friends.

Our cousin Mary Hervey was often at Sunday lunches with my grandmother. She was a woman of great religious faith and was one of Montreal's foremost interior decorators. At the turn of the century, Cousin Mary had studied interior design in Paris. She decorated my Montreal apartment for me when I attended Law School at McGill. When I gave a house-warming party for family and friends, I invited Cousin Mary, too, but warned her that I had a plan. When everyone commented on the beauty of the furnishings and my good taste, with a twinkle in my eye I claimed I had done it all on my own. Only at the end of the party did Cousin Mary receive the credit due her when I revealed the truth.

Her small apartment on Milton Street, in central Montreal just east of McGill University was a wonder. It was furnished with antique silver and elegant Louis XIV furniture. After she died, her belongings were auctioned off. When the auction took place, there was a lineup, mostly of her former clients, on the sidewalk in front of her flat. My beloved Aunt Rooney stood in for me, and I am still the proud owner of Cousin Mary's china. Much of her furnishings went to the Montreal Museum of Fine Arts, where they can be seen today.

I went to grades one and two at Argyle School not far from our home. Recenty, when I was at a nursing home visiting a friend, an elderly lady in a wheelchair nodded at me, and I stopped to talk with her. She told me that she had worked as a teacher in the Westmount School District, which at one time included my old school, Argyle. We both agreed how important it was for children to be stimulated in their early years by good teachers and I told her how lucky I was to have had such a wonderful teacher in grade two. I started to extol her virtues, and even mentioned that I used to bring my teacher flowers from time to time. I noticed a quizzical look on the old lady's face and she asked me the name of the teacher. "Her name was Miss Scroggie," I answered. She reached out, took me by the hand and exclaimed, "I am Miss Scroggie." We both choked up and began to reminisce endlessly.

Wind-up gramophones were in vogue and radio was at its height. *Little Orphan Annie* was standard evening fare and you could tune into the *Chrysler Amateur Hour* from Chicago, with Major Bowes. Who could forget the famous introduction, "Around, around the old wheel goes, and where it stops, nobody knows."

Young contestants from all over the United States would travel to Chicago to perform on the *Amateur Hour*. If they performed badly, Major Bowes would ring a gong and the luckless contestant would have to leave the stage immediately, sometimes crying. You could sense the inevitable after a wrong note or two, before the sounding of the gong and a "better luck next time" from the Major. Whenever I misbehaved, my father would admonish me with, "if you don't behave, you'll get the gong." On other occasions, he would threaten to send me to Shawbridge, a youth detention centre in the Laurentians, north of Montreal.

In the summer of 1933, my father dressed up as Major Bowes for an Amateur Hour at the Brome Lake Boating Club. He built a wooden wheel and a crank handle, mounted on a rack, that he turned as he yelled out, "Around, around the old wheel goes ..." Dad rang the gong with glee, much to the consternation of proud parents who imagined their offspring having some degree of talent.

This was at the time of the Great Depression. In mid-town Montreal, in freezing weather, worried men would wait in soup kitchen line-ups, anticipating a hot bowl of soup. Many rode the rails in search of any kind of work, which usually didn't materialize. Hardly an evening passed without one of these homeless men, sometimes even World War I veterans from Dad's company, knocking on the door of our house. My parents made sure they were fed before giving them a ticket for a bed and breakfast at the Salvation Army. In the country, in the early morning when I went to clean out the barn, I could hear the rustling of hay above me in the loft, as men stirred. Soon they would walk to the highway, their earthly possessions at the end of a stick, slung over a shoulder.

It was from de Casson Road that my father and I went to the six-day bicycle races at the Montreal Forum. After school one day, I dropped by the Forum to see Howie Morenz's casket placed at centre ice. Then there were the American Cup races between the *Endeavor* and the *Rainbow*, and who could forget the Louis-Schmelling fight? I had a guest, Peter Cameron, visiting me, and we were allowed to stay up for the fight. How disappointed we were when Schmelling went down for the count early in the first round, after which we were sent to bed. I had an added reason to be disappointed since Peter and I had a bet. He bet on Louis. I bet on Schmelling. The winner won the right to whack the loser over the backside with my mother's wooden yardstick. I got whacked, and it truly hurt since I was clad in only thin summer pyjamas.

Another more serious event involved my mother herself. In mid-winter 1933, I saw the city's nightlights for the very first time as my mother and father drove me to the Montreal General Hospital. I was to have my eyes straightened and was thankful because the children in the street persisted in throwing snow in my face while shouting, "Cross eyes! Cross eyes!" I was miserable and was led to believe by the jeering kids that I was, at least, in some quasi state of retardation. Once at the hospital, I was put to bed and my mother explained that when I woke up after the operation the next day I would have a hard time seeing. This unnerved me a bit, and I started to question her. She then produced a handkerchief and put it over my eyes, letting in a small amount of light, while explaining that was about how things would be after the surgery. Straightening eyes was a bigger deal in those days than it is now. Dr. Stuart Ramsey was to perform the operation. It was his first attempt at straightening eyes and, subsequently, he kept a picture of me on his office desk. The fact was, after the operation, I was plunged in total darkness for three weeks and began to panic and despair. I accused my mother of deceiving me. I had also heard the famous story of a young law student. He had come to the same hospital to have a diseased eye removed. Unbelievably, the surgeon took out the good eye, after which he left town. The student spent the rest of his life in total darkness.

When I got home, the bandages were removed and as long as the stitches were in I saw double. On the first Sunday after my home-coming, Dr. Ramsey came to take out the stitches. I remembered the anesthetic at the hospital and the suffocating smell of ether. I asked him to promise not to put me to sleep, and to the best of my knowledge, he was going to comply with my wishes. I was made to lie down on the chaise longue in my mother's bedroom and before I knew it, a mask was put over my face. Then came the horrendous smell of ether as I drifted off. This second deception annoyed and puzzled me, but as I grew older, I understood a little better the actions of my mother and the doctor.

How can I forget my seventh birthday? The winter before, I had been seriously ill and moved to our summer cottage with my mother, who bought a pair of rabbits for me. By the time of my birthday on August 5, 1935, we had close to twenty small rabbits and didn't know what to do with them. Dad had a solution. He got over a dozen shoeboxes, put lettuce in them and drilled holes in the lids. At each child's place at my party was a box which occasionally moved. When the children opened them up, they were ecstatic. This was not the case with the parents when they came to pick up their kids. By 9:00 p.m., almost half the rabbits had been returned. Subsequently, Dad and I did a tour of the town, visiting irate parents who were attempting to construct enclosures for their new-found pets. Unfortunately, while hunting for the rabbits before my birthday party, we lowered the rabbit hutch on one of them. The next day, we held a very formal burial service with the dead rabbit in a box being wheeled in a wheelbarrow into the woods by my sister as my father, dressed in a dark overcoat, tolled a dinner bell. We read passages from the funeral service and the book of common prayer.

Today, when a business man promises "to get back to me within a week," I normally take it with a grain of salt and some degree of cynicism. I was well trained in my early years not to count too much on promises. Mr. Rice, the photographer on Sherbrooke Street, was the first culprit. He said if I sat still for him he would give me a rabbit. I really sat still and never budged; no rabbit was forthcoming. A so-called gentleman farmer said he would give me a bull calf if, after a week, my mother reported on "my good behaviour." For two solid weeks, I assumed saintly and angelic characteristics. It was obvious to me my mother had to report my good behaviour to the farmer. I even monitored the phone call, but never got my bull calf.

During the summer of 1936, Grandmother Heward sent me a fine tent for my eighth birthday and we pitched it in the woods behind Rockwood Cottage. One night I invited my friend, Bobby Minty, to sleep over with me in the tent. Bobby and I made our way to the tent with our oil lanterns. As darkness fell, Bobby became alarmed. He was convinced he could hear a bear outside the tent and insisted upon returning to the cottage. I pleaded with him, but to no avail. Soon we threaded our way down the path back home to the cottage and my parents put us in twin beds in the guestroom. A problem soon arose. Rockwood Cottage was well over 100 years old. Mrs. Minty, Bobby's mother, had spent her holidays there many years before in her youth.

That night she phoned to see if she could come over to see the cottage and reminisce. My parents agreed, but Bobby didn't want to admit to his cowardice. As his mother arrived at the front door, with great drama Dad rushed Bobby and me into the cupboard of the guest room and slammed the door as Mrs. Minty began her conducted tour of the cottage. When she entered the guest room with my parents, Bobby and I held our breath. Fortunately for us, an inspection of the cupboard was not in the books, and a little while later, Mrs. Minty left and we were home free. To this day, I don't know whether or not she was informed about her son's desertion of the tent.

Both in Montreal and in the country, we children, I would do things I would later regret. When I was seven years old, I was given my first bicycle with a large wicker basket attached to the handlebars. Once in the country, I decided to save up enough money to buy a small radio, but I was making little progress until I hit upon an idea. I went around the house and gathered together discarded objects and, with my parents' permission, headed off to the village on my bike to peddle my wares. I did a disgraceful thing for which I am still ashamed. Putting my bike down on the lawn in front of a rundown house in the middle of the village, I saw an elderly man in the window. I picked out an old worn-out fly swatter from my basket and then committed the unpardonable—I limped across the lawn in order to evoke sympathy from the old man. Once in the living room, he opened up a small tin aspirin box and gave me ten cents for the useless fly swatter. I felt somewhat guilty, but was ecstatic. By the time my birthday came in August, I didn't have nearly enough money for the radio, but my parents produced a small one just the same.

The legendary Peck's Bad Boy of our neighbourhood was Hugh Welsford (he went by the name Boydie). He got into serious trouble, costing his father quite a sum of money, when one washday he paraded down the lane with a pair of large shears and visited a number of backyards where clothing was hung out to dry. He systematically cut the legs off long underwear and the arms off shirts. On another occasion, one evening my parents went over to the Welsford's to play bridge. It was early summer and Boydie came to the living room to kiss his parents and mine goodnight. Dad sensed something would go wrong—it did. After a hand or two of bridge, the house was plunged into total darkness, and my father noticed Boydie flying out the front door putting fuses in his pocket.

In 1942, during the summer, Boydie and his mother came to visit us at Meadowlands, our farm in Knowlton. While Mrs. Welsford and my mother were chatting in the living room, Boydie and I went to look at our horses in the paddock beside the barn. As one of the horses approached the railing where Boydie was standing, he mounted the railing and jumped on the horse's back. The horse ran to the centre of the paddock and proceeded to get into a kicking match with another horse. The two horses squared off back-to-back and let fly with their hooves. As Boydie screamed bloody murder, the beast on which he found himself came up with a series of bucks. Boydie was sent flying. He hit the ground and quickly crawled under the railing, putting an abrupt end to his bronco-busting days. Boydie went on to have a successful career in business.

In the early years at Rockwood Cottage in Knowlton, we had a black and white piebald pony we loved named Daisy. She delighted in bucking terrified children from her back. The unique thing about Daisy was that she pulled a black Irish gig with two oil-burning lanterns on each side of the front seat—the back seat faced backwards. Whenever Daisy trotted us into the village, eyes would turn and people would wave. In the winter time, we stabled her with a farmer we knew well, named Harry Bannister. In the winter of 1935, he called my parents in Montreal to say Daisy had glanders and had to be put down. Needless to say, there were tears.

Animals play a large part in the lives of children and my sister and I were no exception. Our dog, Jack, was a purebred wire-haired terrier. Jack was a fighter and attacked neighbourhood cats and dogs with abandon. One evening, dad came home with Jack stretched out dead on a toboggan. He had been hit by a car.

When I was seven years old, Mother bought my sister and me two beautiful Persian kittens who grew into magnificent cats. Fuzz, the female, was mine. She was pure black and gave birth to a litter of kittens on the day of the Coronation of King George VI and Queen Mary. When we arrived home from a fireworks display at the

In my Sunday Eaton's suit, Winter, 1936.
Photo by Rice, Montreal.

As a member of the Royal St. Lawrence Sea Scouts,
winter, 1941.

Westmount Athletic Grounds, we found that Fuzz had placed her litter, one by one, in my mother's shoes in her cupboard. Mother used the pregnancy of Fuzz and the subsequent birth of her kittens as a sort of sex lecture for her seven-year-old son.

One fall afternoon, when I was ten years old and convalescing from an appendicitis operation in our home on Rosemount Crescent, Fuzz visited me on my bed and I combed out her lovely coat as she purred with approval. A few minutes later, after she left the room, I heard a screech of brakes from a passing taxi—I never saw Fuzz again.

Buzz, the male, belonged to my sister. He was a beautiful tortoise-shell-coloured giant. Buzz came to an even worse end. One spring evening in 1937, mother and dad were visiting friends to play bridge. We had a milk door near the back of the kitchen which was also used for letting the cats in and out of the house. That evening I heard Buzz crying by the milk door. I let him in and he came and sat on a big stuffed chair by the piano, where I was playing, then I noticed a pool of blood and guts on the chair. Buzz was in agony. I called my parents and they rushed home and took him to the vet. Buzz had been shot by our neighbour who was a bird fancier.

Then there was my horse, Annabelle. She was a dual-purpose horse. I did chores at Meadowlands farm with her, where she pulled a large, yellow wagon. Sometimes I would saddle her up for an evening ride. In the winter of 1940, George Rogerson telephoned my parents in Montreal to tell them that Annabelle had to be put down. She was sold for mink meat, and a couple of weeks later, the money was forwarded to my father. Dad offered me the money rather abruptly. I refused it with much emotion and with support from my mother. I had the impression that mother disapproved of the way my father handled the matter.

On Sundays, I would be dressed up in an Eaton's suit for church. The high starched collar squeezed my chubby short neck and left a red mark. Dad always had real trouble attaching the collar studs. He would stand on my feet, forcing me to keep still. At the age of twelve, my Eaton's suit was changed for a Marlboro suit, which still included the hard collar. At the same time, my grandmother made changes in the letters she addressed to me. Instead of Master Heward Grafftey on the envelope, there was now the more adult, Esquire. On most mornings, Dad would put huge amounts of greasy brilliantine on my unruly hair to control what he called my cock-a-hoop. Then he would say: "Off you go! You look just like Rudy Vallee."

St. John the Evangelist Church was situated in the heart of the city and was the seat of High Church ritual in the diocese. Early bishops never put a foot in St. John's because of its Anglo-Catholic leanings, which included lots of chanting and immense quantities of incense. One day I was passing by the church with a friend from law school, John Pepper, who had gone to a Jesuit school. I brought him to the door. He would not go in, but when I showed him the sanctuary and high altar and explained our ritual and beliefs, he murmured to himself, "So near and yet so far."

St. John's School, at the turn of the century, was located in the church. Dr. Fosbery, the organist, had come out from England and founded the school, which my uncles attended. The school later moved out to huge grounds in Nôre-Dame-de-Grâce in the west end of the city. It was to be called Lower Canada College, and my Uncle Chil, by then a lawyer, incorporated the original LCC charter. The old saying that the Anglican Church is "the Conservative Party of Prayer" surely applied and applies to St. John's. An aura of distinction and upper-class privilege was there for all to see and feel.

I have clear recollections of Lower Canada College, where I was enrolled at the age of nine in Grade Three.

The authorities at LCC had a contract with the Montreal Transit Commission, so that two busses and drivers were at the school's disposal. They were old clunkers—castoffs from the twenties. They burned oil excessively and when the drivers shifted gears going up the side of Westmount Mountain, students had to hang on for dear life as the engines roared and the bus lurched forward. The busses left the terminal before 8:00 a.m. and picked up the boys at designated stops en route. By the time they reached me, most of the seats were full. One driver had the habit of occasionally bypassing groups of waiting students, leaving them stranded and speechless on the sidewalk. If you missed the first bus, there was always the second. If you missed the second bus, you were forced to travel by normal bus or streetcar, usually arriving late for school. This subsequently involved punishment which, more often than not, included a good caning. At that time, teachers and senior students were authorized to administer the beatings. I was an exuberant kid and got more than my share. One night, Dad saw me heading for my bath and asked why I had red stripes on my bottom. I am sure he knew why and I was truly humiliated. Some teachers and boys were truly sadistic and I would feel quite faint after their senseless thrashings, after which they would suggest: "Tonight, you will have to eat your supper at the mantelpiece." Stephen Penton, who eventually became headmaster, liked to recount an incident when he beat the daylights out of me. He took me into his living room study in the junior school to administer "six of the best." After he administered the cane, I clutched my backside and ran to the first door I could see and opened it; it was a cupboard; I tried another door. It opened into the bathroom. I tried a third door; it opened into an adjacent bedroom. Finally, I opened the door into the hallway and fled. Penton recounted the story more than once with raucous laughter.

Pit Péron, the French teacher, usually caned in a fit of temper. He administered his torture in the hallway, usually after he had ejected the student from class. The idea was to bend down facing the walls. The hallways were narrow and Pit couldn't get a full swing at you. At the end of his canings, the back of his hands were often red and bruised. If you had time, you could put a wallet in your back pocket to lessen the impact of the cane.

Then there was Sergeant-Major Cutbush, ex-British Army with a clipped moustache. He was the gym teacher. In my first year Cutbush would line up the boys in the gym. He would then position himself behind the line of boys and then drop a springboard on the floor used to jump over boxhorses. At the sound of the crashing board, the more nervous boys, including myself, would jump around to see what had happened. Cutbush would single us out and tell us to wait in his office. On the walls near his desk there was a selection of canes. He would permit each student to select a cane with which he would satisfy his urge—unbelieveably he had given each cane a special name. As I bent down to touch my toes, he would always say the old cliché: "This is hurting me more than you." I never believed him for a moment. One teacher administered his beatings with a strip of brake lining from a car; the imbedded pieces of metal would often break the skin of his victim. In recounting these caning episodes to various macho friends and acquaintances, many would comment: "Heward, you probably deserved every bit of it." Whether this was true or not, the canings only increased my sense of rebellion. For me, at least, they never constituted a preventative measure and they failed to make "a man of me." As a result of all this, I never, to the best of my recollection, hit my children. For me, physical violence, like patriotism for some, constitutes "the last refuge of a scoundrel."

Who of my generation could forget bolo bats and yo-yos? In the early 1940s, they appeared in the fall of the year in schoolyards and halls. Attached by a long elastic band to the bat was a hard, little rubber ball. Competitions were held, and there was always one or two students in each class who could perform miraculous tricks with the simple apparatus. The same story applied to yo-yos. Groups of students performing clumsily with their bats or yo-yos would cluster around the star performers in admiration. When the bolo bat fad was at its height I attended a baseball game with my Dad. What a sight to see thousands of little rubber balls on the end of long rubber bands popping out en masse from the stands!

Other memories involved marbles in springtime and chestnuts in the fall. When the last stubborn patch of snow disappeared, early spring signalled the advent of the alley season. Small hollows were dished out of the fresh, wet earth and everywhere youngsters could be seen on their hands and knees pushing their marbles towards the open hole, while an excited crowd shouted encouragement.

In the fall, we would throw stones into towering chestnut trees to loosen the chestnuts. Prickly, green covers encased the shiny, dark brown nut. We would drill a hole through the nut and attach it to the end of a long string before wrapping the other end of the string around the palm of our hands. After these preparations, two contestants could face each other. If you swung and missed the other fellow's nut, it was his turn to swing on your nut. If you scored a hit, you got another try. Whoever was first to break the other fellow's nut, won. I kept a large stack of chestnuts in my top drawer. For some reason or other, I covered each nut in a sticky grease substance, feeling such treatment would strengthen the nut. Nothing ever substantiated my odd theory based on total ignorance.

At the same time, a favourite song among my friends was "I like coffee, I like tea, I like the girls and the girls like me. Tell your mother to hold her tongue. She had a boy when she was young." Girls would sing it while skipping. Kids, even those with with no musical talent, would enthusiastically bang out this ditty on the piano, in much the same way they would play " Chopsticks."

The family toasting my grandmother Efa Heward at her
home on Peel Street, Christmas, 1952.

CHAPTER TWO

My Father

On October 1, 1948, when I was twenty years old, my father, William Arthur Grafftey, died suddenly of a massive coronary thrombosis at the age of fifty-seven. Some days later, at the service on Sunday, October 17, 1948, Rod Berlis, the minister of the Church of St. Andrew and St. Paul in Montreal, paid a brief tribute to my Dad in which he said, "I am anxious to pay tribute to one of the most beloved leaders in our parish who has passed from the church on earth to the church in heaven.

"William Arthur Grafftey has gone from us. His death has shocked and saddened our people as perhaps no other event in recent years. This is all the more remarkable since Arthur had been a member of our church only a comparatively short time and was ordained to the highest office in our church, that of elder, less than a year ago.

"Arthur Grafftey was one of God's true gentlemen. How embarrassed he would be to hear those words! You see, he was one of the most utterly unassuming and unself-conscious men I have ever known. I don't think he ever knew how great his courage was in World War I. I don't think he ever knew how his sense of humour lifted our spirits. I don't think he ever knew how profoundly he influenced hundreds of lives in this city. I don't think he ever knew that he was one of the most beloved men in Montreal.

"When Arthur Grafftey went from us, humble workers in his factory and his farm knelt to pray at his casket. The night watchman at his factory spoke for many others when he said, 'I have not only lost my boss, I have lost my best friend.' Distinguished leaders found an unwanted mistiness in their eyes and were unashamed. And this great sanctuary was crowded with people from every faith—and every walk of life. Never was there a more impressive tribute to the power of a good man."

My father was born on Tupper Street in mid-town Montreal and was the youngest of five children—two older brothers and two older sisters. After attending Montreal High School, my Dad went on to McGill University.

He played all sorts of instruments in various groups at McGill, notably in the "Glee and Mandolin Club." I know he played the drum in the band that performed at football games. On one occasion, he was meant to travel by train with the team to Queen's University in Kingston, but he didn't have enough money. Incredibly, he pawned his father's Sunday suit. On the ride back from Kingston, he won enough money from cards and shooting craps to reclaim his father's suit, only to find that the pawnbroker had sold it. Dad said the ensuing confrontation with his father simply couldn't be described in words.

College for Dad must have been somewhat of a lark suited to his exuberance and his sense of fun and downright mischievousness. In 1913, the year of his graduation in Engineering from McGill, the luxurious Ritz-Carleton Hotel had just opened its doors and royal visitors from all over the world were visiting the hotel at regular intervals. That's all the encouragement my father needed. He went to Malabar's, which for many years rented theatrical costumes and uniforms, and rented a King's uniform for himself and a Queen's outfit for a lady friend. The Trenholme family, who owned Elmhurst Dairy in Montreal West, had a lovely open landau and six black horses. Dad organized them for the event. Then a half-dozen friends obtained uniforms and fine motorcycles. At the appropriate time, my father and his Queen left the McGill grounds and headed west on Sherbrooke Street in their elegant carriage, drawn by six shiny black horses, accompanied by a formidable motorcycle escort. By the time they reached the front of the Ritz, hundreds of onlookers had gathered on the sidewalks. The hotel personnel were not prepared for such an event and the ensuing confusion it caused.

Sometime after my father's death, I met one of his college classmates who told me that at graduation time, my father really went too far. A photographer from Notman's Studio came to take the 1913 Engineering graduating class picture on the front lawn of the university campus. It took many minutes to get the class completely still. The photographer then pulled the traditional black hood over his head, getting ready to squeeze the flashbulb. The bulb never flashed—Dad broke ranks, tackled the photographer and headed down Sherbrooke Street with the camera over his shoulder and his classmates in pursuit. What happened after that I never heard.

Father had been wounded twice in the war and was awarded the Military Cross and Bar. As he lay in his bath, I could see the holes in his legs and thighs and a large, blue tattoo on his left leg. He told me he was on leave from the front in London and barely remembered getting tattooed.

A letter dated June 9, 1915, in Montreal, to his sister, read:

Just a short note to you and the boys before I leave for England. The 42nd leave tomorrow morning about 1,100 strong. We have a good strong body of men and I am very proud to be with them. I am sending a photo under another cover and hope you will like it. Will you please see that brother George has one too.

Mother is behaving perfectly great under the circumstances and it is no hardship for me to leave home when she looks at things in such a good common-sense way.

Father has helped me again financially, and I am OK again for the whole trip. Everybody has been very kind to me before my departure, and I could hardly get all the presents into my trunk. I will do my best to try and keep you well posted as to my whereabouts, but if I fail in writing you will know that my work would not permit me to. I do not know what the next year or so will bring about, but whatever comes, I am prepared to try and do my best. I will think of you all every day and will look forward to coming back when all is over.

Best of luck, dear sister, to you and the boys.
With much love,

Art
Canadian Expeditionary Force (C.E.F.)

The week after my father's funeral, there appeared in the *Montreal Star* an editorial by Ewen Irving entitled, "First Man In." The Belgian city Mons was the last city to fall at the end of World War I. My father was the first Canadian soldier and officer to lead his company into the city. D Company captured the historic city whose name is indelibly linked with the beginning and the end of the 1914-18 struggle. Dad's uniform was kept by the authorities to be placed in the museum at Mons. The editorial went on to say that "a modest man, Mr. Grafftey told his story reluctantly, but it had to be told. Once he told his story under compulsion and in dramatic circumstances on the witness stand on April 24, 1928 at the trial of Sir Arthur Currie's libel action against the publisher and editor of the *Port Hope Guide*." The crux of the libel against the commander of the Canadian corps was the assertion that he needlessly sacrificed the lives of Canadian troops in the taking of Mons. Apparently the editor of the paper felt that Currie continued the fight knowing the armistice was imminent. At the time, Currie was principal of McGill University and he made it known he wanted to sue for libel. Dad and a small circle of friends counselled Currie against such a course of action, but the general insisted on 'defending his honour' and pursued his course. My father was cross-examined at length on the witness stand in Coburg. Many of his brother officers and friends subsequently told me his testimony was central in obtaining a favourable verdict for Currie. Currie was exonerated, but the whole matter virtually broke his heart and he died soon thereafter.

As a little boy, I remember the funeral procession leaving the university grounds and proceeding along Sherbrooke Street. I watched with my mother from a balcony along the route. Dad marched behind the horse-drawn caisson which was carrying the flag-draped coffin.

Black boots were placed facing backwards in stirrups attached to a saddle on one of the horses in the parade followed by a steady line of veterans, often limping; some tragically wounded by the horrors of the war. Currie's widow lived on at the Ritz in Montreal. I often saw her sitting alone in the lobby in the following years. In my twenties, I developed a most pleasant friendship with Sir Arthur's talented and charming granddaughter, Lucy Durnford.

Dad's respect for the red-tabbed British generals wasn't very great. On leave from the front, he went to hear lectures at the British Staff College in Aldershot. Dad, like Winston Churchill, was appalled at the official disregard for the lives of ordinary soldiers. The generals were going by the tactic books prepared for the Boer War. No machine gun protection on the flanks was provided for the advancing infantry as men fell like tenpins under enemy fire. Dad spoke up in disgust saying he would never expose his men to such lunacy. His only reward for his observations and forthrightness was a stern lecture and reprimand.

My father rarely talked about the war, but on one occasion I was told about his heroism. After my father married Eva Black, he saw a lot of Walter Molson, who had married Eva's older sister, Mary Kingman. Mary's family were temperance people. Her father insisted that Walter Molson sell all his stock in Molson's Brewery (which he did) before he could have his daughter's hand. Walter had served in the Black Watch with Dad and had been severely wounded in one of his shoulders. Sometime after my father's death, I visited Walter in the Montreal General Hospital a week or so before he, himself, died. He told me that as he lay wounded in France, in no man's land, two German soldiers appeared out of nowhere and started to kick him. They soon retreated under fire. My father, witnessing this incident, crawled over 150 yards, mostly on his belly, over mud-soaked terrain, lifted Molson over his shoulders and carried him back to safety. Walter Molson reached out over his hospital bed and took me by the hand. "Heward," he said, "you should know that your father saved my life."

The war ended for my father on a relatively humorous note. He arrived home in Canada to be greeted by my grandfather at his home in Westmount. Grandfather Grafftey was an alderman for the city in

My father Arthur Grafftey as young officer in Montreal, 1914, before going to the Front.

charge of lights and playgrounds and he had put up in lights over the front door: "Welcome Home, Arthur." Upon greeting my Dad, he said, "What would you like us to do for you, son?" Dad replied, "First of all, please take down the lights."

After the first Great War, my father and his brother, Stewart, joined with their father to work at the Montreal Lumber Company. My grandfather founded the company at the turn of the century. It initially supplied the wood for the sidewalks of Montreal. Two things saved the company during the Great Depression: Canadian National Railways expropriated the company's land and the resultant cash infusion staved off disaster, and my father secured a contract to supply lumber to the Quebec Northshore Paper Company, a subsidiary of the Ontario Paper Company. The lumber he sold to the paper company was for much of the building being completed at the new town site of Baie Comeau. The Ontario Paper Company was, in turn, owned by the Chicago Tribune. Newsprint from Baie Comeau was shipped to *The Trib* in Chicago and to the *New York Daily News*. Col. Arthur Schmon headed the Ontario Paper Company, and at the helm of *The Trib* was the legendary Col. Bertie McCormick. Dad often described to me his meetings with these two men. Brian Mulroney sang for Bertie McCormick as a youth, as he sang for Ronald Regan as an adult.

In order to supply Baie Comeau, Dad set up a collection yard for his lumber across the Gulf of St. Lawrence at Matane. The lumber was purchased from small mills on the Gaspé coast. When Dad visited these mills, he was treated like royalty by the owners. I went with him as a boy. From Cap Chat we would travel to Mechins and Petit Mechins, where we would be greeted with open arms by the mill owners, Wilfred and Antonio Verreault. The last visit would be with Charles Nadeau at Port Daniel. Dad would bring along his mandolin and play it in the evenings. One song always met with laughter and approval. It went, "Hello Mademoiselle, voulez-vous danser. Non, monsieur, j'ai mal aux pieds." We would be offered small glasses of whiskey-blanc, served on a tin tray. It was hard to drink, but courtesy meant we downed it with a smile and without a blink.

Many of these mill purchases were shipped up to our yard in Montreal. The method of transportation used in the 1930s, 1940s and 1950s no longer exist today. The lumber was shipped by schooner, equipped with sails and an auxiliary engine. They were normally manned by a captain, river pilot, cook and, at the most, one or two other hands. The schooners would arrive at the Lachine Canal Basin beside our yard from mid-summer until autumn. The *Donalda L,* made of wood and painted dark blue, was my favourite schooner. The elderly captain, Jan Madsen, a small, elderly, quiet-spoken, pipe-smoking Norwegian, kept a magnificent library of books by the bridge. His cook was a real chef. Jan and I had many good meals on board, and as we sailed up the river he would usually talk about his latest reading ventures.

There was a host of characters at the Montreal Lumber Company. Old Harry Brown, hired by my grandfather, was the secretary-treasurer. He would sit on a high stool with half-moon glasses set on his nose and his books spread out before him. Harry was a hard-line teetotaller. One Sunday, my mother and father invited him and his wife for lunch. He sipped the hot consommé and asked my mother what was in it. She confessed she had added a drop or two of sherry. Much to our embarrassment, Harry Brown berated my mother, who was speechless. Another incident nearly broke my father's heart. Mr. Brown was in charge of purchasing stationery and before one Christmas, a stationery salesman brought him 40 ounces of the best scotch whisky. Brown acted promptly. He took it to the bathroom in the basement and emptied the bottle into the toilet. Dad had followed him down the stairs and witnessed the proceedings in horror. Whisky was by far my father's favourite drink.

Then there was Leo Belittle, the night watchman. He would arrive at 5:00 p.m. with his shaggy police dog on a tight lead. The dog had a menacing growl, as did the dog that accompanied the night watchman at a neighboring plant across Basin Street. Tragedy struck them both. Around midnight each night, Leo's friend would go down the street for a coffee and snack. One night, upon returning to duty, the friend was attacked and killed by his own dog. Affected by the horror, Leo quickly got rid of his man-eater, but he, too, unfortunately, came to a sad end. One night, after I had taken over the company the telephone rang. Thieves had broken into the offices and tied Leo to a chair by the punch clock. They broke into the safe and found no money. In their frustration, they beat him savagely and he died soon thereafter.

Time, it is said, is a great healer. It also distorts past realities. We only remember the good times involving those whom we love and are now gone. It seems that bad times fade away and are virtually forgotten. Thus it is with my father. When I think of him, I smile and sometimes laugh, for that was what he did most of the time. "We must carry on" was an expression he used often. He must have picked it up in the trenches between 1914 and 1918. Nietzsche wrote: "he who strideth across the highest mountains laugheth at all tragedies. Perhaps I know best why man is the only animal that laughs; he alone suffers so excruciatingly that he was compelled to invent laughter." When I read these lines I think of my father and his friends. They had witenessed, first hand, the killing and the tragedy of World War I. They too, were compelled to invent laughter.

My father had a temper. It didn't flare up often, but when it did all hell broke loose. He would bellow at me from time to time, "Be a man's man, and don't hang on to your mother's apron strings." This, however, never lessened my love and respect for him. It seemed to me that I was more bookish and had a greater artistic leaning than he had. I don't think this troubled him as much as it did me. As I got older and went through something of a socialistic stage, I asked him one day why he didn't, from time to time, invite our janitor for dinner. Dad retorted with, "When did the janitor last invite *me* to dinner?"

When my aunt, Prue Heward, the well-known Canadian artist, would bring me a house gift while visiting our summer cottage, father would needle and tease me since the gift would often be a coloured silk handkerchief or a sweet-smelling lavender lotion. He felt that artists' paintings should be like real-life photographic reproductions. "Aunt Prue never measured up," he exclaimed while putting his engineering instruments to her landscapes in order to inform me that she had no sense of real-life measurement and perspective. I was always somewhat bemused and never really argued the point. When I did protest, tempers flew.

Dad, as if to counterbalance the overwhelming influence on my life of my mother's side of the family, mentioned with pride the achievements of his own family circle. This included my cousin, Doug Dadson who became Dean of the Ontario College of Education; his brother, Dr. Stewart Dadson, a renowned geologist who made a major gold discovery in northern Ontario; and, as already mentioned, his Uncle Joseph Stewart and his grandfather, the legendary Baptist missionary and minister, Alexander Stewart. In his latter years, Alexander Stewart was a neighbour of Alexander Graham Bell in Brantford, Ontario. Bell would invite him for Sunday lunch and, before they ate, would ask him to go down to the barn in an attempt to communicate over what Bell called a 'telephone.'

My father loved to organize the kids in our neighbourhood. He put together a street hockey team and we got trounced. We didn't have a chance against one of the players on the opposing team, Johnny Pearson, who would later play for the Boston Bruins. He scored against us at will. In the country and in our backyard in the city, father built a pitcher's mound for me and a home plate for himself. After arriving home from work or at the country for the weekends, he would call for me, "Let's go and throw."

In the spring of the year at our farm, Meadowlands, melting water from the snow would pitch down the sides of the hills, often overflowing the mountain streams. That would signal the approach of our annual bottle races. Dad would assemble as many children as possible. Each child would put his name on a paper and seal it in a bottle. We would gather at the top of the hill and, altogether, put our bottles into the stream. The owner of the bottle that first arrived at a checkpoint in the meadow below was the winner. The smile on Dad's face was truly delightful as hoards of children scrambled, screaming down the sides of the hill, often prodding their bottle loose with a stick.

Being a graduate engineer from McGill, he was a great help to me in my mathematics and science studies. Sometimes he would try and teach me how to read a compass he had brought home from the war. He would take me out to the fields at Meadowlands, but the results were minimal. I never caught on, and to be honest, I wasn't very motivated.

Meadowlands was situated on a bay on Brome Lake in Knowlton, Quebec. It was our home during the summer and on winter weekend holidays. During World War II it was a centre of much activity. George Rogerson, a local who lived with his family in a cottage on the farm, was our farm manager, and he was my boyhood friend and confidante. On Sunday mornings, I would churn ice cream for dinner. On Saturday George would prepare four or five chickens for his family and ours, for Sunday dinner. The beheading of the chicken involved the axe over a tree stump. Once the axe fell, George would throw the headless chicken into the air. To my amazement, it would fly around briefly, wings flapping, before hitting the ground. George and Dad, supervising farm activities, became great friends. I rather think he related to George as he would have to his company sergeant-major in World War I. The farm had originally been owned by the Hon. Sidney Fisher, a bachelor and Sir Wilfrid Laurier's Minister of Agriculture. My mother was left a handsome legacy by her Uncle Frank in 1939 and with it she bought the farm from Philip Fisher, nephew of Sidney and president of the Southam Company. He had married Margaret Southam and lived at Alva House beside our farm.

Over the years, the Fisher's could not have been nicer to me, especially after the tragic death of my mother. 'Alva' was, and is, a beautiful estate. Sir Wilfrid Laurier and his shadow cabinet had their very last meeting on the front lawn before he left office. The royal family used it during the Olympic Games of 1976; there are photos of them on the spacious lawns at Alva. The whole royal family gathered there, the only time they were so together outside the United Kingdom.

The farm was the source of great pleasure—the greatest being the sugar bush. One year I tapped a few trees around the house and boiled the maple sap on the kitchen stove. The sticky vapour condensed on the walls and the kitchen stove was declared out of bounds for the next year when I tapped considerably more trees in the nearby woods. Nobody told me about boiling procedures and George Rogerson purposely remained mute. I got my hands on a huge round metal vat and hung it over a great fire at the edge of the woods. Instead of pouring in a little sap at a time, I filled the vat to the very top. I started the procedure in mid-afternoon. By eight p.m. the water was luke-warm; by ten p.m. it had come to a boil. At 3 a.m. I came down the hill with one gallon of very dark syrup. As I passed the farm house, a light went on. George appeared on the veranda and made all sorts of caustic remarks to the effect that "city slickers" had much to learn about sugaring. The next year, Dad and I got serious. Mother had given us permission to go ahead. I took a $500 war bond to my bank in Montreal and put it up as collateral for a loan. With the proceeds, I made a down payment for the equipment. We had an old workhorse, Ajax. George had felled many logs in the woods and, with Ajax, we pulled the logs to a nearby field where they were neatly stacked. I made a further down payment at a local sawmill, which sawed and dressed enough lumber from our logs to build the sugar cabin. This involved a third payment to Harold Sanborn, a master carpenter. George and I helped him build our sugar house at the edge of the woods.

By the spring of 1945, we were ready to go. My father instructed me in rudimentary accounting, and together we set up the books. I was sixteen years old, and during the school break at Easter, helped George collect the sap as Ajax pulled the gathering tank through the woods. Boiling and taking off the sugar from the front of the rig was another pleasure. The steam would rise and pour out of the cupola on the roof. Watching the sap boiling on the rig in the sugar house, together with George and my father, brings back wonderful memories.

The first year we tapped 375 trees and made 150 gallons of high quality syrup. Government regulations made us weigh each gallon (13 pounds, 8 ounces per gallon) and grade by colour. The grades were "A" (Canada fancy), "B" (Canada Light), "C" (Canada Medium) and "D" (Canada Dark). The latter was sold to a tobacco company who used it in their manufacturing process. Dad sold the rest with ease to the family, friends and working colleagues at his lumber company. The first year we paid off the bank and equipment supplier, and the sawmill. The second year was equally as good, and we paid off Harold Sanborn. Dad taught me how to keep the books and, at the same time, he instructed me on the fine points of his balance sheet and annual reports at the Montreal Lumber Company. By the age of twenty, after working one summer at the Royal Trust Company in their investment department analyzing annual reports, thanks to my father and his training, I had a good grounding in practical accounting. In short, the sugar camp endeavour constituted my most constructive and happiest association with my father. It was great fun and I learned a lot.

These were, however, sad years for my father. My mother's suicide in the fall of 1943 left him in a depressed state until the time of his remarriage in late 1945. During my last years in high school, I worked long hours in the summer on a farm three miles away. I would bicycle back and forth. During the crop seasons, I would sometimes get home as late as 9 p.m. Sunday, I couldn't sleep in as I was an alter boy at our Anglican church in the village. The big Brome Fair was always held on Labour Day weekend and we all had our jobs. I was in charge of sugar products, Dad and George Rogerson took care of the pigs and chickens, George handled flowers and vegetables, and my sister would ride and drive in the horse events. She won many ribbons. Dad, George and I never did all that well, but, oh God, did we enjoy ourselves, even if fair time involved a lot of work.

It was in the country where I observed Dad's gambling instincts. He had marched off the number of paces between our front gate and the Fisher's front gate at Alva and he would challenge the guests to a guessing game. Each guest, including Dad, would put down on paper their guestimate of the number of paces between the gates. The guests, unaware of Dad's built-in advantage, never came close to winning and Dad would collect. The only mitigating circumstances relating to this quasi-dishonesty involved the fact that his winnings were regularly deposited, with more than a little showmanship, when the plate was passed at Sunday services.

Another gimmick of his involved the rail crossing in the Town of Farnham. Farnham was a railroad town just a little over half-way between Montreal and the farm. Sometimes the barriers went down at the crossing, causing an interminable wait as the freight train went by. Horns would honk as the traffic backed up. Over a period of time, Dad calculated the odds as to whether the barrier would be up or down. When the odds were firmly in his mind, he started his betting procedure on subsequent trips with fellow passengers. They, together with their fellow victims and marchers between the gates at Meadowlands at Alva, were unaware of Dad's devious tactics. Once more, he collected his winnings. Once more, they were deposited on the Church plate.

I rather think he was happiest worshipping in our lovely Anglican Church in Knowlton. He would bellow out the hymns, sometimes to our youthful embarrassment and always to the chagrin of my mother. Dad loved music and played the mandolin very well. How often he would ask, "Son, go and fetch my bazoo." He would pour himself a whiskey and we would gather around him for song and laughter. George M. Cohan was one of his favourites. Dad played his mandolin and sang for the troops in the trenches between 1914 and 1918.

Occasionally I would be allowed to stay up late at night when he played it on Montreal radio stations. He once entered a competition for Fitch's Shampoo. The best ditty got a prize, but Dad never won it. His submission, which he accompanied with his mandolin, went this way: "I bought a bottle of Fitch Shampoo—it made my son look slick—we really were so happy cause Fitch's did the trick. Try Fitch Shampoo, try Fitch Shampoo, try Fitch Shampoo—diddly, diddly, diddly, do."

Once at the Brome Lake Boat Club, Dad wasn't very popular. He sang "Old McDonald Had a Farm" with his mandolin at the annual stunt night. Unfortunately, he decided to roam the countryside before the event and collect animals for each verse of the song. My sister and I were forced to remain backstage and release a dog, cats, ducks, chickens, suckling pigs, turkeys, etc. into the crowd. The directors were not amused. If the sound of laughter is the hallmark of freedom, my father was truly a free man. To put it simply, most of the time it was fun to be with my Dad.

During my teenage years, my queries on matters sexual were met with the kind of silence typical from his generation. On the other hand, he must have known that I was learning, bit by bit, by the simple process of experimentation.

I acutely remember where I was the night President Franklin Roosevelt died. I was sixteen years old. A very attractive girl on my street asked me to help her with her mathematics homework. School girls in those days wore extraordinarily short skirts, and I had been fantasizing about her for some time. She was alone in the house when I arrived, since her mother was away at work. We proceeded upstairs to her bedroom to start the homework. This didn't take long and, in no time, we were in bed together. It wasn't an entirely satisfactory first experience for me, particularly when I heard the front door open and her mother calling up as she made her way upstairs. I had but one option—the window on the second floor. I threw my clothes and shoes outside into the garden below. Completely naked, I jumped out onto the balcony and dove into the muddy garden below just as the girl's mother reached the top of the stairs. I could hear the shouting and commotion behind me as I sat below dirty, bruised, and somewhat bemused. I managed to dress myself and, totally dishevelled, pushed myself through a line of thorny bushes onto the sidewalk in front of the house only to be greeted by my father who was out for a walk. "Oh, God," he exclaimed, "what were you doing?" Apparently he had seen the clothes and shoes flying out the window, followed by his son. He turned his back on me and entered our house. He must have mentioned the incident to my sister because she taunted me the next morning as I listened to President Roosevelt's funeral ceremony on the radio.

Later on that spring of 1945, my zeal for experimentation never slackened. My bedroom was on the third floor of 69 Rosemount Crescent. Across the hall from me was the bedroom of the young nurse who looked after our guest child from England, Susan Douglass. The nurse was very young and pretty and the proximity of her bedroom played havoc with my teen age fantasies. One Friday evening, I could no longer withstand the temptation across the hall. I went to her room and clumsily propositioned her. She was horrified and ordered me to "take the door" and the next day, she informed me that she had called my Grandmother Heward to tell her about my advances. My nightmare was complete—I was scheduled to go to my grandmother's for Sunday lunch after church. Following a sleepless night, I appeared at 3467 Peel Street at the appointed hour. Grandmother was as cheerful as ever. To this day, I do not know whether or not the nurse really made her telephone call.

After the sudden and tragic death of my mother, my grandmother took a special interest in my activities, an interest that frequently involved her authoritarian directives. On another occasion, my indiscretion failed to escape her notice. When I slept over at Peel Street, I would see her bedroom light go out when I mounted the stairs in the wee hours. In 1955, when she was in her ninetieth year, I stayed over at Peel Street the weekend before Christmas. I was out practically the whole night and got totally bombed. Once in bed, I knew the jig was up. The room spun. The bed rocked like a ship at sea. I didn't make the bathroom, and scored more than one direct hit on Granny's gifts neatly wrapped and stacked in my bedroom. Time was flying and I, too, flew into action, depositing sheets and blankets into the dirty laundry. Hardly had I stretched out on the bare mattress when grandmother awoke me for 8:00 a.m. communion. The ride to church was pure torture. When I knelt beside her, the whole church pitched forward. Later on at breakfast, she was unusually silent. I persisted in deluding myself that my nocturnal activities had passed unnoticed by my elderly grandmother. Such was not the case. A year later, I asked her, "Would you like me to stay with you over Christmas, Granny?" "I think not," was her abrupt reply. Later on I was to learn she had discussed my performance of a year earlier with my Uncle Brian. He laughed and exclaimed, "You nut! So you thought you were fooling the old lady." I should have known better.

I have already alluded to my grandmother's authoritarian streak. Her husband died on May 16, 1912, leaving her with eight children and without much financial support. She directed the family with an iron hand, in many ways arising out of her own past Victorian age.

I remember shopping with her on Saturday mornings. I would sit beside Danny, the chauffeur, who was separated from the back of the vehicle by a glass window that went up and down. With a push of a button, Grandmother would bark out orders over an intercom telephone held in her hand. One day she demanded, "O'Connor, are you chewing gum?" "Yes, mum," was his subdued answer. "Spit it out immediately," she demanded. Danny rolled down the window, turned his head and out went the gum.

I was one of the first people in Montreal to own a television set—the rest of my family only owned radios. For the coronation of the Queen and Prince Phillip, I invited many members of the family, including my grandmother, to my apartment to witness the crowning of Queen Elizabeth. In those days, there was no direct television broadcast; we waited for the film to be flown from the United Kingdom. Grandmother came with an exquisite picnic, packed in wicker baskets. During the prayers, in the middle of the ceremony, the CBC announcer made running commentaries in a low voice. This enraged my grandmother, and she demanded that I telephone the CBC immediately to silence the impious announcer. Naturally, I hesitated, but she persisted. I then pretended to put in a call from the next room. Miraculously, and by coincidence, the announcer mercifully fell silent. Grandmother gave me a smiling nod of approval for my supposed powers of persuasion.

In the winter of 1945, I met my father's friend, Dr. Louis Reford. Reford never practiced medicine. He had inherited a large fortune from the Reford family shipping business connected with the Cunard Lines. He lived in a mansion with exquisite gardens at the top of Drummond Street in Montreal's square mile. He was instrumental in raising a lot of money for Wilder Penfield's Montreal Neurological Institute, but most of his time was spent drinking at the University Club. He was truly eccentric. While not attempting to be a middle-age swinger, he was a pioneer of sorts. Rolling his own cigarettes, Reford grew first-class marijuana in his Drummond Street garden. When he would offer me a smoke from his silver case, the pot-filled cigarettes were arranged at one end. He would put his finger over them to prevent me from indulging. He and I got on really well, and he asked me to call him Uncle Louis. His wife, Jean, disapproved of his antics and I surmised, with reason, that their marriage was in pretty poor shape. Uncle Louis had good season tickets for the Montreal Forum's Canadian hockey games. His seats were situated in the south end right behind the goal. By the time we reached the Forum in his chauffeur-driven limousine, Uncle Louis was always pretty tanked.

Spectators stared at him in amazement as he bellowed all through the game. Before he took his seat, he blew up for comfort a small, tire-shaped orange rubber cushion. One evening, he so harassed Mike Karakas, the goalie for the Chicago Blackhawks, that Karakas banged his stick on the wire netting behind the goal appealing to the referee to admonish Reford.

Reford's claim to fame was his Canadian stamp collection worth well over one million dollars and easily the foremost collection in the country. He had six pairs of the rare Canadian stamp—the 12 penny black which he discovered in an attic across the river on Montreal's South Shore. My father was a prominent philatelist who specialized in the Pence issue named "The Small Queen's Head." The Pence issues were printed before Confederation in 1867 and were used by the citizens of the Colonies at that time. Reford was leaving his collection to McGill University, and Dad was charged with cataloguing it. On many occasions, late in the afternoon, he would get an urgent call from Reford's secretary. Explanations weren't needed. On arriving at Reford's mid-town office, Dad would find Uncle Louis passed out on an office sofa; he had removed his stamps from a safe and they were scattered everywhere. It took my father some time to put them in order and pack Uncle Louis off home. After Reford died, Dad took the part of his collection not deeded to McGill to sell at auction in New York.

Early in 1948 my father was truly annoyed with me. He wanted me to travel and broaden my horizons during the summer break. Instead, I took a job at the Royal Trust Company. He was furious. I guess he sensed the real reason for my staying in Montreal—I had a serious girlfriend. As it turned out, it was a blessing in disguise that I remained in Montreal for the summer. About a week before I returned to Mount Allison, following an early supper at Murray's Restaurant, Dad and I went to see the Montreal Royals play at Delormier Stadium. They were a great ball team and were leading the International League. Jackie Robinson was the club leader, and how Dad loved to see him play. The Royals were the primary farm club for the Brooklyn Dodgers. On their way up, great stars like Robinson, Duke Snyder, and Roy Campenalla played in Montreal. Towards the end of the game, Dad headed for the men's room. He was gone for what seemed to be an interminable time and I was becoming concerned. When he returned to his seat, he was pale. When I pressed for the cause, he confessed to having had a slight heart attack, forcing him to lie on bathroom floor. It was an ill omen for things to come—sooner than I cared to think.

After the game, Dad and I parked outside the home of my aunt and uncle where I was staying. It was one of those conversations that started out casually, but two hours later we were still having a wonderful father and son exchange. He felt I was very ambitious and that I had the intelligence and drive to fulfil my ambitions, but, at the same time, he had some serious misgivings. "Heward, I fear you are a bit of a buffoon, like me, and no one is going to take you very seriously." I remember the advice he gave me that night: "Work hard and play hard."

The next day before setting out to Mount Allison in my Austin, I drove to the home of my father and stepmother, Eva, to say goodbye. He came out to the front steps and gave me a cheerful wave. A few days later, October 1, 1948, I drove from Sackville to Moncton with two friends to have supper and see a movie. Probably around the same time in Montreal, my father was writing a letter to me. On the drive home, stretched out on the back seat because I was tired, a funny thought crossed my mind: wouldn't it be bad if I had to return on the same road that very evening. Little did I know what was in store. Once in bed at the university residence, there came a loud knocking at the door. Irving Koven, a renowned prankster, said I was wanted on the phone on the floor below. I ignored him. He kept knocking. I continued to ignore him, even when he persisted: "Seriously, Heward!" My roommate, Ted Rainnie, said he felt I better go. So, I complied and went to the telephone. My Dad had died of a massive heart attack—at the age of twenty, I was a fullfledged orphan.

Dad, humorously, claimed he was a member of the "Two-strike Club." Membership dictated that two coronary attacks were required for entrance, and the third was meant to kill you. On the night of October 1, 1948, he got up from the bridge table, announced the imminence of strike three, and died soon thereafter. Within a short time, I was driving back to Moncton in the middle of the night.

The Moncton Airport was fogbound. The next morning flight was completely booked. I asked the ticket agent to see if someone would kindly, under the circumstances, give up their seat. She said that only I could make the request to the passengers myself before the flight. I surely didn't feel up to that, and settled into a lobby seat for the long wait. When dawn approached, as I sat with my head in my hands, the agent informed me she had a seat for me. The next question was whether the aircraft would be able to fly. Mercifully for me, about a half-hour prior to departure, the rising sun burned off the fog. Soon I was home. The letter Dad wrote me was on a silver tray with a stamp on it. He had intended to mail it that day, but because it was raining, did not.

Part of the letter reads:

"… Your course sounds frightfully interesting. All your subjects appeal to me, also your work on the Debating Society. I am giving your interest in lumber some consideration. I recall when I left engineering and went to the Montreal Lumber Company my Dad was disappointed because he felt I should steer for something better. I feel much the same about you. However, we have time to give the subject most careful thought. In the meantime, you have a full year's work ahead."

Well over a thousand people from all walks of life crammed into the Presbyterian Church of St. Andrew and St. Paul. Since marrying my stepmother, Eva, Dad had become an elder in her Presbyterian Church. He had been born into the Baptist faith, but his regimental padre, during World War I, was the renowned George Kilpatrick of the United Church. After marrying my mother, he worshipped in the Anglican faith—he had run the denominational gamut. Once I mentioned all of this to him and questioned him about his central belief. He said, in the end, he thought he was a 'confusionist.'

Soon after my return to Mount Allison, I received a beautiful letter from George Kilpatrick. I don't know whether he had been speaking with my father, but he reiterated some of the same sentiments

"Don't let the love of your father's memory beget in you the idea that you ought to carry on his business. Unless your heart lies in it, that would be a great mistake. Everyone has his own gifts, tasks and aptitudes. His vocation should give him a chance to express them. I knew a man who had a genius for railroading whose life has been a failure because he allowed a strong-willed father to make him a lawyer. You'll do best what you like to do. Thank heaven the day is gone when any form of honest work is considered socially demeaning. So choose a field which you are drawn to and don't be in a hurry. You may have to find out your real line by trial and error. You know that I loved your father. As his son, you bear a great heritage. He would not have wished for you a lot of money, social position or power. But just a place where you could live out what was in you and help others. It was in his relation to others that he found satisfaction and joy."

In the mid-seventies I travelled to Thunder Bay to address a political meeting. Before it began an elderly gentleman approached me outside the hall. "Are you the son of Major Arthur Grafftey," he asked. "Yes I am," I replied. "Then let me shake the hand of the son of the finest and bravest man I have ever known! I was his company sergeant in the First Word War."

Since my father's death, I have often had a dream. It is nearly always the same. We go out for dinner and after the meal is over, we sit and chat. I ask him how he is and what he is up to and he fills me in on his latest activities and asks me the same. I tell him about my hopes and aspirations, then I wake up with a feeling of well-being, ready to face another day.

CHAPTER THREE

My Mother

On the afternoon of November 25, 1943, I had completed my school classes. I was a five-day boarder at Lower Canada College, and most of the other boys had gone home. I was talking with one of my fellow boarders in the hall outside the teachers' common room, when the Headmaster, Dr. Penton, approached me. At school, I always got into my fair share of trouble and, while I was not sure of what I had done wrong, I anticipated some sort of admonition. I did not have to wait long outside the Headmaster's office. Dr. Penton told me to step inside and take a seat opposite his desk. Immediately I could tell from his tone of voice that I was there for an important reason and that it had nothing to do with misbehavior on my part. "Heward," he said, "you know your mother has been very ill." "Yes," I replied, "but she's getting better and we hope she'll be home for Christmas." My reply obviously perplexed Dr. Penton. He turned uncomfortably in his chair and looked away from me. His head slowly moved around again and he confronted me eye to eye. I sensed the worst and my initial reply to him constituted a little bravado buoyed by false hope. He continued, "I hate to tell you, Heward, but your mother died suddenly this afternoon." I was devastated; after a few moments of silence, I asked, "How are my father and sister?" Obviously, he did not know. Then he added, "Don't be afraid to cry." I wasn't about to break down in front of him. He said that my aunt, Barbara Heward, had telephoned him with the news; that her husband, my Uncle Brian, would pick me up in a few minutes and that I should pack my belongings.

I don't know if Dr. Penton gave the news to Hugh MacLennan

before breaking it to me in his office. Maybe it was just a coincidence, but Hugh, my dear friend and beloved teacher, was standing outside the Headmaster's office as I left. I rushed into his arms and told him what had happened.

Soon my Uncle Brian arrived. He was two years younger than my mother and they were virtually inseparable. He stood by silently with tears in his eyes as I packed some clothes from my boarder's cubicle.

My mother died in Hartford, Connecticut at approximately 2:30 p.m. on November 25, 1943. She was a resident at the Institute for Living, renowned for its excellent psychiatric care. The Wednesday night before, my Dad and sister could not contact her by telephone as Bell employees were on strike. They had called her regularly at a given time each Wednesday evening. My mother was, reportedly, very upset at not receiving a call. On Thursday evening, she was to visit her cousins, Paul and Fanny Monroe, in Hartford; they normally invited her to dinner on Thursday evenings. I was told that this Thursday my mother seemed to be outwardly in high spirits. She intended to do some shopping with a nurse attendant before visiting her cousins. My mother was a resident in Terrence House on the grounds of the institute. When she and the nurse were in the lobby on their way to leave for shopping, my mother said she had left her purse in her room and would go upstairs to get it. The nurse said she would accompany her, but my mother insisted on going upstairs alone. When many minutes went by and my mother did not reappear, the nurse hurried upstairs. She found my mother dead by her own hand. How did it happen? To this day, I do not know and do not want to know. There was one exception. One night, when I was in my mid thirties, after more than one drink, I phoned my Aunt Rooney Nares. I knew she knew the details of what had happened. My aunt said to call or visit her the next morning if I still wanted to know. I didn't, and let the subject drop.

My uncle drove me directly home. I found my sister and father in a state of deep shock and dismay. Dad and my Uncle Brian made plans to go by overnight train to Hartford to bring my mother's body back to Montreal. After spending some time with my sister and dad, I was driven to my grandmother's on Peel Street. Many members of the family had gathered around her in the upstairs living room. I embraced her. In her grief, she said to me, with tears in her eyes, "Heward, dear, pray God you never outlive your children." She had already lost two daughters before the death of my mother.

My sister and I spent the night with my Aunt Barbara Heward and her four children. They lived down the street from us. I remember waking up early the next morning. When something is really wrong in our lives or we have experienced a tragic or unfortunate event, we are often immune to the sad thoughts brought on by these happenings for a few merciful moments after awaking. Thus it was with me as I awoke in a strange bed on Friday, November 26, 1943. After a few moments of blissful repose, a sense of uneasiness set in. Then it occurred to me what was wrong and I remembered my mother was gone. As a smaller boy, some years before, lying in bed before falling off to sleep, I had contemplated the probability that some day I would lose my mother and father. The very thought filled me with much terror and sadness. Little did I know at that time how soon I would be confronted with the death of the mother I loved and adored, a mother who loved me in turn, disciplined me, brought me to good books, encouraged me in my academic pursuits, influenced me by her good example and high moral standards and who, with my father, nurtured my spiritual needs.

Her funeral was set for 3:00 p.m on Saturday afternoon at our church St. John the Evangelist. The day before the funeral, while my father and Uncle Brian were in Hartford, I went with my Uncle Jim Heward to the cemetery offices to make sure my mother's grave was prepared at the family plot.

I do not recall any other events during the morning and afternoon of the day before the funeral, but I can't forget what happened that evening when the train arrived at Montreal's Central Station with my father and Uncle Brian. They had accompanied my mother's body from Hartford. My uncle was in a bad state. The Canadian customs officer at the border insisted on inspecting a number of suitcases containing my mother's belongings. Dad explained the situation to him, but this did not deter the officer. At the sight of my mother's clothes and personal articles, my uncle broke down. On the way home by taxi, I sat beside my father. He was not the kind of man to display his emotions, and I was surprised, but pleased, when he slipped his hand into mine and held it firmly as we drove home in silence. Members of both sides of my large family had already gathered in our home before my father, my sister and I arrived. I went right upstairs to my bedroom to be alone for a while. Soon I saw a hearse park in front of the house and my mother's casket was carried along the pathway leading to the stairs before our front door. I could hear the commotion in the downstairs hall as my mother's body was placed in the glassed-in conservatory beside our living room. She and I had spent many happy hours there growing and arranging flowers and plants we bought at the Atwater Market or at greenhouses on the South Shore across the river. My grandmother and her children, my uncles and aunts, followed the casket into the house. Grandmother was dressed in black, including her overcoat and hat, and, in the Victorian tradition, she would remain in deep mourning for two years. This included a black border around her notepaper. She was visibly distraught and literally stumbled along on the arms of my Uncle Chil and Aunt Rooney. I could hear her mumbling: "Oh, Nonnie, my dear beloved little Nonnie." I went down-stairs. The casket was closed and my grandmother arranged a blanket of white calla lilies over the top and sides of the casket. She was acting in good faith, but there was no question in her mind that this prime space on the casket was reserved for her. Oddly enough, I don't think the matter ever entered into the minds of my Dad and his children. That's just how things were. Granny Heward was the undis-puted and loving head of the family.

I sat at our dining room table beside my dad's older brother, my Uncle Stewart, whom I truly liked. He must have thought I was sleepy or in pretty bad shape for he kept giving me karate-like chops in the back of my neck. My Aunt Rooney told me the casket would remain closed and that she had put a transparent veil over my mother's face and a red rose over her folded hands.

Aunt Rooney handed me a red tin box with fruit painted all over it. The paint had not dried. There were cookies inside with a note from my mother dated Thursday, November 25 that read: "Heward, I painted this box and baked these cookies for you today. Enjoy them.

My mother, Honor Grafftey (second from the left),
as a Red Cross worker, France, 1916

All my love, Mommy." When all the family and guests had parted, I went to bed only to awake in the middle of the night. I tiptoed down into the conservatory. Youthful curiosity and a desire to see my mother's face for the last time overcame me. I pulled back my grandmother's flower blanket from the top of the casket but looked away just as I had the top of the coffin half open. My heart pounded, then I remembered what my aunt said the night before and thought maybe my mother's face had been terribly disfigured. I changed my plans and slowly lowered the lid of the coffin before closing it and returning upstairs to my bed for a little more fitful sleep. Little did I realize at the time that I would never lose sight of my mother's face in my mind's eye or of her voice in my inner ear.

On the morning of my mother's funeral, the house was quiet and still, with the exception of the singing and playful noises coming from Susan's room. Susan was our four-year-old guest child from England. My father and mother welcomed her to our home during the summer of 1940, and she would stay with us until Christmas of 1945.

I was not surprised that my mother produced the painted tin box for me as she was always good with her hands. In the final weeks of her stay at the Institute for Living, the staff were absolutely astounded at the results of her work in handicraft classes. This led them to believe she was making a good recovery and might soon be discharged. I was not at all surprised at my mother's exceptional accomplishments in this field. In World War I, she became a full-fledged mechanic and paramedic. She was able to change tires and adjust the engine on the ambulance she drove bearing the wounded and dying from the front lines. She could paint landscapes. Her mother and maternal grand-mother, Eliza Jones, made most of the clothes for their children. On the third floor at Peel Street beside my aunt's art studio, my grandmother would sew by the hour on an old Singer sewing machine operated by her feet, which rocked a wide metal pedal back and forth. My Uncle George Grafftey gave my mother a modern Singer sewing machine as a wedding present. It was operated by electricity and my mother merely had to touch her foot on a small pedal attached to a black box-like apparatus on the floor. On coming home from school, how often I heard the rat-tat-tat of my mother's sewing machine located on the stair landing. My mother made most of my clothes for me. While they were magnificent, I did not like being singled out from other little boys who were dressed in store-bought clothes. My mother's talent for sewing meant family and friends received marvellous gifts at Christmas and birthdays. Christmas was a time of extraordinary celebration for my mother. Her gifts to others included beautifully embroidered silk scarves with initials, suede gloves, knitted socks, and ordinary and sleeveless cable-stitched sweaters. After she died, I kept many things she made for me over the years, especially her beautiful sweaters and scarves. She taught sewing and handicraft at a Montreal orphanage where she was one of the directors. In the summertime on the veranda at Rockwood Cottage in Knowlton, I remember so well groups of my mother's lady friends gathered about her, sitting in a circle, as she instructed them in knitting and handicrafts.

On the morning of her funeral, flowers arrived at the front door of our house. I was in charge of arranging them in the conservatory and of putting the cards that accompanied them in a glass bowl in the living room so that Dad could write thank-you notes. I remember my Uncle Brian coming into the living room. He looked exhausted. He leaned on the mantle piece and wept openly for a number of minutes as the rest of the family stood by in silence. After a light lunch, I went up to my bedroom to change into my dark suit. As I looked out my window, the hearse, flower cars and limousines drew up in front of the house and parked. It was a dark grey November day. The ground was covered with a light layer of snow, enough, unfortunately, to make snowballs. Two of the drivers from the funeral home, undoubtedly feeling nobody was watching, gathered snow from the top of the wall beside our front steps and proceeded to pitch snowballs at each other.

St. John the Evangelist was packed. Once my mother's casket reached the top of the steps leading to the front door, the blanket of calla lilies was removed and replaced by a simple purple shroud with a gold cross embroidered in the center. This was, and still is, church practice. It was a good practice that recognized that poorer parishioners could not afford expensive blankets of flowers and that rich and poor are equal in the sight of God.

Rossetti's "Snow on Snow." It begins with, "What shall I bring him poor as I am? If I were a shepherd, I would bring a lamb...." As the funeral cortege wound its way north up Park Avenue on its way to Mount Royal Cemetery, many onlookers, unknown to us, bowed their heads in respect as we passed by. I appreciated it very much, but still felt I was having a bad dream. Death and funerals, like accidents, I thought only happened to other people—not me.

After the burial, the family returned home for high tea. Little Susan had remained at home. She was sort of a saving grace. She always called my father Artie. When Dad was settled in the living room, she rushed up to him and said, "Artie, did they put Nonnie in the ground?" Dad put his arms around her and squeezed her and said, "Susan, darling, Nonnie is in the arms of Jesus. She is suffering no more and some day you will meet her again." He released her and she ran off to play.

Dad said I should return to school as a boarder the next Monday. This I did, but it was hard. I remember that Monday at recess. The boys fled the class and left me alone as if I had leprosy. I sat alone in the classroom during recess, but remember one boy coming back early. He came up to me, extended his hand, looked me in the eye and said, "Heward, I was so sorry to hear about your mother." God had entered into the heart of this boy and he helped me break the ice in a very real way.

The next weekend I was allowed to return home. At around 4:00 p.m. as I approached the steps in front of our house, there waiting for me was my old Sunday school teacher from the nearby Church of the Advent, the Reverend Sydenham Lindsay. Father Lindsay was an exceptionally fine priest and a great Christian. I attended Sunday school classes in the afternoons when I was between the ages of five and nine. He was an excellent teacher. When I arrived at the front door, he asked if I would like to go down to the church with him and pray. After informing our housekeeper that I would be away with him until supper time, I left for the church, accompanied by Father Lindsay. How wonderful he was with me as we talked together in one of the front pews near the altar. To this day, I use the prayer he gave me. It went, "Dear Lord Jesus, Please bless my mother and give her joy and

Mother with our World War II guest child, Susan Douglass,
on the front lawn at Meadowlands, Knowlton, Quebec,
summer, 1942

peace in paradise with thee."

For my dad, my sister and me, the next months were inexpressibly sad. When I arrived home for the weekend, I would often find my dad sitting alone in the corner of the living room with the lights dimmed and a whisky and water in his hands. At other times, he would pace up and down the living room.

Collectively and individually, I think we all felt guilty about my mother's suicide. Even when faced with the facts of mental illness, family members must invariably cope with this sense of guilt after a suicide. They ask and say to themselves what did I do or not do to cause this terrible tragedy. In my own case, as I lay in bed at night, I recalled all the troubles I gave my mother and bad things I said to her during times of confrontation. In my current work relating to accident prevention, I have often noted that the families of accident victims invariable must cope with a similar burden of guilt.

It is said that suicide victims often signal their intentions one way or another in conversations. In my mother's case, it was only in retrospect that I realized she was calling for help. Sometime before she went to Hartford, she said to her sister, my Aunt Rooney, "If anything ever happens to me, please keep an eye on the children." While she might have been crying out for help, little could be done in 1943 to come to her rescue. Drug therapy, which might very well have saved her today, was in its infancy. The only apparent experimental treatments for her were electric shock and hypnotism. To compound matters, I subsequently discovered she was suffering simultaneously from schizophrenia and manic depression. Her suffering was unbelievable and intolerable. I witnessed it first-hand and never want to see anyone tortured in this way again.

I am not attempting to rationalize my mother's death and suicide, but she was the victim of a horrible mental disease that could not be cured at the time. She saw no light at the end of the tunnel. For her, things were hopeless, and as far as I was concerned, she committed what I choose to term an act of self-inflicted euthanasia. Many will say I am playing with words, but if my mother had acted in the same way during the terminal stages of cancer, her act would hardly be classified as suicide.

Up until the summer of 1942, when I was thirteen years old, my life seemed pretty normal and extraordinarily happy. Yet, at this time, I could detect that the foundation of this happiness was shifting onto shaky ground. My father, mother, sister and I were driving along back country roads near the farm early one evening around the beginning of July 1942. I don't know whether my sister and father noticed it, for there was no family argument or anything like it at hand. I could see that my mother, for some inexplicable reason, was in a dark black mood. In fact, while she didn't say much, I could detect she was despondent. This puzzled me, for I did not know why. There seemed to be no real reason for it as far as I could see. Nothing, to my knowledge, had gone wrong at home. Yet, even at this early date, I sensed the worst and knew my dear mother was very sick.

During the next weeks and months, she grew progressively worse. In the fall of 1942, she was getting regular psychiatric treatment. When school resumed in the fall, I returned as a five-day boarder. At the beginning of December, I was in a school play and upon returning home around 10:00 p.m. on a Friday evening for the weekend, I could detect something was terribly wrong. My mother had taken to her bed and my father and other members of the family had gathered around her bedside. I rushed to her bedroom door, but was told not to go in. I could see the look of consternation on the faces about her bed.

Before Christmas, my mother was hospitalized and my father became totally despondent. Christmas had always been the highlight of the year for my mother. Dad bought me a new Fedora hat for Christmas and I was excited to show it to my mother. After church, we drove to the hospital. Once we were in her hospital room, my mother merely stared at us. I asked her how she liked my new hat, but she never replied. Much to my horror, I realized she didn't recognize me, my father or my sister. We left her room in silence. It was not a very happy Christmas.

In mid-winter, she was moved into a psychiatric institution. In early March, I was home with a bad case of flu and mother insisted on coming home to take care of me. She stayed for two or three nights and things seemed totally normal again. She was cheerful and loving, and we had a great time just being together. Then on the third afternoon, she came into my room and bent over the bed and kissed me. She had tears in her eyes. Her face was contorted, agonized and deeply sad. I could easily see how terribly she was suffering. "Heward, dear, I shall have to leave you and go back to the hospital." In a moment, she was gone.

For a while, she seemed to get a little better. By the time the summer arrived, she seemed well enough to go back to the farm at Knowlton. We were to be sorely disappointed when she had to return to the Royal Victoria Hospital in Montreal where she could receive electric shock therapy and hypnosis. My sister bade her good-bye on the driveway at Meadowlands. My mother hardly ever wore dark sunglasses, but on this occasion she did—I believe she did it to hide the tears and sorrow in her eyes. Little did we know she would never come back.

After returning to Montreal, it was decided she would go down to the Institute for Living in Hartford. In mid-July, my sister and I drove to the city to stay at our grandmother's home on Peel Street and say good-bye to our mother. When we visited her at the hospital before she left for Hartford, she was in good spirits, but I sensed she was only putting up a front. She walked with us to the top of Peel Street at the corner of Pine Avenue and waved good-bye. I proceeded down Peel Street, walking backwards, returning my mother's waves. As I descended Peel Street, I could see less and less of her. At one time, she was only visible from the waist up. Then I could only see her head and shoulders, and finally only her head with her hand waving over it. Soon she was out of sight. I would never again see her alive.

CHAPTER FOUR

Prudence Heward

My Aunt Prue led me into the world of art with sweetness and dedication. I would watch her working with charcoal and oils in her Peel Street studio. She would take me to exhibitions at the art gallery in Montreal and talk to me about colour and form as we walked together on Mount Royal. Little did I realize how privileged my youth was in this sense—that I was being led into the world of books and literature, music and the visual arts by a caring and loving family. Only as I grew older did I realize what I was being given by my parents and aunts—that my youth, in this sense, was extraordinary. Now when I look at my books, my piano and my paintings in the living room, I remember my family with praise and thanks. I cannot begin to imagine my world without these gifts bestowed upon me.

In 1994, the National Film Board produced "By A Woman's Hand," a fascinating documentary on Aunt Prue and two of her great friends from the Beaver Hall Group, Sarah Robertson and Ann Savage. The Beaver Hall Group was made up mainly of excellent women painters. I say excellent because they were not a group of part-time amateurs gathering together informally—much of their work was by any standards outstanding. Only now are they beginning to receive proper recognition. I met so many of them in my grandmother's upstairs living room in her home on Peel Street where my Aunt Prue lived and had her studio. I met and heard of others, too; not all of them were in the Beaver Hall Group. How can I ever forget my Aunt Prue and her friends A.Y. Jackson, Arthur Lismer, Marion Scott, John Lyman, Clarence Gagnon, Gordon Webber, Ethel Seath, Nora Collier, Lillias Torrence Newton, Isabelle McGlaughlin, André Bieler and his wife Jeannette, Mabel Lockerby, Annie Savage, Kay Morris and Sarah Robertson.

In the summer of 1961, A.Y. Jackson visited my home in Knowlton. I had first met him at my aunt's memorial exhibition at the National Gallery in Ottawa in the early spring of 1948. Subsequently, I invited him on many occasions to dine with me at the Parliamentary Restaurant in the late fifties. At that time, he lived in centre town Ottawa. Before visiting me in Knowlton, he had opened an exhibition of Canadian paintings at a small art gallery in the nearby town of Cowansville. While he was with me, I showed him some of my Aunt Prue's paintings. We were standing before one of her sketches in my bedroom when I asked, "Alec, was my Aunt Prue one of our best women painters?" He became slightly irritated and replied, "Heward, forget the woman part of your question. In my opinion, she was the very best painter we ever had in Canada and she never got the recognition she richly deserved in her lifetime. I wanted her to join the Group of Seven, but like the Twelve Apostles, no women were included."

My Aunt Prue was born July 2, 1896. She originally studied under William Brymner at the School of Art and Design of the Art Association of Montreal. Around 1922, she received her first public recognition and in 1928, the Group of Seven invited her to Toronto to show two of her paintings, *Jones' Creek* and *Torina*, in their exhibition at the Art Gallery of Ontario. She was thirty-two. The next year, her magnificent *Girl on the Hill* won the Willingdon Art Prize and she became the focus of national attention. Later, in 1929, her painting *Rollande* would establish her international reputation as a figure painter. In 1933, she became a founding member and vice-president of the Canadian Group of Painters.

My early recollections of her when I was a little boy are very clear in my mind. When I was just five years old, I remember she liked to tickle me. She would approach me with outstretched hands saying, "Tick tock, wind up the clock." I would flee. She stayed with my grandmother on Peel Street. I have already described my formidable

Grandmother Heward. She cared for my Aunt Prue in every way, giving her the freedom to paint. Aunt Prue had her living quarters and studio on the top floor on Peel Street. It is hard for me to describe the third floor at Peel Street. Her studio was at the back of the house overlooking a yard. As soon as we reached the top of the stairs, we could smell the pungent odor of her oils. As far as I can remember she always painted standing up, blocking out broad strokes of charcoal on her canvasses. Watching her mix her oil paints on her palette with a knife-like object was fun for me. Her bathroom was covered with murals, as were some of the walls in her bedroom. Her bedroom was truly magnificent. By the windows, facing Peel Street, was a narrow chaise longue, with a mattress and pillows, set over the radiators. Aunt Prue would rest there sometimes, reading the *New Yorker*, but more often books, lots of books. She was a voracious reader. It was easy to see that from her conversations. Between the windows were mirrored panels over which she had painted magnificent designs of flowers and vines. Her boat-like bed, painted silver, was unique. With a gray and chartreuse colour scheme with accents of red, the room had an art deco look, including the chrome and black lacquered furniture, and her desk near the entrance to her room. The total effect, while simple, was unique. I vividly recall the elegant style of her dress at family reunions. Her avant garde taste invariably engendered snide remarks from the more conservative members of the family.

At her beloved Fernbank, near Brockville, Aunt Prue slept in a screened porch overlooking the river. After her death, when I visited my grandmother, I would sleep there, too. At night, you could hear the swishing noise from boats approaching the bay in front of the house. Just before a boat would reach the bay, you could see the lights behind the trees. Then it would pass by and soon disappear on the other side of the bay. Less than a minute after it passed, I would hear a swishing noise from the shore as the waves from the boat washed up on the rocks. If, by chance, two boats passed each other in the middle of the bay, they would blow a noisy welcome to one another when they were side by side. Across the river was northern New York State. Aunt Prue told me that the cove by grandmother's house was called Smuggler's Cove. During Prohibition, booze was smuggled from the cove to New York. She said you could hear the rattling of bottles at night. I remember, as a tiny boy, seeing the RCMP and FBI gun boats patrolling the river.

When André Bieler was in Paris, he lived and worked on the Left Bank. When in Paris, Aunt Prue lived on the more conventional right bank and crossed over to the other side to study and paint. Bieler felt that the Right Bank represented her more conventional well-to-do family background, while the Left Bank represented her artistic temperament. To an extent, he was right. While Aunt Prue always communicated with me on a sensitive, artistic level, she never hesitated to correct my table manners and discipline me in the mould of her privileged and conservative background. As she lived with her mother, I could expect no less.

She was physically frail but strong-willed and had developed her own points of view on many subjects. Her strength of will and character showed in her paintings. I would like to think that she, along with my father, encouraged me to be an independent thinker to the extent I could be.

Robert Swain, Director of the Agnes Etherington Art Center in Kingston, Ontario, in a foreword to the book entitled, *Expression of Will: The Art of Prudence Heward*, wrote, "The story of Prudence Heward is one of struggle, life-offering vitality and pathos. The brittleness and frailty of her personal existence is in utter contrast to the power of her art, which, when encountered, leaves an indelible impression." Robert Henri wrote, "See things not as they are, but as you see them." Aunt Prue, like the impressionists, believed strongly in this dictum.

Aunt Prue had her first art lessons at the age of twelve. During World War I, she went overseas with my grandmother and worked for a time with the Red Cross.

Much of her career developed between the two great wars and during the Depression years. The Depression and the civil war in Spain affected her thinking and the thinking of many of her artistic friends. I remember how she and a few of her colleagues painted murals on the walls of the old Russian Samovar cabaret in downtown Montreal. Like the lovely murals at Peel Street, I imagine they have disappeared. During this time period, the Beaver Hall Group came

Aunt Prudence Heward, circa 1928.
Photo: Hugh Cecil, London

into existence. She and other artists shared space on Beaver Hall Square. Unlike the Group of Seven, they had no specific manifesto. The majority of the group, with the exception of John Lyman and a few others, were women painters. In Montreal and Toronto, a basic conservatism surrounded artistic taste. In the 1930s and 1940s, my aunt's nudes were not allowed to be hung in the Montreal Museum of Fine Arts. They were strictly forbidden.

When I was young, she would often talk to me about her work. We would visit exhibitions together where she would give me much information and many insights. It was with her that I developed a love for the French impressionists. Around that time, A. Y. Jackson had gone to Europe on a mandate for our National Gallery in Ottawa. He advised the Bennett government that most of the old masters were out of Canada's price range, but that he could pick up scores of the impressionists for a song. Much to his and my aunt's bitter disappointment, the Cabinet turned thumbs down on Alec's proposal. Today, the impressionists are surely out of Canada's price range.

I also accompanied my Aunt Prue to Sunday afternoon concerts of the Montreal Symphony at His Majesty's Theatre. But mostly she went alone because she never knew whether or not her guests really liked classical music and this made her uncomfortable. She knew my love for the symphony and how we enjoyed the concerts together! After they were over, we would walk along Sherbrooke Street and drop by the Ritz-Carlton Hotel for tea, cakes, and sandwiches. On the floor above us, in an alcove overlooking our tea area, a string quartet sawed away. She encouraged me to run upstairs with requests from both of us. Aunt Prue loved Brahms, and wanted me to know and love his works. I often listened to his music with her in my grandmother's second floor living room on Peel Street. Today, whenever I play Brahms' "Intermezzi" on the piano, I think of her.

At Fernbank, I sometimes accompanied my Aunt and her friends on their "picnic sketching trips." What fun they were. More often than not, Aunt Prue completed her sketches quickly and some time before the others. When everyone had finished, they would compare notes and show off their work to each other. Their observations were always kind and supportive and the atmosphere was friendly and close.

After Sunday lunch at Grandmother's, I often walked on Mount Royal with Aunt Prue, accompanied by her dog. My aunt sort of swayed from side to side as she walked. Stopping from time to time was the highlight of these outings. She would point out a tree to me asking, "Heward, what colours do you see on the trunk and branches?" I would answer, somewhat impatiently, "Gray and blackish gray." "Look again," she replied. "Pretend you are mixing your paints and look harder. Don't you see some blue, some mauve, some white?" At a second and third glance, I saw what she meant. Just as great musicians and composers hear sounds and tones we lesser mortals have difficulty hearing, she had to look only once to see the subtle mix of colours. In much the same way, Glenn Gould would later take me into the countryside and stand by a pasture and ask me to listen to sounds that he heard and that, initially, I did not hear. Only after much prodding and encouragement, could I begin to hear what he heard in the first place.

In the late winter of 1936, Aunt Prue completed a figure painting of me. This involved many sittings in her studio. By that time, she had gained an outstanding reputation as a figure painter, especially of young children and teenagers. As opposed to portraits, so revered by the Montreal English-speaking establishment, figure painters did not, so it seemed to me, strive for an exact photographic likeness of their subjects. Their more informal treatment highlighted the artist's impressions and insights into the subject.

My sessions with her were truly memorable. I had a well-earned reputation for being a somewhat mischievous and hyperactive child. Some of the family named me "Peck's Bad Boy." With such encouragement, I dutifully tried to satisfy their expectations. Aunt Prue bribed me. She knew I loved flowers and plants and said that at each sitting I could take home one of her plants if I sat still and behaved. I cannot ever remember taking home a plant. The sittings were so very long and Aunt Prue would stand and look at me for an eternity, then she would turn around and dab her brush on the pallet before touching the canvas. Again, she would turn and stare at me. It all seemed so painstakingly long and deliberate for a restless seven-year-old. As each sitting came to a close, I had long since abandoned any expectation of a plant reward. My Aunt Prue would confirm her refusal of a plant, often after long and sometimes tearful pleadings on my part.

In early July of the summer of 1936, Aunt Prue gave my picture to my mother on her birthday—it now graces a wall in my house. While Aunt Prue painted quickly when it came to sketches and landscapes, the same cannot be said of her approach to figure painting. In this latter instance, she was so deliberate that it seemed to me "an eternity passed" before each work was completed. This fact, combined with the shortness of her lifespan, limited her output and production. She often said to me that the painting of hands offered her a huge challenge that she often wrestled with.

When I was ten years old, I was leaving a church hall after seeing a movie. My mother came to pick me up and told me Aunt Prue had been injured in an automobile accident. Her friend, Blue Haskell, swerved his car on Peel Street and hit a tree. Aunt Prue hit her head on the windshield and broke her arm as she stretched her hand out against the dashboard trying to lessen the impact. She also broke her nose. I visited her often in the hospital. She was physically frail to begin with and this incident did not help. The accident occurred about eight years before her death and was one of a few factors that hastened her end when she was struck with severe asthma. She was a smoker and enjoyed her cigarettes. Her generation was not really warned about the hazards of smoking and artists of her day were not aware of the dangers of fumes from paints and solvents. These fumes in her studio, especially in winter when the windows were shut, were obviously bad for her health and lungs. Lorne Bouchard, a Montreal artist with the eccentric habit of painting in his car with the windows shut, would eventually die of lung cancer. Fortunately, today, artists have much more information available to protect themselves from the hazards of toxic fumes.

Another factor that I know hastened Aunt Prue's end was my mother's tragic and untimely death in 1943. My aunt was totally devastated.

Aunt Prue and I shared many happy times. Driving with her was always an experience. Her first car was a yellow Chevrolet convertible with a rumble seat. Later, she bought a classy gray-blue Hudson convertible. She drove fast and sometimes carelessly and never seemed to believe she should be in the outside lane when turning left, much to the annoyance of other drivers. She liked the top down on the convertible as much as possible to get the sun. At Fernbank, she would sun herself in the nude in front of the boat house. From time to time, when I was a small boy, she would catch me peeking, but her scoldings were hardly convincing. Was I her favourite? I cannot tell and really don't care. I know one thing, however, we loved each other and we communicated well.

When I was six years old, fighting for my life at the Children's Memorial Hospital, she came by to visit me regularly. On one visit, she said she would be walking on the mountain by the back of the hospital on the following Sunday afternoon. I had often taken the same walk with her. She showed me a red handkerchief she said she would use to wave at me. I said, "But Aunt Prue, there is such a crowd up there, how will I know where you are?" There was a huge high chimney-like incinerator outside my window behind the hospital. She said she would stand as near as possible to it and be there at 3:00 p.m. on the dot. The next Sunday afternoon was bright and sunny and the nurse wheeled my bed to the window facing the mountain at a few minutes before 3:00. As the hour approached, my excitement mounted. I was somewhat apprehensive. The mountain road was thick with skiers and walkers. It was exactly 3:00 p.m. At first I could not pick out my Aunt Prue. But in no time, I could see her by the edge of the road facing the hospital, waving her red handkerchief in the air. I waved in return fighting back the tears. I could tell she could see me. She stayed for at least five minutes just staring towards my window, then she was off with her dog, Spot, a wire-haired terrier.

Aunt Prue was very attached to Spot. He died at Fernbank and I was with her when she buried him in the woods near Smuggler's Cove. It was a sad and solemn moment. Spot was replaced by a Cairn terrier named Sandy. She had Sandy for only a few years. He came to a tragic end. One late spring day, Aunt Prue was painting in her third floor studio on Peel Street. The window was open and Sandy was sitting at her feet. A dog barked in the yard below. Sandy literally flew through the open window and plunged to his death on the pavement below.

Prudence Heward (wearing hat, centre), attending session
of the Kingston Conference, Queen's University, 1941.
National Archives of Canada

Sandy was replaced by another fine Cairn terrier named Andrew. Andrew outlived my Aunt Prue. I don't believe my grandmother really liked dogs. Nevertheless, she kept Andrew with her as long as he lived—I am sure in memory of her daughter, Prue.

Aunt Prue had a number of ardent male admirers and spent many happy times with them, sometimes walking on the mountain, sometimes visiting the theatre or going to art exhibitions with them. I liked them all, and they included her cousin Frank Heward, John Fry and Blue Haskell.

When I was sixteen and had finished my third year of high school, I had to have my tonsils removed for the second time. In June I was admitted to the public ward M at the Royal Victoria Hospital. There was no air conditioning in those days, and it was oppressively hot and humid. After the operation, Aunt Prue visited me often; 3467 Peel Street was nearby. One day, she brought me a large bottle of eau de cologne and before leaving, she gave me a good rub. Unfortunately, there were some Navy veterans in the ward I had come to know. They witnessed my aunt's visit and their teasing never ended. One veteran stood over my bed and laughed, "Did auntie rub her little boy with eau de cologne—oh, how sweet!" I was not happy. This event reminded me somewhat of her visits to Knowlton. She would always bring me a present. I came to expect it and anticipated her visits with much pleasure. The gifts always had an original and artistic flavor to them, much to the chagrin of my father. One weekend she arrived with three beautiful handkerchiefs all of different colours—one bright red, another dark green and the third bright blue. After I opened the box in front of my aunt and my parents, I remember Dad saying, "What an odd present for a young boy, Prue. I want my boy to be a man's man, not a sissy." I liked the present, but was uneasy with my father.

In the late spring of 1945, as the war in Europe came to an end, the house we were renting at 69 Rosemount Crescent in Westmount was sold and we had to move out. I was a five-day boarder at my school at that time and I stayed with my grandmother and Aunt Prue on the weekends. All the spare rooms were full so I had to sleep on a couch in the upstairs living room. During this time, I saw a lot of my Aunt Prue. She was quite depressed after the death of my mother, but we did a lot together. I remember one Friday evening walking a few blocks from Peel Street to a downtown theater. We saw Humphrey Bogart and Ingrid Bergman in *Casablanca*, and we both loved it. During the next few days after seeing the movie, I arranged my own version of the song, "As Time Goes By," made famous by the movie. Aunt Prue loved to hear me play it. To this day, I play it often and think of her always.

During my weekend visits to my grandmother's in the spring of 1945, it was apparent to me that Aunt Prue's health was beginning to deteriorate. She would stay in her bed until quite late in the morning, cutting into her painting time considerably. She struggled with, and worred about her bad health. Aunt Prue depended on her mother and often said to me, "What will ever happen when mother goes."

Around this time, an event took place that pleased my aunt. The students at the University of Toronto had an annual budget that allowed them to purchase a Canadian painting to be hung in Hart House. They decided to purchase one of her beautiful figure paintings. It hangs there to this day. Recently when I was in Toronto, I visited Hart House in order to see the painting. It is magnificent. The students of that day chose well, and in so doing, they made my Aunt very happy.

Aunt Prue was meant to go to Arizona in the winter of 1947 to see, as she wrote, "what it will do for me." Her attacks worsened and instead of going to Arizona, she went with my Aunt Rooney and grandmother to the Hospital of the Good Samaritan in Los Angeles, California for further treatment. Before the end, I would phone her in Los Angeles from Sackville, New Brunswick. She pleaded with me to write often, but warned me that she was too weak to reply. In the last letter I wrote to her, I said, "Dear Aunt Prue, Soon you will be painting again and someday you will get the recognition you so richly deserve. Don't forget that J. S. Bach received little recognition in his day and that someday Canadians will recognize your work for what it is." Not long before going to Los Angeles, Aunt Prue wrote, in a letter to A. Y. Jackson, that if she could no longer paint she would die. She died on March 19, 1947.

CHAPTER FIVE

Wilder Penfield

October 31, 1934 is an easy date for me to remember. Two events occurred that would be etched in my memory forever. It was Halloween and, at six years old, I was about to attend my very first Halloween party where, for the first time, I would meet a man who would become my friend and encourage me in my life's work.

On this day, my sister and I left de Casson Road on our way to the Wilder Penfields' at 4302 Montrose Avenue. This meant walking up stone steps at the end of the street near where we lived before proceeding along Montrose Avenue to our destination. The Penfields had a lovely house constructed of light brown brick with cream-coloured wood trim and a sloped roof of black slate. By the time we reached their front door, my sister had talked me into a state of near panic. Dusk was falling and she insisted on pointing out witches swooping down from the sky on their broomsticks. She told me that the pumpkins staring out from living room windows were watching my every move. By the time we reached the Penfields' front door, I was nervous and over-excited.

My sister and I had become friends with the two youngest children in the family, Priscilla and Jeff. Their parents, like mine, placed much importance on learning other languages at a young age. We all attended Mlle Loisselle's French primary school situated in the basement of the new Sherbrooke apartments on the southeast corner of Bishop and Sherbrooke Streets.

They and their governess, Fraulein Bergmann, would arrive around 8:30 each morning in front of 2 de Casson Road where my sister and I joined them for the twenty-minute walk to school. Fraulein was meant to help the children brush up on their German. Sometimes my father would join us for the walk to school along Sherbrooke Street. We passed the high stone walls and historic towers of the Sulpician Catholic Seminary. The year 1934 was deep in the middle of the Depression and my father walked to save bus fare. Accompanying us to and from school was the Penfields' red Irish setter, Don, who had a habit of running away, causing many delays en route. He later drowned in Lake Memphramagog one summer while attempting to reach the children who were in a boat.

By the time I was six, I had already established my credentials as a mischievous kid. I was well aware that the Germans had been the enemy between 1914 and 1918, and that German soldiers had wounded both my father and my uncle. Before setting out on foot for our first walk to school with Fraulein Bergmann, I received a stern lecture from Dad about keeping my mouth shut and keeping any possible anti-German sentiments and prejudices to myself. "Who was he to talk?" I thought. I had never heard him or any of his military friends say a good word about the Germans. Suffice it to say, my behavior was exemplary.

The Penfield Halloween party was soon in full swing. Not long after we had cleaned up the ice cream from our plates, I feared for my life. A witch, in pointed black hat, suddenly appeared on the stair landing. She made menacing gestures and screamed incomprehensible threats at the children below. My fear knew no limits and my panic was total and extreme as I ran from the hallway into a small adjacent room. The room happened to be the doctor's study—the very room where he had been informed that he was being awarded the Rockefeller grant that was so instrumental in setting up the Montreal Neurological Institute which opened in 1934. As I ran into the study, the doctor was standing there and I jumped right into his arms. He settled into a big armchair and proceeded to console me while holding me on his knee. The witch turned out to be his oldest teenage daughter, Ruth Mary. He used the same tact and consoling genius with me that he used over the years with countless patients and their families, calming the fear and panic that had overcome me. He succeeded in his efforts and I soon returned to the party.

Some twenty-four years later, in the summer of 1958, I arranged a meeting between Prime Minister John Diefenbaker and Wilder and his colleagues from the Institute. The meeting, held in the Prime Minister's office, had to do with federal assistance for the Institute. When the meeting was concluded and the House of Commons went into session, Diefenbaker signalled for me to come and sit beside him. During the conversation, he said, "Heward, you must have been proud to have introduced me to Canada's greatest citizen since Confederation." Today I ask myself, "What do Canadians really know about Wilder Penfield? Do they really know who he was and what he did?"

Wilder Penfield worked on the function and dysfunction of the brain, and in 1934 he founded the landmark Montreal Neurological Institute. His research would bring him to one of the central problems that face the scientist and the philosopher—the link between brain and mind and, consequently, human behavior. Wilder was intrigued with the problems of thought and memory and their relation to brain activity, a concern he often discussed. He struggled throughout his career to advance our knowledge of his chosen field. His "Montreal procedure" for the treatment of epilepsy is known and practiced world-wide. He was a pioneer in the mapping of the brain and he continually wrestled with the question of the scientific basis for the existence of the human soul.

Penfield's concern for his patients was legendary. Brain surgery is a traumatic experience for those in need of it. He met at length with patients and their families before and after operations, helping them overcome their fear and guiding them through the trauma. Mary Roach, his anesthetist and operating room assistant, related that when he completed an operation of many hours' duration, Wilder would be totally exhausted and disorientated. Staff at the Institute would have to guide him to a taxi and give the driver precise instructions on how to get to 4302 Montrose Avenue.

Was Wilder Penfield a genius? My short answer is yes. He described himself as a plodder, which in many ways he was, but his discoveries were as important as those of Einstein or Freud in their respective fields.

No Man Alone, completed by Penfield just before his death in 1976, asserts the importance of the team effort approach during his years as director of the Montreal Neurological Institute. Penfield insisted to me and to others that this book was in no way meant to be an autobiography. I think he protested too much, for *No Man Alone*, in many ways, is autobiographical in the truest sense. From it, we get many insights into his past and beginnings.

Wilder Graves Penfield was born on January 26, 1891 in Spokane, Washington, U.S.A. to Charles and Jenny Penfield. Jenny was formerly a Jefferson. The Jeffersons were what might be termed "society people." From his mother, Wilder inherited a deep religious faith, a sense of stubbornness, determination and drive, a desire for study and education and the search for excellence in whatever he did. His father was another matter. His father, Charles Penfield, was the local general practitioner. According to Wilder, he would neglect his patients—he had a severe case of wanderlust, often going into the wilderness for weeks at a time with guide and tent. When Wilder was eight, his father left his mother. At first, the young boy was led to believe this would be merely a temporary arrangement, but his father had left for good and the separation would be permanent. That same year the family moved to Hudson, Wisconsin, where his Grandfather Jefferson looked after him, his mother, his brother and his sister. It would be fair to say that Wilder was somewhat bitter over the departure of his father and he rarely, if ever, wrote or talked about it. His father's behavior was something the young boy put behind him, but it surely left its mark.

I have always been fascinated by the influence of strong-minded and able women on sons who go on to subsequent fame. Winston Churchill comes to mind, as does Franklin Delano Roosevelt, Harry Truman, Dwight D. Eisenhower, Bill Clinton and a host of writers, artists, composers and inventors. From his mother he got, in part, his sense of stubbornness, conservative values, the belief in a sound schooling and education and spiritual direction. He did not believe in a detailed plan of predestination prepared for each of us, but he believed that God had a role for each of us to play, and that if we nurtured our spirituality and kept it alive, He would point the way. One of my own prayers, "Use me, oh God, for thy purposes," was also surely one of Wilder's exhortations. As time went on, he became less and less convinced that the Church as a bricks and mortar institution constitutes the mainstay of our spiritual existence. He felt our activities outside the four walls of a church should be the hallmark of our spirituality and God-inspired activities. As his work progressed, the relationship between the brain and the mind and man's spirituality truly captured his attention. His study of the brain and of human memory only reinforced his conviction and belief that man was fundamentally a spiritual animal, and that there is a God.

His mother had great influence on his outstanding educational achievements. In the summer of 1904, when Wilder was only thirteen, his mother went to the Presbyterian Church in Hudson to hear a young student talk about the Rhodes Scholarship program at Oxford. Later that evening, sitting on the porch at home, she told Wilder about the talk and strongly suggested that he prepare himself to win a Rhodes Scholarship later on. That same year, his mother started the Galahad private school with a small group of friends and associates, two miles from Hudson, overlooking the St. Claire River. Wilder graduated from it first in his class, and was captain of the football team. Then it was on to Princeton. It was there he believed he could obtain a Rhodes Scholarship more easily than at other Ivy League universities. While the scholarship went to someone else, Wilder was eventually awarded his scholarship while at Wisconsin.

On leaving Princeton, he attended Merton College, Oxford. At Oxford Sir William Osler, one of Wilder's heroes, helped him accelerate his studies so that he might enter third-year medicine at Johns Hopkins. Wilder married Helen Kathleen Kermott on June 6, 1917 in Hudson, Wisconsin. From Oxford, he entered John Hopkins University for his final year in medicine and in June 1918, he received the degree of Doctor of Medicine.

Penfield was a surgical intern at the Peter Brigham Hospital in Boston. The hospital's chief surgeon was the legendary Harvey Cushing, who proved to be a great influence on him. Subsequently, there were years of work, study and research in England, France, Germany and Spain. At the Presbyterian Hospital in New York City, he met William Cone, a National Research Grant Fellow. Bill Cone was born in Connesville, Iowa and would go on to Montreal with Wilder to be his lifetime associate. While in New York, Wilder travelled to Spain and spent four and a half months in Madrid. The methods he learned there were to point the way for him in making a contribution to neuropathology, neuroanatomy and clinical research. Studying and working under Santiago Ramón y Cajal, he examined and analyzed brain cells. This experience was important in the setting up of the research arm of the Montreal Neurological Institute and the subsequent treatment of epilepsy.

After his return to New York, Wilder received the invitation that came to be known as the "Montreal offer." On June 25, 1927, Dr. Edward Archibald, the professor of surgery at McGill University, met with Penfield. He wanted Wilder to come to Montreal. On a subsequent visit to Montreal, Wilder met the distinguished Jonathan C. Meakins, professor of medicine, also at McGill, and the Dean, Charles Martin. After an interlude of study and research in Germany, Wilder accepted the Montreal offer, and in 1928 Bill Cone decided to move with him. As Wilder wrote in 1928: "... and so the Cones and Penfields converged on Montreal."

My first meeting with Wilder that Halloween day in 1934 was at a time when his life was virtually in midstream. He was 43 years old and already a man of great repute and distinction. His first application for a Rockefeller grant to establish the Institute was turned down, but then Alan Gregg of the Rockefeller Foundation, came on the scene. Wilder told me time and time again that this was a period of great anxiety for him. The Rockefeller Foundation had been seriously considering Philadelphia as a centre along the lines of Wilder's plans. Gregg subsequently visited Wilder in Montreal and, on a Sunday, lunched with the Penfields and their children in their home, after which they went to the study by the stairwell. Wilder was encouraged from this conversation. Later, the City of Montreal and the Province of Quebec offered financial assistance for the proposed Institute and in April 1932, the Trustees of the Rockefeller Foundation awarded an endowment grant of $1,232,000 for the Montreal Neurological Institute proposal. Years later, Gregg would return to Montreal to proclaim that this endowment was easily the most successful initiative of the Rockefeller Foundation in the medical field. This endowment was central for long-term planning, and years later Wilder would expound to me on his philosophy on endowments as opposed to one-shot grants. His ideas eventually influenced my work as federal Minister of Science and Technology in 1979 and 1980.

When I first met the Penfield family, they were just settling down into their new environment. Early in March 1929, six months after their arrival in Montreal, Helen noticed an ad in the *Montreal Star*. A farm was for sale on Sargent's Bay on Lake Memphramagog, some 80 miles from Montreal. This wooded inlet appealed to the Wisconsin rural background of both Helen and Wilder and would provide a restful retreat for him and his family—a retreat from the many burdens of his new work. The first summer, they rented a campsite and a small cottage on Lake Memphramagog. Wilder loved to relax and swim and fish in the lake. Later that summer, they visited Sargent's Bay and were overwhelmed by its beauty and surroundings. Soon thereafter they purchased a farm that was about to be sold at public auction. It included 233 acres and three-quarters of a mile of lakefront and they named it Magog Meadows.

There was a separate wooden building for the children with a large play area downstairs and sleeping quarters upstairs. My sister Ann frequently visited her friend Priscilla there. Helen organized and directed activities for the children with skill and imagination. Their Presbyterian background was never forgotten. Wilder and Helen nurtured a strong spiritual life and belief. There was no church conveniently located nearby, but this provided no excuse for escaping Sunday worship. There would be hymn singing with prayers and bible reading on the veranda of the main cottage, where there was an old, wooden, upright piano. As Wilder read from the Bible, the children would look towards the lake where they really wanted to be.

At first, they farmed Magog Meadows. Soon deficits mounted and farm activities claimed too much of Wilder's time. Farming was abandoned, but over the years, a family compound grew up around the original cottage. Additional cottages would house Helen and Wilder's married children and grandchildren.

Back in Montreal, my sister and her friend, Priscilla, jokingly referred to Wilder's dream come true, the Montreal Neurological Institute, as "Penfield's Palace." This new, modern structure sat atop University Street, above Pine Avenue.

In 1935 we moved from de Casson Road to 69 Rosemount Crescent, and my sister and I often visited the Penfields since we were so much closer. In 1936, Priscilla came down with tuberculosis. Treatment in those days meant lots of fresh air—often cold air. I remember when walking as a child on the mountain on Sunday afternoons seeing the children afflicted with tuberculosis at the Shriner's Hospital set out on open balconies in their beds, covered with red blankets. The Penfields built a balcony for Priscilla on the second storey at the side of their house. When we visited with her in the cold of winter, there she was in bed clad in a black overcoat and toque. Priscilla had inherited the congenial and kind temperament of her parents.

At my old school, Lower Canada College, "speech night" was an annual event where prizes were awarded for academic excellence. Citizens of note were invited to give speeches. In 1941, when I was thirteen years old, I was awarded a prize for high marks during my previous school year. I could choose the book to be awarded to me. Then, my ambition was to become a doctor. The book the headmaster selected for me, after I told him I wanted a book relating to the practice of medicine, was entitled, *The Young Man and Medicine*. That year, Wilder was the guest speaker, and his speech was memorable. He talked about brain function in relation to language learning and how it was preferable to learn other languages at a young age. He said that our brain functions in such a way that the optimum time for learning languages was during our early years. When the time came for me to receive the prize from my hero, I was full of joy and pride as I walked to the podium. He greeted me with a broad smile and put his hand on my shoulder. He kept me with him much longer than most of the other prize recipients. I refer to Wilder as my hero, for at the age of thirteen, I was absorbed with the ambition to become a doctor and I knew my neighbor was no ordinary doctor. I embraced him with enthusiasm and he knew it, and I rather think he was somewhat bemused with his young friend.

At the end of 1952, Wilder was awarded the Order of Merit, the highest civilian honour in the Commonwealth. Prime Minister Mackenzie King was the only other Canadian so honoured. There are only twenty-four holders of the Order of Merit at any one time. Although possible recipients are suggested, the award is given strictly at the King or Queen's discretion.

I have many fond memories of visits and encounters with the Penfields but by far the most important visit I had with Wilder took place in June 1958, just after I was first elected to the House of Commons. Wilder and his staff had prepared extensive documentation in order to receive endowment assistance from the federal government for the Montreal Neurological Institute. His secretary forwarded it to me for study and to arrange the necessary appointments in Ottawa. I set up a meeting with Prime Minister Diefenbaker and Health Minister Waldo Montieth. On the appointed day, Wilder, accompanied by Bill Cone and Francis McNaughton (they called him St. Francis at the Institute), arrived by train. I was on hand to greet them at Ottawa's Union Station. Wilder was in a happy and expansive mood. I was still in my twenties and I could tell he was proud of his young friend. We were truly a mutual admiration duo. As he approached me on the platform, I noticed Wilder's limp, caused by his leg injury in World War I and exacerbated by countless hours standing during long operations. He was tall and big-boned, and swayed from side to side as he walked, reminding me of older farmers from my riding whose bones and frames were worn from long hours of toil on the land. I could tell he was glad to see me. His colleagues, McNaughton and Cone, could not have been nicer. Bill Cone exuded much charm and civility.

We went from the station to my office, where I briefed them and they me on the upcoming meeting with the Prime Minster and Health Minister. We then went for lunch at the Parliamentary Restaurant. During the meal, Paul Martin came over to chat. Penfield had many contacts with him as Minister of Health in the St. Laurent government. On January 26, 1957, Penfield reluctantly accepted Martin's request to do a speaking tour in India.

After lunch, we went to the Centre Block office of Prime Minister Diefenbaker, who was accompanied by his Health Minister. The meeting in the Prime Minister's office was most cordial. Diefenbaker was meeting Wilder and his colleagues for the first time, and the atmosphere was very pleasant. Montieth and his officials had obviously studied the documentation I sent to them, documentation that requested long-term endowment assistance for the Montreal Neurological Institute. The bad news was that Diefenbaker had to inform Wilder that the federal authority could not commit funds in perpetuity on an endowment basis. The good news was that the grant to the Montreal Neurological Institute for 1958-59 was greatly increased over past annual grants. The Prime Minister and his Minister also informed Wilder that future requests for annual grants would be viewed with great favour and that officials from the Montreal Neurological Institute could count on a sympathetic hearing from Ottawa. I think Wilder was pleased with the results of our meeting. I also think he knew from the very beginning about the problem Ottawa had with the question of endowments. When we left Diefenbaker's office, reporters had gathered. One reporter from the *Montreal Star* insisted on being informed about the nature of the meeting. Wilder remained silent. The reporter volunteered that J. W. McConnell, the owner and publisher of the *Star* had given much financial support to the Institute and that Penfield should be more forthcoming. Wilder merely smiled and went on his way.

When we left the House gallery and walked to Union Station, Wilder expanded on his theories on endowments for long-term scientific research. He insisted that only such endowments could ensure stability in research initiatives. He was adamant on this point, and I never forgot his lecture. Before I waved good-bye at the station platform, he thanked me most warmly for my efforts. Back in the House, Diefenbaker thanked me profusely for my work in preparing and arranging the meeting.

When I was named Minister of Science and Technology, I remembered Wilder's views on scientific research and endowments. When I assumed my post in October 1979, I found the research establishment at the university level in Canada in a state of discouragement and disarray. Research and laboratory equipment was generally worn out and outdated. Researchers were truly demoralized. The Natural Science and Research Council fell under my authority and was responsible for university research grants. While I was well aware of the impossibility of invoking assistance by way of endowments, I hit upon another course. The course involved "the five-year plan" whereby Ottawa made the usual one-year grant plus the guarantee that for the subsequent four years, Ottawa would spell out its firm intentions without giving a legal endowment commitment. My initiative was received with tremendous enthusiasm by the Canadian scientific community and proved to be a true and long-lasting success. This move was to be my single most important accomplishment during my short-lived term as science minister. It was influenced by Wilder, and I only wish he had been alive to witness his protégé in action.

At the time of my meeting with Wilder and his colleagues in 1958, it is fair to say that many Canadians considered him the greatest Canadian since Confederation. What made him great? What nurtured his genius? He was devoted to the establishment and work of the Montreal Neurological Institute. His personal leadership, before and after the founding of the Institute, is legendary. This leadership and sense of teamwork was initiated in his youth and was reinforced on the football fields of Galahad and Princeton. Penfield often claimed that the team approach was responsible for his many successes. This is true, but he was always the captain of the team and gave it indispensable leadership.

Wilder was a pioneer in what has come to be known as "the brain dominance theory." The left side of the brain constitutes our logical and verbal centre. Herein is our super computer, our memory and learning bank. The right hemisphere is the more creative, intuitive one. While Wilder claimed he was a plodder, he also drew enormously on his right brain capacity. He always had a holistic picture of what he wanted to do and be in life. We are told that great athletes have many psychological advantages over their less endowed colleagues. They visualize and internalize winning. They actually sense and picture and feel the final victory long before it arrives. They behave like winners. Wilder always kept his vision and values before him. He knew what he wanted, and went after it. The plans had been in his mind's eye for years. He was able to articulate his vision and enlist the support of Alan Gregg, which led to the Rockefeller endowment funding. The values on which he based his life were indispensable to his greatness and genius. Wilder was not narrow-mindedly religious but his spirituality was the very bedrock for his balanced life. His life was centred on the spiritual principles of decency, honesty, integrity and truth as he saw it. His balanced life included his family and recreation and emanated from his principle-centred spirituality, and in turn this gave him his strength and enormous serenity. Every time I was with him, I sensed these qualities. When I left Wilder, I was always spiritually refreshed, even when our encounter was brief.

Wilder had much to say about retirement. He hated the word, and I daresay, the reality. Governor General Georges Vanier persuaded Wilder, now in semi-retirement, to take on the leadership of the Vanier Institute of the Family. His leadership of the Vanier Institute in the 1960s proved to be rocky, to say the least. In 1972, after I completed my book, *The Senseless Sacrifice: A Black Paper on Medicine*, I visited Wilder at the Institute. He was not pleased and he gave me a stern lecture: "All you do is criticize. Where are the solutions?"

In the years between 1968 and his death in 1976, I saw a lot of Wilder and Helen. In the summer of 1968, I drove over to Magog Meadows for afternoon tea. He showed me the little cabin house where he did much of his writing, a second career he took very seriously, writing both fiction and non-fiction. But most of all we talked. He told me about being consulted long distance from Los Angeles a few weeks before as Robert Kennedy lay dying in the Hospital of the Good Samaritan after his brutal assassination. Wilder said, on being told of the nature of the wounds and the damage done, that he knew it was a hopeless situation and relayed his opinion to the callers. He also informed me about the drug developed at the Montreal Neurological Institute during World War II to combat seasickness. Seasick marines, overcome by nausea, were sitting ducks for enemy fire when they landed on the shores of Pacific islands. At Cartierville, just outside Montreal, the roller coaster at the Belmont Amusement Park served as experimental equipment for the new drug.

I told Wilder a story having to do with my constituency office. Andrew Marion lived near Magog Meadows and carried out work on Wilder's property. Marion travelled to Knowlton as he was looking for compensation for a back injury caused by a falling tree. At the beginning of the interview, he told me he had been treated and operated on at the Montreal Neurological Institute. At the end of the interview, I wanted to ascertain that it was really at the Institute where he was treated. I put the question, "Where were you operated on, Andrew?" Then came a superb malapropism. I love malapropisms, and had a great aunt who unknowingly committed at least two per day. In reply to my question, Andrew said, somewhat taken aback, "I told you already, the Montreal

Wilder Penfield in his office at the Montreal Neurological Institute.
Courtesy of the Montreal Neurological Institute.

Neurotical Institute." Wilder was amused. In the ensuing years to 1976, I travelled from time to time to Magog Meadows, usually for afternoon tea.

In 1972, an event involving his writing career took place—an event that was amusing but extremely embarrassing for me. In the years preceding my re-election in 1972, I had been practicing law in a perfunctory way, and writing.. Above all, I was campaigning for re-election to the House of Commons. Frank Lowe was the editor of *Weekend Magazine* which was a supplement placed in weekend editions of newspapers across Canada. I wrote over a dozen articles on current affairs, many of them cover stories for *Weekend*. Frank was my editor and he was truly superb. He also wrote a daily column for the *Montreal Daily Star*. He was a thick-set gnome of a man with reddish hair. He always had a twinkle in his eye and loved martinis. Unfortunately, he was also in excruciating pain from a back ailment and died soon after my re-election.

Frank was involved in organizing a get-together of writers and authors in Old Montreal. At the time, an author was considered to be anyone who had written and published one hardcover book. Wilder and I qualified for an invitation and we both accepted. The gathering of writers was a boisterous and boozy affair. Conversation was mostly incoherent, and I suspect Wilder wished he were somewhere else. I was standing beside Frank Lowe when he engaged Wilder in conversation. Frank had had more than one martini and was in a mischievous mood. "Doctor," he said, "I have read everything you have written about second careers. I have heard your comments on the subject and have been truly impressed. I have taken your remarks so seriously that, after much consideration, I have decided on my second career." "What is it?" Wilder earnestly demanded. Frank replied with the usual twinkle in his eye, "I am taking up neurosurgery." Wilder wasn't at all amused.

The 1960s and early 1970s were not easy for Wilder. It would be too facile to say that he was out of touch with the times, but the upheavals of the mid-1960s upset his sense of conservative values deeply rooted in his youth in Hudson, Wisconsin and thereafter. Long hair and pot-smoking shocked him. Listening to his pronouncement as head of the Vanier Institute for the Family, Wilder reminded me of the present Pope.

Bending his principles to satisfy what for him were alien ideas, was something he would never entertain. His notions of an orderly world were being seriously challenged, and this made him unhappy and sometimes cranky. He was not a typical establishment man, but he revered established principles, which were the very foundation of his life. He was not alone in his age group in his unhappiness over the times.

Life for Wilder was not always easy, and he had his share of sorrow and tragedy. His father's departure had been traumatic. Finances had been a problem until he became established in Montreal. He faced death and was seriously injured in volunteer service in World War I when he was a student. Yet, the real tragedy of his life was reserved for his later years. Bill Cone committed suicide by taking cyanide in his office at the Institute. He had hinted about this possible course of action to his wife, Avis. Like others, I was shocked to hear the news. It is hard to speculate why he did this. He was a classic workaholic with few extra-curricular activities, with the possible exception of bird watching. He and his wife had no children. Was he totally exhausted? Was he frustrated by the pain and suffering he saw so regularly? He was a perfectionist and he hated failure of any kind, especially the failure of his patients to get well again. Bill Cone was a truly gracious and friendly man and we often talked together. Avis was a ball of fire. Was their marriage in trouble? Who could tell? One thing is certain, Bill was deeply disappointed when he was not considered to succeed Wilder as director of the Montreal Neurological Institute. The post was to go to Ted Rasmussen. Cone was virtually Wilder's indispensable right-hand man, but Wilder never dreamed that Bill wanted the job with all its administrative demands and public relations activities. He thought, with some reason, that Bill was a hands-on surgeon dedicated to the well-being of his patients. This was true, but, nevertheless, Bill was very unhappy that he was not, at least, consulted about the succession. Is it possible that he had spent so much of his life giving to others that, when faced with an inner crisis himself, there was nothing left to help him over the hurdle. Again, it is hard to speculate. Wilder helped arrange the funeral. He was devastated. It was possible to hide the death of Guido Cantelli from Toscanini, but it was impossible to hide the facts of

Bill Cone's death from Wilder. Wilder's sadness nearly plunged him into a state of despair.

My last get-together with Helen and Wilder was both amusing and more than a little embarrassing for me. In the summer of 1973, I ran into Wilder and Helen on the street in the middle of our village of Knowlton and invited them back to our house for coffee. He gladly accepted and my wife Alida was a gracious hostess. Wilder noticed our beautiful Siamese cat, Lent, nursing her new litter of kittens. He and Helen loved animals and he got down on his knees by the cat basket and was enthralled. Joy was written all over his face. He glanced at Helen. It was obvious to my wife and me that they would love to have one of the kittens. Before I knew it, my wife asked, "Would you like to have one?" After exchanged glances, they both answered together, "Oh, yes." During the conversation that followed an insurmountable problem arose. Helen volunteered that they would have to get the cat declawed because of their furniture. My wife was aghast. She showed them a scratching post in the kitchen covered with carpet, where our cats did their scratching and even produced the cat's nail clippers. But Helen was adamant—the claws were to be removed. My wife was equally resolute. The irreconcilable standoff was embarrassing. When it came to cats' claws, I was not a man of principle. My wife claimed that nails were integral to a cat's character and personality— a virtual defense mechanism. The doctor and I stood silently on the sidelines and there was a period of agonizing silence before conversation was resumed. The Penfields left without their kitten.

After 1965, Wilder encouraged me in my work in the area of motor vehicle safety and the prevention of highway deaths and injuries. While he always had supported my political career, he never hid his disappointment that I had abandoned my wish to become a doctor, when I showed him, at the age of seventeen, my high school graduation book, which read in part, "Heward, good luck on your road to Parliament Hill." On July 1, 1965, with the assistance of Réal Casavant and Alex Brown, I prepared an all-party brief on motor vehicle and highway deaths and injuries which we presented to Prime Minister Lester Pearson. This marked the beginning of my efforts to reduce the carnage on our highways.

Wilder was very supportive. He was all to aware that over 75 percent of highway deaths and injuries involve the head. The Montreal Neurological Institute was full of accident victims with serious head injuries.

In the winter of 1966, Ralph Nader invited me to Washington, where I presented a brief to the U.S. Senate Commerce Committee on the subject of safety standards for the manufacture of motor vehicles. My testimony was carried over the U.S. and Canadian networks and, upon my return, Wilder congratulated me for my work. He displayed a real interest in my safety initiatives. He truly encouraged me. He arranged for me to address a black tie dinner of doctors and medical faculty and students at McGill on the subject of motor vehicle and highway deaths and injuries

Wilder had a great influence on my work in this area of preventive medicine. For years, Wilder's concern with the relation between the brain, mind and human behaviour was of great and vital interest to me, especially in my work in safety initiatives. It is my great hope that between now and the end of the century we will make major inroads on the world-wide epidemic of death- and injury-producing incidents, sometimes called *accidents*. To do this, we shall have to gain a greater understanding of the relation of the brain to *human behaviour* as we ask the question, "Why do people get into accidents and injury-producing situations and what can we do to reasonably influence human behavior in order to save lives and reduce injuries?" The answer is not easy. To date, superficial assumptions have produced minimal results. In conversation, I told Wilder that we must take an epidemiological approach to the challenge, with the motor vehicle as the microbe, the driver as the agent and the road and surroundings as the environment. He agreed with me and had much advice to give. As he mapped the human brain, he encouraged me in my research. My ongoing work on safety is due in no small part to his encouragement and mentoring.

On a spring day in 1975 I saw Wilder and Helen walking slowly, ever so slowly, arm-in-arm. We exchanged friendly greetings. Sadly, I realized for the first time that my hero was only human. He had visibly aged. It was the last time I saw him alive. Soon after, Helen and Wilder decided to leave Montrose Avenue and move into the Glen Eagle Apartments on the slopes of Mount Royal overlooking the city. Some time later, the doctors discovered a malignant tumor in Wilder's stomach. After an exploratory operation, chemotherapy was recommended, but Wilder decided against it.

Wilder died in a bed at his beloved Institute on the morning of April 5, 1976. On the next day I had the sad privilege of informing the House of Commons of his death, which unanimously passed my motion expressing "the gratitude of the Canadian people for the life and work of Wilder Graves Penfield."

I drove to Montreal from Ottawa to attend Wilder's memorial service at St. Andrew's United Church in Westmount. Upon entering the church, Crosby Lewis, Penfield's son-in-law, thanked me profusely for my remarks in the House. It was a lovely service. I attended it with Hugh MacLennan. Wilder must have known that two of his greatest admirers sat side by side in the church wishing him well as he entered into the Kingdom of Heaven where a special place was surely reserved for a very special man.

CHAPTER SIX

John Diefenbaker

John Diefenbaker was the most complex individual I ever met. I saw a lot of him and met with him often over a period of twenty-three years, from 1957 until his death in 1980. He was bigger than life. His changing moods made it impossible to characterize him—his life often seemed to waver between tragedy and tragi-comedy. We are inevitably faced with the question—how did a Prime Minister with a record number of 208 seats in the Commons in June 1958 lose his majority and return to the Opposition benches five short years later in early 1963?

During elections he had incredible energy and was a star performer on the hustings. As Tommy Douglas once said, "Dief could smell a vote a mile away, but couldn't administer a popcorn stand." There was much truth in Tommy's observation and many of us know by now that the ability to win an election and the ability to govern are not one and the same thing. Another positive characteristic of Dief's personality was his complete honesty in a material sense. With a couple of notable exceptions, his ministers and their aides knew better than to steal from and plunder the public coffers as long as Dief was around. No money scandals plagued John Diefenbaker's administration.

Over the years, as a young high school and college student, I saw Diefenbaker from the visitor's gallery performing in the Commons. I also heard him speak at the Canadian Club at the Windsor Hotel in Montreal in the fall of 1956 where successive Progressive Conservative leadership candidates were invited to address the club. Then I saw him during the 1956 convention in Ottawa where he won the party leadership. I first met him in person at a party gathering at the Windsor Hotel in Montreal in late February 1957. He was, by then, the new leader of the party and I had been named the new Progressive Conservative candidate for Brome-Missisiquoi. At our first encounter, he greeted me with piercing eyes and a firm handshake and said, "Congratulations, I hear you're a winner."

In mid-August, 1965, when Diefenbaker was once more Leader of the Opposition, he visited three Quebec ridings including my own. During his stay at my home and in my riding, I could not help but observe many of Diefenbaker's characteristics, both positive and negative. His visit lasted less than 48 hours, but his performance and so many of his traits displayed during the visit will be forever etched in my mind.

In August a few weeks before the writs went out for the federal election, Diefenbaker came to the eastern townships in Quebec. At the time, the party held eight seats in the province. When I heard of his planned swing through my area, like my other seven colleagues from Quebec, I was not overjoyed at the prospect of his visit. The conventional wisdom held that Dief, as Leader, was not a political asset in Quebec. To a large extent, his campaigning in my part of the country proved this assumption to be incorrect. Even in Quebec, he was still popular in the small towns and rural areas where they liked his fighting style and his championing of the underdog. In short, Dief was a formidable campaigner. This summer visit involved three ridings, starting with Standstead held by René Letourneau, my own riding of Brome-Missisiquoi, and Nicolet Yamaska held by Clément Vincent.

It was a bright and sunny afternoon when I met our leader at the Town Hall in Magog, in René Letourneau's riding. After the usual ceremonies with the Mayor and his Council, Diefenbaker signed the golden book. The next stop was at the local Dominion Textiles plant. As Diefenbaker stood in the courtyard inside the factory gates, it soon become apparent that something had gone wrong. There was no one in the courtyard to meet him. Whether it was poor advance planning on the part of the leader's office or a calculated snub orchestrated by senior officials at Dominion Textile I shall never know. Two or three years later, I learned that senior officials at Dominion Textile, had become totally disenchanted with Diefenbaker. As Diefenbaker paced up and down in the courtyard, surrounded by the national press, I could sense trouble brewing. He was incensed. Finally, a minor official emerged from the office complex beside the factory area and the tour got underway. It did not take long for Diefenbaker to observe the working conditions at the plant. They were not good and resembled conditions prevalent in 19th century England's textile mills. Diefenbaker mumbled his displeasure to me about the conditions more than once during the tour. After the tour was over, reporters gathered around the leader in the outside courtyard. They, too, had heard his comments inside the plant. One reporter asked, "Mr. Diefenbaker, what were your impressions of the working conditions you just saw?" Then all hell broke loose as Diefenbaker went into full flight. "Never in my life," he roared, "have I seen men and women obliged to work in this way. I could not believe I was touring a Canadian factory in the 20th century. Working conditions there are unacceptable," he continued as he turned and pointed towards the plant. "What a disgrace!" were his final words as he paced out of the courtyard through the plant gates. The press had their story. The headlines the next day in the *Montreal Gazette* read, "Dief slams working conditions at Dominion Textile plant in Magog."

Next on his agenda was a reception for town officials, union and business leaders and the party faithful at a local motel. Diefenbaker and his party were meant to stay there that evening before moving into my riding early the next morning. During the reception, one of the leader's aides approached me and asked if the leader could change his plans and proceed to Knowlton that same evening, have dinner with my wife and me, and stay the night before campaigning in Brome-Missisiquoi. I naturally agreed, but had to call my wife and advise her of the change in plans. One of my organizers agreed to drive my car back to Knowlton while I accompanied John and Olive Diefenbaker in his car, during which time I briefed him on plans for his stay in Brome-Missisiquoi. Diefenbaker was in high spirits and in a fighting mood. He was doing what he liked best and what he was best at doing—campaigning.

Once in our house, it was easy to see he was relaxed and ready to hit the campaign trail. My wife prepared steaks on the grill in the garden behind our kitchen, where we ate at a long table with benches. Diefenbaker devoured a good seven or eight cobs of corn with much butter. He told one story after another, but by far the most interesting part of our conversation dealt with his many appearances before the Supreme Court of Canada and his series of victories in appeal. I found it unbelievable, but he told me that these achievements in the law gave him more lasting satisfaction than his position as Prime Minister. He warned me, "Never forget, Heward, crucifixion is the fate that awaits most politicians." I could not help but feel he never ceased to see himself as the ever-oppressed underdog fighting against those he called *them, the powerful.* Olive and my wife chatted quietly together and, after dinner, went for a good walk, leaving Diefenbaker and me to talk in the living room. As the federal election was near at hand, I tried out one of my policy initiatives on him. I wanted him to articulate the idea of a property-owning democracy where the ministers of his future government would develop policies encouraging farmers to own their own farms, families to own their own homes, small business men to own their own businesses and Canadians in general to invest in Canadian enterprise. I told him I felt democracy was well served when Canadians, living in freedom, were encouraged by policies designed to give them a private property owning stake in the country. On his way upstairs to bed, he said he would give it some thought. I wasn't optimistic for, as Opposition Leader, he preferred to attack and bait Lester Pearson, in particular, and the Grits at large. Before going to bed, we visited the kitchen. He asked me to leave some milk for him in the fridge and a glass on the table as he always drank a large glass of milk before his early morning walk. He said I could accompany him on his walk if I wished, but that I should know he was a very early riser.

Before going to bed, I set my alarm for 5:30 a.m. On rising the next morning, I headed to the swimming pool for a few laps before what I knew would be a heavy day of campaigning. I had only been in the pool about ten minutes and, after completing a number of good laps, I rested for a moment at the deep end. There was John Diefenbaker sitting on the diving board with a glass of milk in his hand. "Let's go," he barked. I didn't really have time to change and merely put on a large sweatshirt and running shoes with no socks. My wet bathing suit completed the picture. Soon we were off through our stone gates, turning left and pacing towards the village at high speed as Diefenbaker counted his steps, 1, 2, 3, 1, 2, 3. It didn't take me long to realize that John Diefenbaker was still popular, especially with the rural English-speaking electors of my village. I always thought the local milkman was a Grit, but was mistaken. As we headed past Coderre's Feed and Grain Depot, the milkman stopped his truck, got out and ran towards Dief with his arm outstretched crying, "John, John, you're my man." After an animated conversation, we were on our way again. Countless early risers, French- and English-speaking, greeted my Leader with warmth and enthusiasm. We turned off Main Street onto a side street. I could see a light in Harry and Irene Seal's kitchen. They were in their late sixties and were among my avid supporters. Irene, especially, worked very hard for me during and between elections. I ran up their driveway and entered by the kitchen door at the back of their home. Irene and Harry were having their morning cup of tea. A picture of Diefenbaker and the Queen hung on the wall beside the kitchen table. Before I could ask them if they wanted a visitor, there was John standing in the kitchen doorway. Irene and Harry sat speechless. Then Irene sprang to her feet crying, "John, John," as she put her arms around him. John Diefenbaker elicited this kind of frenzied loyalty from supporters from coast to coast.

Soon we were back home at the breakfast table in the dining room with Olive and Alida. Halfway through breakfast, the phone rang. It was Ryland Daniels, Chairman of Dominion Textiles, calling from Montreal. He had just read the *Gazette* headline and was incensed. He claimed nobody had advised the plant manager in Magog about the leader's proposed visit and that was the explanation for the non-welcome. I said I knew nothing about the mix-up, as Magog at that time, was not in my riding. Daniels never spoke about conditions inside the plant and was by no means reconciled when I hung up the telephone. I told Diefenbaker about the nature of the call and he merely smiled. I detected a little look of triumph and self-satisfaction on his face.

After breakfast, Diefenbaker appeared at the top of the steps outside our front door. Members of the national press had gathered in the driveway. Diefenbaker taunted them saying, "If you got up earlier, we could have had a brisk walk together in the village." I was reminded of Harry Truman's early morning constitutionals, accompanied by the press. Diefenbaker jostled individual journalists from his perch on our front steps and answered their questions. Then we were off to the Brome Lake duck farm where he addressed thousands of ducks, standing on a box in the middle of their pen, asking them to vote for me. Bystanders bent over with laughter. He told the assembled press that duck support was largely responsible for my impressive majorities and successive victories. Our next stop was Cowansville and the traditional visit with the Mayor at the Town Hall where, once more, he signed the golden book and inspected the local band.

In 1963, Justice Minister Davie Fulton had informed me that a medium security penitentiary would be constructed in my riding at Cowansville. By the time of Diefenbaker's visit, it was nearing completion. The Leader and his party made a scheduled visit to the site. Paul O. Trépanier was the architect for the penitentiary and a good Tory blue. He greeted Diefenbaker upon his arrival and conducted him on a tour of the buildings. Diefenbaker entered one of the cells. Trépanier thought it would be funny to push a button and lock Diefenbaker and me in the cell. As the metal doors closed behind us, Diefenbaker looked decidedly uncomfortable. He, in fact, was not amused. Diefenbaker always had a sense of his office and did not appreciate anything that, in his opinion, compromised his dignity. When the doors opened, he made a hasty exit with a stern look on his face.

We still had many hours of campaigning left that day, but before resuming our itinerary, we drove back to Knowlton to my sister and brother-in-law's farm at Meadowlands. Arne, my sister's husband, was the local veterinarian. They had invited the Diefenbakers and their entourage, the press, some local party supporters and neighbours for a luncheon buffet at the farm. I knew how much John Diefenbaker liked mushrooms. Slack Brothers were famous mushroom growers in the nearby town of Waterloo, and Irving Slack, the owner, made sure we had a good supply. Arne had concocted a wonderful recipe for mushroom pies and they were delicious. Dief was ecstatic, and I have never seen so many pies devoured so quickly by all the guests.

Our next stop was the Monastery of St-Benoit-du-Lac on the shores of Lake Memphramagog. The monks always gave me a wonderful greeting as I had been able to get a number of things done for them in Ottawa. There was always an individual polling station at election time at the monastery, and it was easy to see after the votes were counted that I had a majority of the monks on my side. Fathers Walton and Thibodeau always discretely put in a good word for me. After our arrival, we lined up outside the refectory before the Abbot appeared and, as is the custom, poured holy water over our hands from a silver pitcher. Once inside, I couldn't help being amused watching the staunch Baptist Diefenbaker eating in silence beside the Abbot on a raised dais at the end of the hall. One incident caused me some embarrassment. Silence is the golden rule during the meals as prayers are chanted and homilies read. The journalists in attendance took notes at the table, talking and laughing in loud voices. Some of the monks didn't look very happy. After the meal, Diefenbaker attended an early evening prayer service in the monastery's chapel before speeding back to Knowlton for an event scheduled in the hall of the village's Roman Catholic Church of St. Edouard's. We were running late and the parade of cars kicked up a lot of dust as we sped over the rural back country dirt roads. The reception for Diefenbaker at the church hall was warm and enthusiastic. Annette Fleury, one of my ablest supporters, headed up the organization of the event, which included coffee, sandwiches, cookies and cakes. Diefenbaker was at his best moving through the crowd asking people to repeat their names and signing autographs for many young people in attendance. It was a happy event, and during the reception, the national press interviewed me on my safe car activities, since I had initiated an all-party brief on the subject on July 1 of that year. I guess the Diefenbakers wrongly assumed I was a staunch monarchist for, on arriving home, they gave

Alida and me a signed copy of a book. It was entitled, *The Mountbattens: The Last Royal Success Story*, by Alden Hatch. It still sits in my library unread.

Soon we were off again, this time to Clément Vincent's riding of Nicolet Yamaska. It was about a two and a half hour drive from Knowlton. Vincent was a very successful dairy farmer and was superbly organized. He was also Mayor of the small parish of St. Perpetue, with a population of about 500 souls. The evening rally was to be held at the Town Hall. Vincent realized that his town's small population could not sustain a well-attended meeting. He bussed in supporters from the rural areas. When Diefenbaker arrived at the Town Hall around 8:00 p.m., over a thousand people had gathered in and around the hall. It was standing room only. "How," he asked Vincent, "did you ever do this in your small town of 500 people?" Vincent just smiled. He and I delivered hard-hitting stump speeches, followed by Diefenbaker with his terrible French. Jean-V. Dufresne, the respected journalist from Montreal's *La Presse* was in attendance. He must have been thinking of Jesus and the parable of the loaves and fishes multiplied by miracle to feed the multitudes. Dufresne had a wonderful sense of humour and next morning, the headline in *La Presse* read, "Le miracle du St-Perpetue."

During this 1965 visit to the three Quebec ridings, I witnessed Dief at his fighting best. I saw the full kaleidoscope of many of the characteristics responsible for his rise and fall.

It must never be forgotten that when Dief took over his party in 1956, we only held four seats in the Province of Quebec. When he lost the leadership some eleven years later, he left the party with eight seats in my province—twice the number we held in 1956. Subsequently, Stanfield's two nations stance reduced us to two seats, Joe Clark's community of communities ultimately ended up giving us one seat, Mulroney completed the disastrous route of the party in Quebec and Canada. In this light, Diefenbaker's Quebec track record is somewhat better than the one accorded to him by conventional wisdom.

John Diefenbaker was a Progressive Conservative in the truest and best sense of the word. In the 1957-58 minority parliament, he moved forward progressively on social issues such as pension legislation. On the economic front, Don Fleming, as Finance Minister, invoked conservative economic policies to reduce government spending.

Again on the positive side, John Diefenbaker was a House of Commons man. This honour goes to few people, a name that comes to mind is the venerable Stanley Knowles. Diefenbaker could hold the House spell-bound for hours at a time—he was pure theatre. He could stand with his hands firmly grasping his sides, leaning forward and then pointing with his arms stretched before him and with his eyes darting across the floor of the House. He could be sarcastic; he could be funny; he could be melancholy and grave. Whatever the occasion demanded, he normally rose to it. His sense of humour was legendary. In his office after telling a joke, he would slap his thighs and roar with laughter.

Once on the hustings in British Columbia, two Doukhobor women appeared before the speaker's rostrum and stripped themselves naked. Diefenbaker stopped his speech, glared at them and said, "I know what those are. I was brought up on a farm." Sometimes the joke was his very own, made up spontaneously. This didn't stop him from laughing even harder. Who can ever forget his famous television interview in Kingston in the late 1960s. Flora MacDonald was working with Dalton Camp to unseat him as Leader. When asked by the interviewer what he thought of Flora, he looked puzzled and feigned surprise at such a question. Then after a calculated pause, he replied, "Flora, oh Flora, she's the finest lady who ever walked the streets of Kingston." There was one downside to his humour. If he thought the joke was particularly good, more often than not, you were obliged to listen to it on more than one occasion.

He was an inveterate storyteller. His generation liked good storytellers, and he was among the very best. His storytelling involved good theatre. He would often rise from his seat and act out his story, sometimes with amazing mimicry and superb intonation. If his acting was directed at someone he didn't like, his performance could be devastating.

On one occasion, I well remember Diefenbaker's sense of theatre directed at someone he didn't like. Peter Regenstrieff, in his column for the *Montreal Star*, predicted trouble for the Diefenbaker government long before the 1962 elections. Regenstrieff also foresaw the rise of Réal Caouette and his Social Credit Party in Quebec, and he stated his views time and time again in his column. Caouette and his party made major inroads in Quebec during the 1962 elections, proving Regenstrieff to be correct. They also reduced my majority in Brome-Missisiquoi by thousands of votes. Before the 1963 elections, Regenstrieff came into my riding and provided me with some invaluable polling data and advice about recapturing the Créditiste vote. Acting upon this advice, during the 1963 campaign, I met the Créditistes head-on in those parts of my riding where they had done well and increased my majority by a wide margin.

Later in the summer of 1963, Regenstrieff was in Ottawa and I invited him to have dinner with me in the parliamentary restaurant. We got on the elevator in the Commons lobby; we were alone. The elevator stopped on the fourth floor and Diefenbaker entered. He totally ignored us, giving the impression he felt no one was accompanying him. He held his head high, his eyes staring at the ceiling of the elevator. We reached the sixth floor where the restaurant is located. As the elevator doors opened, Diefenbaker looked directly at me and said, "I see you are with your friend, Mr. Ribbentrop." Dief's favourite insults invariably involved mixing up and confusing somebody's name when addressing them. Regenstrieff, who was Jewish, was infuriated at this reference to the Nazi leader. I was terribly saddened at Diefenbaker's unkind and ill-considered insult.

One of Dief's favourite stories involved Winston Churchill. Churchill admired Diefenbaker and his fighting qualities. At Diefenbaker's last Commonwealth Prime Minister's Conference held in London, England in the early winter of 1963, the Commonwealth Prime Ministers gathered at Churchill's residence at Hyde Park Gate for a black tie dinner. Lord Louis Mountbatten was also in attendance. Churchill had never really forgiven Mountbatten for accepting the post of Viceroy of India, given to him by Clement Attlee after World War II. To make things worse in Churchill's view, Mountbatten presided over the dissolution of this last jewel of the Empire. At the dinner, Churchill was in an irascible mood. Harold MacMillan was sitting on Diefenbaker's left. Just before the time came for brandy and cigars, Mountbatten announced that he had to leave. He was standing at the door at the end of the dining room. MacMillan whispered into Diefenbaker's ear, "Winston is about to misbehave." Churchill looked up and glared at Mountbatten. At the same time, he barked in a loud voice, "Harold, Harold, who is that man?"

John Diefenbaker had a deep faith and was a devout Baptist well familiar with his Bible. Biblical quotations came readily to him, to be used on appropriate occasions.

Little known is the fact that he was a voracious reader. He would leave the Parliamentary Library late on a Friday with many books in his arms. Normally, they would be returned by the next Friday, completely read. He was well informed and a great resource for me. On more than one occasion he would suggest good reading material for me relating to the subject at hand. If Mulroney boasted to his friends that he never read books, this was not the case with Diefenbaker. He was also a speed reader. In the early winter of 1959, I prepared a four-page brief for him on federal/provincial relations. Once in his office, I sat across his desk and handed him the brief. He glanced at it, quickly flipping over the pages, tossed it aside in little over a minute and resumed our conversation. I was more than a little disappointed that my sacred offering was dispatched with such speed and nonchalance. My disappointment was alleviated and I was somewhat encouraged when, in the ensuing conversation, I soon realized he had read and digested every point outlined in my memo.

With all these traits and characteristics in his favour the question must be asked again "Why did he and his government fall from grace so quickly?" Political commentators and historians have already analyzed the question to death. Peter Newman is notable for his lofty conclusions in this regard. The answer to the question is complex, but I have come to a number of conclusions, some more obvious than others.

Diefenbaker shared the same fate as Pierre Elliott Trudeau. Few people were neutral or lukewarm about him. You either hated or loved him. Characteristics and factors that brought him down were many. Some are now legendary. Soon after John Diefenbaker took over the reins of power in 1957, it was easy to see he was not about to cast off his role of Leader of the Opposition. Even as Prime Minister, he attacked and continued to act as Opposition Leader. Too many years to the left of Mr. Speaker were responsible for this state of affairs and Diefenbaker was frankly unable to make the transition. After the 1958 elections, I sat in what was referred to as the rump with 208 members. Many Progressive Conservative members had to sit on the Opposition benches. I sat directly opposite Diefenbaker and witnessed his attacking style from across the floor of the House. It was anything but prime ministerial.

He often referred to his adversaries as *they*. Who were *they*? They happened to be, for the most part, old-line right-wing Tories who never liked the populist prairie lawyer in the first place. They had to accept him as their new leader. After all, he had led the party to power after twenty-two years in the wilderness. He had reason to dislike these Neanderthal reactionaries. One old dowager in Montreal during the convention that named George Drew in the mid-1940s, told me that a name like Diefenbaker would never do to take the electorate. He referred to them loosely as the Establishment, whether they were Grits or Tories, and he was constantly at war with them and they with him. It is ironic that, a few years later, it was the more left-wing so-called red Tories who eventually engineered his downfall. On New Year's Eve of 1958, a television network program showed Olive Diefenbaker taking a group of journalists around 24 Sussex Drive. She felt the public should have a look at the prime minister's residence. The same old dowager already referred to, thought the televised tour was in bad taste and referred to Olive as being rather common. This small event, however, spelled trouble ahead.

John and Olive Diefenbaker were inseparable. While Olive was a loving and supportive wife, she was also, to a great extent, a bad influence on him in many ways. Whether or not it was written down on paper, she kept an enemies list before him which only served to increase his paranoia. Just after my marriage, Olive Diefenbaker invited my wife to 24 Sussex Drive for afternoon tea. Alida arrived back in our apartment late in the afternoon, visibly shaken—she was obliged to listen to a litany of stories about supposed plots within the party and about unsavory individuals not to Olive's liking. With the wind in the government's sails and 200 seats in the Commons, my wife had expected to hear about happier events.

An incident took place just a few months before Diefenbaker died which summed up, in some ways, many of the characteristics that typified his attitude to the very end. I was sitting in the lobby in the House talking with him. He told me about his youth in Saskatchewan. He wanted to attend a baseball game in Saskatoon, but couldn't afford the ticket. He soon found a solution to his problem. He went beyond the wooden outfield fence and began to watch the game through a knothole. Before long, a security guard came by and gave him a hard kick in the pants, resulting in a shiner around his watching eye. I had the impression, by the way Diefenbaker recounted the story to me, that he felt *established authority* was always kicking him in the pants. Because of this, he carried a lifelong chip on his shoulders, always referring to those who did the kicking as *they*.

His inability to make the transition from opposition to government was plagued by yet another factor. The party in opposition had made few, if any, plans for a potential transition to power. Diefenbaker had virtually no guidance from a transition team or from a well worked out transition plan. As in policy formation, his approach to the transition was hit or miss.

With 208 MPs it was hard for Diefenbaker to keep his caucus occupied and happy. His efforts in this regard were notoriously unsuccessful and his performance when it came to interpersonal relationships, especially with caucus members, was disastrous.

There was yet another factor that led to his eventual demise. Three of his senior ministers played prominent roles in the 1956 convention that named Diefenbaker Leader. Léon Balcer walked out of the convention when Diefenbaker finally won. Balcer felt Fleming was more acceptable to the Quebec electorate as he could, at least, read a French speech. Fleming and Fulton were opponents to Diefenbaker in the leadership race. I felt Diefenbaker never had the complete loyalty or support of either of these three ministers. Furthermore, Diefenbaker found it hard to understand Quebec. He got off to a bad start by naming no Quebec MP to a senior Cabinet post, and the advice he received from his Quebec ministers was questionable to say the least. Fulton's handling of the loggers' strike in Newfoundland where he wanted to use the RCMP as strikebreakers caused his Prime Minister much grief. Diefenbaker remembered the RCMP being used as strikebreakers during the Winnipeg strike at the time of the Depression and would not agree with Fulton's stand. Fleming was constantly at war with the provinces on financial matters. He was also unnecessarily combative and partisan in the Commons. His mandate culminated in the firing of Coyne as Governor of the Bank of Canada and the eventual devaluation of the Canadian dollar during the 1962 election campaign. These three ministers who opposed his leadership ambitions in 1956 severely wounded his government in the following five years.

The devaluation of the Canadian dollar in the 1962 general election confirmed Diefenbaker's suspicion of the bureaucracy. Devaluation occurred in the middle of the campaign without Cabinet approval and cost the government many seats.

Diefenbaker was a one-man show and paid very little attention to policy matters. He would announce policy on the run either on the hustings or during a scheduled speech between elections. Invariably there was little or no Cabinet consultation. Mid-way through his 1958 mandate, it was an open secret that frequent and interminable Cabinet meetings were plagued with indecision and temper tantrums by the Prime Minister. Many of his Cabinet colleagues were beginning to have serious doubts about his stability and ability to govern.

Tommy Douglas was largely correct in his assessment of Diefenbaker's administrative and organizational abilities. Every time I entered the Prime Minister's office, I witnessed chaos. Sometimes you could hardly see his head as documents and papers piled up on his desk. More often than not, he couldn't shut the top of his desk in the Commons, which was stuffed with paperwork of all kinds. Now and again, he would throw the overflow on the top of his desk and summon a Commons page to remove it. All this, coupled with his poor handling of people, was central to his eventual demise.

I am entirely convinced that if nothing else had brought

Diefenbaker and his government down, his handling of people and interpersonal relationships alone was enough to seal his fate. An old joke circulated among the caucus long before Diefenbaker's first majority mandate ran out. It was said that if every Tory MP who had been given an unfulfilled promise for a promotion or position by Diefenbaker, was asked to stand up in caucus, over half the membership would jump to their feet.

My own story illustrates the point in a clear and unmistakable way. In mid-June 1959, the Prime Minister asked me to accompany him to the City of Granby just outside of my riding. Granby's legendary mayor, Horace Boivin, had organized a 100th anniversary celebration for his city and Diefenbaker was to take part. I met the Prime Minister at Montreal's Central Station in the observation car of a private train that was to take him to Granby. Seated in the car was the Prime Minister, his wife Olive reading a copy of *Chatelaine*, and his press secretary Jim Nelson. After the greetings were over, I handed Diefenbaker a briefing book which I had prepared for him. The book contained a short history of the city and surrounding regions and a contemporary description of local industries and activities, including the well-known Granby Zoo. I also included pictures, together with biographical notes, of local dignitaries and others I assumed he would meet during his visit. Soon after my arrival, the train pulled out of the station and, after a few minutes, Diefenbaker had completed his reading of my briefing book. The train slowed at Chambly, where around 100 local citizens had gathered to greet the chief. Diefenbaker appeared on the back observation deck of the car waving enthusiastically, Harry Truman style, at the small crowd of admirers. He was in his element. When the train passed through Chambly, Olive got up and left the Prime Minister, Jim Nelson and me alone in the living room. Diefenbaker began to cross-examine me. He asked me about my activities in the private sector, my educational background and what religious denomination I belonged to. After I answered his queries, there was a long pause before he said, "I shall name you a parliamentary secretary and would like to know if you would accept. I expect to name 16 parliamentary secretaries some time this coming fall." I was truly surprised by his offer and thanked him most sincerely before telling him that it would be a real honour for me to serve in this wider capacity.

Once in Granby, the celebrations quickly got underway. Diefenbaker and his party were met at the train by a Cadillac convertible, its top down, ready to parade him through the city. Diefenbaker asked if he could be driven in another car. He did not like to be seen in expensive and ostentatious motor vehicles. His car in Ottawa was a simple medium-sized blue four-door Buick bought from a dealer in his riding of Prince Albert. Welcoming officials said it was too late to change cars, so off went the Prime Minister beside Pierre Sévigny, seated on the trunk of the car with their feet planted on the back seat, waving tentatively to the crowd. Mayor Boivin proudly showed off the city's parks, flowers and various sculptures from Europe. The Granby Zoo was the first stop. Boivin attempted to have Dief feed an elephant in front of the assembled press corps. Diefenbaker refused the request. Security was poor to say the least. Diefenbaker was visible annoyed when the same drunk accosted him at every stop with pencil in hand asking him to sign a sheet of cigarette rolling paper. Granby was in Shefford County, and even in 1958, it was held by the Grits. Mayor Boivin and the sitting member, his cousin Marcel Boivin, were both partisan opponents and Dief knew it. Dief delivered a speech at the City Hall—his French was appalling and many onlookers, including the press, snickered audibly.

I bade farewell to Diefenbaker, together with Olive and Jim Nelson, early in the evening as they boarded their train. Jim Nelson warned me not to mention Dief's offer of a parliamentary secretaryship before it was announced. With this in mind, I was somewhat astounded, a few weeks later in Montreal, when one of Egan Chambers' workers in his riding of St. Lawrence and St. George said he heard I was to be named a parliamentary secretary. Little did I realize it at the time, but this was just the beginning of a long war I would have for years to come with the party establishment on the island of Montreal. It also sowed the seed of my eventual disillusionment with Diefenbaker as a leader and, what was more important, as a man. I asked myself who planted the story and why?

In late September of 1959, I had attended a conference for

parliamentarians in Switzerland. Back in Ottawa, I was campaigning in a by-election in the section of Ottawa known as Eastview. I received a call at party headquarters in the riding from Gowan Guest, the Prime Minister's Executive Assistant, to come right away to Diefenbaker's office. The Prime Minister greeted me warmly and asked me to sit down. He then announced that he would not be able to nominate me parliamentary secretary that fall and that Egan Chambers had the nod and that I would be named his personal parliamentary secretary a year from then. I was disappointed, especially as I had resigned many good private sector posts in order to assume my anticipated increased workload in Ottawa. The consolation was that I would eventually be named parliamentary secretary to the Prime Minister, a sure stepping stone to a Cabinet post. In 1959, there was much press speculation that I was to be named a parliamentary secretary, but it was not to be that year. Over the next twelve months, time and time again Diefenbaker would take me aside saying, "I haven't forgotten my promise to you." For this reason, I was truly shocked when, a year later, my name was not included in the announced list of sixteen new parliamentary secretaries. I was only thirty-two years old and I was naive about the games of party infighting. What had gone wrong? What had I done or not done? I asked myself these questions as I began to lose a bit of self-confidence, something I usually had in abundance. After the announcement of the list of parliamentary secretaries in the fall of 1960, I met Diefenbaker once more in the rotunda outside the House of Commons. Once more he confided, "I haven't forgotten my promise to you. You'll be named during this parliament." I was puzzled and, for many reasons, more than a little sad.

In the late spring of 1962, when Diefenbaker dissolved parliament for the federal elections, a new list of parliamentary secretaries was made public. My name was not on it. Diefenbaker had broken a promise to me. Later it become apparent that one method he used, hoping to keep his troops and caucus members in line, was to keep them off balance with promises he never intended to keep or could not fulfil. In my case, such a promise was never necessary in the first place. This whole sequence of cynical madness would later boomerang and come back to haunt him.

After the Writs went out for the federal election in the spring of 1962, I was still puzzled and somewhat dejected. At the beginning of the campaign, I was asked to meet with the Leader at a motel in the constituency of Vaudreuil, represented by Marcel Bourbonnais. Diefenbaker's next stop, after a luncheon meeting at the hotel in Vaudreuil, would be my riding. When Diefenbaker completed his lunch at the motel, I met with Olive and him in their suite in order to brief him on his swing through my area. Once again, he looked at me and said, "I haven't forgotten my promise. Anyway, you are slated for bigger things than a parliamentary secretaryship." I paid no attention and Olive seemed very impatient with her husband saying, "Stop it, John. You haven't been fair with Heward." Dief glared at her.

On the way to Cowansville in the car, I sat in the front seat by the driver. Diefenbaker and Olive were in the back seat. In the middle sat my old friend, Bunny Pound, his confidential secretary. He dictated a number of letters to her and then began eating one candy after another, depositing the wrappers on the car floor. As we approached Cowansville, he told me how annoyed he was at his finance minister, Donald Fleming. He charged that Fleming had not informed Cabinet about the possibility of devaluing the Canadian dollar during the campaign. The dollar had been devalued and Pearson and the Grits were having a heyday. The Liberals distributed "Diefendollars" which were dollar bill look-alikes with a caricature of Diefenbaker where the Queen would normally be. They were intended to demonstrate the declining value of our currency under Diefenbaker and the Tories. Diefenbaker told me that we would have difficulty surviving the election. On the outskirts of Cowansville, we were greeted by the town band, awaiting our arrival. A young boy on a bicycle was peddling madly. He had adjusted his gears so as to stand virtually still on his bike in order to get a good look at the Prime Minister. Diefenbaker, watching the boy's frenzied peddling motion while standing still quipped, "He reminds me of our campaign, Heward. No forward motion."

After the results were in, we were reduced to a minority government. We had gone from 50 to 14 seats in Quebec. My own majority was substantially reduced, but I was among the survivors. It was a gruelling campaign—my third in under five years. Little did I know at the time I would fight ten federal elections between 1957 and 1980. Six of these elections resulted in minority governments.

Around the end of July 1962, I received a letter from Diefenbaker asking if I would accept a parliamentary secretaryship and to list my preferences. I did so and added at the end of my reply, "If any of the above are not available, I would consider other ministries with the exception of Finance, which I do not want." About two weeks later, my telephone rang. It was Diefenbaker's office and I was asked to meet the Prime Minister the following week at 24 Sussex Drive. I arrived at his residence early in the morning on the appointed day. Diefenbaker had broken his ankle and seemed very depressed and irritated. His downstairs study and paperwork were in total disarray. He started off by admonishing me saying he got my letter and added, "Why do you not want to be my parliamentary secretary?" I said I had put parliamentary secretary to the Prime Minister at the top of the list. He replied that was not the case and called out for my letter. A maid, the daughter of one of my workers in Brome-Missisiquoi entered the room and greeted me with a smile. She handed Diefenbaker my letter, which was on a small silver tray. He read it and replied, "By the galls, you're right. Would you be my parliamentary secretary and report to my office next week?" I accepted and left Sussex Drive with mixed feelings, knowing working with Diefenbaker would be no bed of roses. Back home in the riding, I decided to relax for a few days before assuming my new duties. Around mid-day, in the middle of the week, I was having a swim before lunch. My wife arrived at poolside saying that the Prime Minister's office was on the phone. Dief came on the line and confided, "I have good news for you. I want to name you a parliamentary secretary. George Nowlan, our Finance Minister, needs a bilingual assistant like you. He doesn't speak French and wants someone to watch Réal Caouette and his Créditistes' funny money policy." I wondered if he was crazy, devious or both. Had he honestly forgotten our meeting the week before? I protested, asking him to look at my letter where I stated that I did not want finance. He lost his temper and roared, "I'm offering you a great opportunity and you are hesitating. If you don't accept immediately, you won't be named a parliamentary secretary and that's that." I swallowed my pride and reluctantly accepted.

Working with George Nowlan and his officials in finance turned out to be an invaluable experience. Dief's parliamentary secretary must have been traumatized most of the time during the 1962-63 minority parliament. When Diefenbaker's paranoia reached its zenith, Cabinet ministers met in private to unseat him. Cabinet members loyal to Diefenbaker, such as Gordon Churchill, approached me in the Commons lobby, asking me to report anything that seemed like a plot. My minister, George Nowlan, was not considered a Diefenbaker fan and was suspected of plotting. Some ministers resigned. Others refused to run again. His policy against warheads for U.S. Bomarc missiles in Canada divided his Cabinet, resulting in the resignation of Defence Minister Douglas Harkness and Cabinet Ministers Pierre Sévigny and George Hees. The confrontations at caucus sessions were hard to imagine and Diefenbaker was becoming totally unhinged. The fates were kind to me and my short stint in finance was a much better and more rewarding experience than I could have ever wished for.

In retrospect, most of my meetings with Diefenbaker over the years had some unusual quality which only served to emphasize, one way or another, his unique characteristics. Midway through the 1957 campaign, he came to my riding. On the day of his arrival, a headline of the Sherbrooke *Daily Record* read, "Grafftey Leads Eastern Townships Push." Half a dozen candidates from surrounding ridings met to greet the Leader at a small hotel beside Orford Lake in the hills of Brome County. At the time, the hotel was owned by Red Charest. I remember a little boy called Jean playing in the dining area. He now sits in lonely isolation in the House of Commons. The meeting was uneventful in most ways. One candidate told Mrs. Diefenbaker he would be happy to give her husband French lessons. She said nothing and did not look pleased. After lunch, all the candidates met with Diefenbaker on the roof of the hotel for a photograph. One journalist asked Mr. Diefenbaker, "Mr. St-Laurent says that in Brome-Missisquoi a very young candidate is knocking on doors bothering people like a Fuller Brush salesman. What do you have to say about that?" "He's running scared and so he should," replied Diefenbaker before lighting into Prime Minister St-Laurent for what he termed his "failed policies." In a few minutes, Diefenbaker and his motorcade were off wending their way through the surrounding hills.

In late August of 1957, Diefenbaker, as Prime Minister, asked to see me in his East Block offices. When I arrived, all hell had broken loose. Derrick Bedson, his urbane and witty Executive Assistant, told me why the P.M. was in a rage. A press leak reported that Roland Michener was to be named Speaker. A combination of circumstances was responsible for Diefenbaker's intemperate outburst. First of all, Diefenbaker would not tolerate leaks of any kind. When they occurred, he went into a total tailspin and demanded that the culprit be rooted out. Secondly, the chemistry between Michener and Diefenbaker was not good. The sophisticated lawyer from Toronto and populist prairie Diefenbaker didn't hit it off. Michener wanted to be named External Affairs Minister and during my meeting with Diefenbaker, I sensed he felt Michener himself was responsible for the leak. When I entered the Prime Minister's office, he was prancing around, shouting and waving his arms in the air. The whole performance didn't seem very prime ministerial to me. We discussed Quebec politics and he indicated that the minority government wouldn't last long and that I should prepare for another campaign in the not too distant future.

Diefenbaker was true to his word. In the early winter of 1958, the House was dissolved and the government came back with a record majority of 208 seats. I really had never stopped campaigning after the 1957 vote, and in 1958, I had the highest popular vote in the province.

After the House was convened and over the next few months, a number of incidents involving John Diefenbaker took place. I can never forget them. In mid-summer Derrick Bedson, decided to leave. Bedson was a cerebral intellectual with a biting wit. Diefenbaker had inherited him from his predecessor as Leader of the Opposition, George Drew. It was easy for me to detect from the very beginning that Diefenbaker and Bedson formed an uneasy alliance. Bedson went on to become Clerk of the Council in Duff Roblin's government in Manitoba. His going away party was held in a reception room on the Senate side of the parliamentary buildings. It was a blistering hot day and, at that time, there was no air conditioning in the buildings. At the end of the reception room, there was a big, high, open hearth with wrought iron fireplace tools at its base. One of our west coast members had a snout full. As I talked to him, he was swaying from side to side, his eyes rolling in his head. Soon, high drama ensued when he stumbled backward into the fireplace and passed out. I, together with a couple of my colleagues, was attempting to free him from his entangled state among the wrought iron when the Prime Minister made his entrance. Diefenbaker passed in front of the hearth, pretending not to notice my embattled colleague fumbling in the fireplace. He passed by shaking hands with his usual, "Hello, how are you?" seemingly oblivious to the plight of one of his backbenchers. At this time, Diefenbaker was a staunch teetotaller. Once Winston Churchill offered him a brandy, and as Diefenbaker refused, stating his views on alcohol, Churchill explained that it was too bad and added, "You're not hurting anybody but yourself." From then on, much to the distress of the national press and others, receptions at 24 Sussex Drive were to be dry affairs with cakes, sandwiches, small eats and soft drinks, but no booze. In the first place, John Diefenbaker was a practicing Baptist and Olive was staunchly opposed to the grape. In his early years in opposition, Diefenbaker enjoyed the odd beer. One day he had received a letter from the ladies of the Christian Women's Temperance Union in Saskatchewan saying how much they admired his opposition to the bottle. Diefenbaker, the consummate politician, never touched a drop after receiving the letter.

That same summer, an event took place which did not show Diefenbaker at his best. Dwight Eisenhower, President of the United States, and the Queen came to Montreal to open the St. Lawrence Seaway. At the opening ceremonies, the Queen and the President sat on the welcoming platform in the front row as heads of state. Diefenbaker, not being a head of state, was relegated to the second row with other officials and he was furious. He made it known that Canada was the host country and that the protocol involving head of state niceties should be waived and ignored. He sat sulking throughout the historic ceremonies shaking his head from side to side.

In the summer of 1958, I received an encouraging letter from

With John Diefenbaker and caucus colleagues in the garden,
24 Sussex Drive, on a hot and humid evening, summer, 1960. Only tea,
sandwiches, cakes, and soft drinks were served—no alcohol—much to
distress of the press corps.

Diefenbaker. Like myself, he realized how very easy it would be for the party membership to become complacent and overconfident with such a lopsided majority. Like myself, he was a grassroots man and both of us had to fight hard over a long period of time to gain our seats in the Commons. The letter dated September 17, 1958, read:

> Dear Heward:
> Now that the first Session of the Twenty-fourth Parliament is over, I take this opportunity to thank you for your part in making it as successful from the point of view of the Government and our Party as I believe it was. I am sure you will agree with me that the record of achievement since we took office on June 21st, 1957, is an impressive one. You will shortly be receiving an extensive outline of these achievements and I would urge that no opportunity be lost to remind your constituents and others of the very substantial nature of the accomplishments of this, the first Conservative Government, in so many years.
> As a party, we have much to be proud of but we must, at all costs, guard against over-confidence, particularly in the matter of constituency organization. In many parts of the country, the organizations which carried us through the elections of 1957 and 1958 are comparatively new and much remains to be done in consolidating the ground gained. I have asked our National Headquarters to undertake (in co-operation with our Members, constituency presidents and former candidates) a complete check of the status of the organization in all 265 constituencies. The objective for the period between now and the opening of the next Session is the establishment of a broadly-based, representative Federal Conservative Association in every constituency in Canada. By this I mean an association:
> a) which will take invite into its membership all who may wish to associate themselves with the future of the party;
> b) which will have an up-to-date written constitution;
> c) which will have a fully elected executive;

d) which will hold regular meetings of both the executive and the association.

Your full co-operation in this with those who are charged with the responsibility of achieving it will be appreciated.

I am, with best regards,
Yours sincerely

He was a true and sincere believer in grassroots input and initiatives. Ultimately, the party brass would turn its back on the importance of organizing at the grassroots level.

During the first year of the 1958 majority mandate, I noticed Diefenbaker's method of Cabinet organization. I am well aware of the British inner-Cabinet tradition where a select number of senior Cabinet ministers meets to decide on major policy initiatives before submitting their proposals to the full Cabinet and, subsequently, to the party caucus. Starting in the late 60s, successive Canadian governments have attempted to initiate the British practice. The result has been, in my opinion, for the most part, an unmitigated disaster. United States presidents govern with a Cabinet of between 12 and 15 Cabinet members. Canada, ten times smaller than the U.S., has, for the past generation, governed with a Cabinet three to four times larger than the Cabinet south of the border. First of all, in my view, the creation of an inner Cabinet creates jealousy and confusion among Cabinet officers. Communication between the inner and full Cabinet breaks down. Ministers not in the inner Cabinet, are often subjected to decisions which are poorly communicated to them and which affect their ministries. The ministers outside the inner Cabinet, invariably have little or no input into the decisions affecting the ministries for which they are responsible. Michael Pitfield, Trudeau's Clerk of the Privy Council, started the process in Canada which ended in the disastrous performance of the Mulroney government with its Planning and Priorities Committee and layer upon layer of Cabinet committees with ill-defined and confusing responsibilities. Diefenbaker avoided this pitfall which was, from time to time, suggested to him. Instead of an inner Cabinet, he relied, informally, on a select handful of loyal friends within Cabinet, friends he felt he could count on and trust. In this group, among others, were Howard Green, Gordon Churchill, Michael Starr and Alvin Hamilton.

Towards the end of the parliamentary session in the late summer of 1958, Diefenbaker crossed the floor of the House of Commons after question period and sat beside me. He asked if I would like to be a delegate to the 13th session of the United Nations Assembly, which was to get underway in December. Naturally, I was happy to accept.

I well remember halfway through my term at the United Nations that Diefenbaker dropped by the Canadian United Nations Mission in New York and attended our morning briefing session. He was starting off on a world tour and was accompanied by his good friend Alvin Hamilton, then Minister of Northern Affairs. As we said good-bye to the Prime Minister, while standing on the sidewalk in front of the Mission as he was entering his car, a workman on a ladder was washing windows on the building. He could not help but notice the commotion surrounding our Prime Minister and asked, "What's all the fuss about?" At that time, Dief was riding high in the polls in Canada. The workman's query rudely reminded me of Canada's place in the scheme of things.

When I returned to Ottawa, I prepared some notes, which I sent along to Diefenbaker. In my memorandum, I related to Diefenbaker that the renowned Canadian journalist, Woodson Woodside, gave me a good, general definition of the purpose of the United Nations when he stated, "The world of today must have a meeting place and this is it."

At first I was puzzled by Diefenbaker's loyalty and attachment to the monarchy. I was puzzled for I felt the British monarchy constituted a form of elitism that should have been anathema to his populist instincts. I wondered if he was playing for the WASP vote. Upon closer examination, I found this was not necessarily the case. Diefenbaker was loyal to and supportive of the monarchy as an institution independent of its British connection. My colleagues from the west explained to me that many westerners had come to Canada from eastern Europe to escape the yoke of Communism. They had been affected by Czarist considerations and, like their counterparts of British origin in Canada, supported the institutions and traditions of monarchy. Some westerners literally chose Canada because of the institution of monarchy. Today, with changed immigration patterns, it is more than conceivable that the institution of a foreign monarch in Canada will soon disappear.

Early in the winter of 1959, an event took place in my parliamentary career which had to be seen to be believed. During Question Period in the House, Lionel Chevrier got into a shouting match with a government minister. The House erupted, with members shouting insults at one another across the floor. The Speaker had lost control. I was sitting quietly in my seat when the Speaker arose from his chair and gravely announced, "If the member from Brome-Mississquoi refuses to remain silent, I shall have to name him." Being named means being expelled from the chamber for the remainder of the day. I had done nothing and when Question Period ended, I left the House extremely annoyed. Lionel Chevrier came up to me and said the Speaker had been unfair. His seat was near to mine and he had observed that I had remained silent during the raucous exchange across the floor of the House. The Prime Minister must have made the same observation, for soon after I arrived in my office, the telephone rang. I was asked to go immediately to the Prime Minister's small office across the corridor at the back of the House of Commons. When I entered, Diefenbaker was in a furious mood. He obviously had little liking for Speaker Michener and roared, "That was unfair—totally unfair. Michener is no longer an impartial Speaker. Such injustice will have to stop." Then, much to my amazement, he asked his secretary in the next office to get the Speaker on the line. Soon I heard the Prime Minister lashing out at Michener before banging the telephone down. "That's that." he snapped as I got up to leave.

Once back in my office, it was not too long before my phone rang again. It was Mr. Speaker. He asked if I would play squash with him at his Minto Club the next day and then have lunch with him and his wife, Nora, in the Speaker's Chamber before the House resumed that afternoon. I don't believe he realized I was in the Prime Minister's office when the phone call had been made. The next day I met Mr.

Speaker outside his chambers. We were driven to his club. It was a bitterly cold day and the squash courts and changing rooms were unheated. Back in the chambers, I had a fine lunch with him and his charming wife. At the appropriate time, he raised his wine glass and I raised mine as he said with a smile, "Here's to you." I felt it was his way of saying may bygones be bygones. Thus came to an end a bizarre episode in my early years of parliamentary life. For a young backbencher, it was pretty heady stuff.

On May 12, 1959, Diefenbaker invited me to accompany him to the annual convocation at my old alma mater, Mount Allison University, in Sackville, New Brunswick. I had graduated from Mount Allison exactly ten years before. We left Uplands Airport in the Prime Minister's Viscount, arriving in Moncton, New Brunswick just under two hours later. During the flight, the prime minister read a briefing manual I had prepared for him for his visit to my old university. On the drive from Moncton to Sackville, I was reminded of the number of times I had hitchhiked to and from Montreal on that same route on university holidays and remembered many landmarks. In a run-down area on the outskirts of Moncton, I noticed a young child squatting in a ditch. As the Prime Minister's cavalcade of cars approached, the child sprung from the ditch, totally nude and, as barking dogs often do, chased our car along the side of the ditch for a number of yards.

At the university, I was presented with formal academic garb to walk with Diefenbaker in the convocation parade. I was filled with nostalgia and very happy. At the reception following the convocation, it was a pleasure for me to introduce officials and faculty members by name to the Prime Minister. During the reception, I had never seen a receiving line move so fast in front of the guest of honour. When a guest appeared before the Prime Minister, he or she was greeted with a smile, a "How are you?" or a request for their name. They were also greeted with a firm, circular handshake moving in a small arc from right to left. This kept the line moving as each individual guest was kept in motion, unable to gain a firm footing in front of the Prime Minister. I saw an elderly lady virtually stumble past Diefenbaker as she was propelled on her way. Returning to Ottawa on the plane later that day, I referred to the record speed of the reception line.

Diefenbaker merely smiled.

We were back in the House of Commons for the evening sitting at 8:00. Diefenbaker spent much more time in the Commons than any prime minister either before or after his tenure.

Later on, in the same year, Diefenbaker called me to his office. He wanted me to campaign in the Saskatchewan provincial elections. He felt it would be a good and broadening experience for me and that I could help out especially in the French-speaking centres. I was to report to party headquarters in Saskatoon in three days. Once there, I was greeted by Senators Pearson and Hynatshyn, father of the future Governor General. The Senators presented me with a bus ticket as long as my arm. The ticket would take me from town to town throughout the province, and I was to stay with local organizers.

The campaign turned out to be an unmitigated disaster. Martin Petersen, the Tory Leader, seemed singularly uninspired. Tommy Douglas, the CCF Premier, was at the height of his popularity and the people of Saskatchewan were not about to turn their backs on him. Often meetings would be cancelled or no one showed up. I would hang around an empty hall with two or three organizers for half an hour or so after the meeting was supposed to begin. When no one showed up, we would lock up the hall and go for coffee. On one occasion, in Delmas, we found the hall locked. It took us a good half hour to locate the caretaker and get the key. Our efforts were to no avail, as no one came to listen. After a couple weeks of campaigning in hot prairie weather, I returned to Ottawa. Diefenbaker wanted to know about the elections, and on the very day of the vote, he invited me for coffee in his small office near the House of Commons. When I sat down, he started to reminisce about his days in Saskatchewan and I could detect a note of great nostalgia in his voice. At one point, he asked, "How are we going to do in the vote today, Heward?" I anticipated the question, but really had not thought out my answer. "We'll get one seat, sir." "Where?" he asked. I was stumped and as I hesitated, he said, "We'll get no seats. Why and where do you feel we'll get a seat?" he added with his eyes fixed on me. Later that night, the Prime Minister was proven correct. We got no seats and drew a complete blank in the Saskatchewan elections. That was not the end of it. For some time to come, each time I would run into the Prime Minister he would quip, "One seat—by the galls—one seat. Where did you get that idea?" He wouldn't let me off the hook, and with flashing eyes, continued to tease me. One slight consolation was in a letter I received from Diefenbaker a few days after my meeting with him. It read,

Dear Heward

I received a letter today from Hector L. Roberge, 822 James Street, North Battleford. In this letter he referred to you in these terms:

"One of my reasons for writing to you at this time is to tell you about the visit we had from Mr. William Heward Grafftey, MP. He delivered a most brilliant address; unfortunately before a poorly attended meeting, and this was most regrettable, as he had a warm and friendly message for all. I was most favourably impressed with this young man from the province of Quebec, and I am sure that he has a great future before him —in fact if I should ever be a candidate I would want him on the platforms to speak on my behalf. He was most eloquent, and honoured us by speaking a few words in French, as well as in English. Sometime when you happen to meet Mr. Grafftey in the House, or in the lobby, please convey to him my personal regards, and sincere best wishes."

Diefenbaker had no children of his own and, at times, I felt he took an almost fatherly interest in my career, writing me most supportive and encouraging letters. That made his performance regarding naming me as a parliament secretary all the more hard to understand and believe.

During a debate in the House in mid-July 1959, I had delivered a relatively partisan speech. When I was finished, I took my seat. Jack Pickerskill rose to reply. He started his remarks with, "Now we have heard from the honourable schoolboy from Brome-Mississquoi." I jumped to my feet and took the bait, hook, line and sinker. Diefenbaker saw how enraged I was and attempted to wave me down and back into my seat. The veteran parliamentarian saw trouble ahead for one of his rookie supporters and he was rightfully concerned. "Mr. Speaker," I roared, "the people of my riding have elected me to this place in spite of my youth. In future, the honourable member from Bonavista-Twillingate should refrain from personal remarks and dwell on the substance of my speech." I slumped back into my seat. The damage was done. Pickerskill rose slowly to his feet and, turning towards Mr. Speaker with a hurt and puzzled look, retorted, "Your honour, we are only wasting the time of the House. The honourable member from Brome-Mississquoi doesn't seem to realize and appreciate that I was speaking more out of envy than anything else." Diefenbaker looked dismayed. I had tangled with a veteran and was bloodied. In a day or so, I received a letter in the mail from Diefenbaker In the first paragraph, he admonished me, but the second part of the letter was full of encouragement and references to William Pitt the younger of England and his youth. I hope I learned from this experience.

In the early winter of 1960, shortly after the opening session of parliament, I was flying back with Diefenbaker from the Canadian Lumbermen's annual convention in Montreal. Diefenbaker hated flying and was nervous. Conversations with him during take-offs and landings were out of the question. His hands trembled as he adjusted his seatbelt and he would stare furtively out of the window. Conversation only resumed when we were safely on our way after take-off or on the runway after landing.

Returning to the House our car stopped at a red light in downtown Ottawa. Diefenbaker lowered his window so that an eager passerby could shake hands. I guess security would not permit this today. After this, I got to know Diefenbaker's chauffeur. He had driven for Mackenzie King and told me that he detested having to tuck the old man and his dog under a fur rug during the winter months. The chauffeur was to be further annoyed by Mike Pearson when he installed a glass barrier between the driver and passenger section of his Buick sedan, thus eliminating the possibility of being let in on state secrets or even more mundane affairs.

The parliamentary session was not long under way when the prime minister spoke to me in the concourse outside the House. He wanted me to write a speech for him, to be given at the opening of the new National Gallery on February 17th. Diefenbaker knew that my late aunt, Prudence Heward, was a well-known Canadian artist.

A few days before the official opening of the new National Gallery, I was asked to deliver my speech to the prime minister at Sussex Drive. I soon learned that I was not the only one to be flattered by a "speech request." Apparently, when he wanted a specific text, Diefenbaker would sometimes ask several people to prepare one. When I arrived, he was lying on his bed with a pair of scissors, cutting out sections from a number of texts that had already been submitted. I handed him my offering. He went through his normal speed-reading routine and soon applied the scissors to my text. On the night he delivered the speech, it was clear that my hours of effort had had little effect on his final pronouncements.

The opening took place at the Lorne Building on Elgin Street. It was a pretty ordinary office building, quite inadequate for a National Gallery, which could not begin to display even a fraction of its collection. At any rate, the Lorne building was merely to provide a temporary home; temporary in this case meant a quarter of a century.

By the spring of 1961, Diefenbaker had been in power for four years. President J. F. Kennedy came to Ottawa on an official visit. It was the President's first visit outside the United States since his inauguration at the beginning of year. During this visit, I began to have serious doubts about Diefenbaker's stability and his ability to lead. On the very day of the visit, many senior members of the government caucus expressed outrage that no provisions had been made for Members of Parliament to meet Kennedy. While they were conferring, I witnessed Diefenbaker storm into the room. He was totally out of control. I can remember him shouting the empty threat, "I could go to the Governor General any time!" While he could not have been serious, he was undoubtedly referring to the Prime Minister's traditional prerogative of dissolving the House and calling an election. When things calmed down, he agreed to have the MPs meet the President in Room 16, the official reception hall beside the Speaker's chamber in the House of Commons. I was told that Diefenbaker often carried on in Cabinet in a similar way. His outbursts and temper tantrums had become legendary among his Cabinet colleagues, who were growing more and more concerned.

Meeting Kennedy was, for me, a truly happy occasion. As I went through the receiving line, a broad smile crossed his face as we shook hands. I guess I looked even younger than my thirty-two years for he said, "Do you get the same deferential treatment I did as a young congressman?" He was surprised when I asked him to remember me to a very dear Kennedy family friend, David Hackett. I got to know David well during my law school years at McGill. During my conversation with Kennedy, Diefenbaker frowned and seemed restless at my lengthy exchange with the President.

Diefenbaker's famous feud with Kennedy is now well recorded. Things went from bad to worse when Kennedy dropped a note on the floor while conferring with Diefenbaker in his office. The note addressed to a presidential aide read: "How do you deal with this SOB?" Unfortunately, after the President departed, Diefenbaker picked up the note and read it. The stage was set for "everlasting enmity" between the Prime Minister and the President. Later on, Diefenbaker would say to me, while imitating Kennedy's New England accent, "I have nothing to learn from this young pup. He won't push me around." Diefenbaker's attitude, for me, was incomprehensible. That the relationship between Canada and the United States could so suffer because of such personal incompatibility seemed unbelievable.

At the end of the day, during the presidential visit, my sister and I went up to the top of the Peace Tower to see Kennedy and his wife, Jackie, drive across Parliament Hill. They passed beneath us in an open convertible. I remember remarking to my sister how easy it would be for a sharpshooter standing where we were to fire on the presidential couple.

Some years later, in March, 1968, I was preparing for a national televised program on poverty in Canada. I was to anchor and narrate the program and had gone to the still photo division of the National Film Board to select some pictures to accompany my narration. While I was choosing some suitable pictures, the head of the unit asked to speak with me. He showed me some beautiful photos of President

Kennedy's visit to Ottawa in May, 1960. Only the NFB were authorized to photograph the presidential visit once the presidential party
reached the Parliament Buildings. The pictures were magnificent.
There was only one problem. After the disagreeable altercation
between Diefenbaker and Kennedy during the visit, when their enmity
had been solidified, Diefenbaker ordered the pictures to the National
Film Board archives. They were not to be seen again. I immediately
selected some of the pictures and organized them in a series starting
with the President entering the main door of the Parliament Buildings
under the Peace Tower until the time he completed his visit in the
Parliament Buildings. I contacted Bruce LeDain of McKim Advertising
in Montreal. LeDain had worked with me on my past two federal
election campaigns. We mounted the pictures around the Canadian
coat of arms and noted they represented Kennedy's first presidential
visit outside the United States. There was a beautiful flow of movement
in the photos and the whole montage was beautifully framed. On a
rainy, early spring morning, I crossed Parliament Hill to the United
States Embassy, where I had an appointment with the Ambassador.
He accepted my gift with great pleasure. It was agreed that on that
very day it would be transported by a U.S. government plane to
Washington and delivered to Senator Robert Kennedy. Senator
Kennedy phoned and also wrote me. He was obviously glad to receive
the pictures and thanked me most warmly and sincerely. At the
completion of the Kennedy Library in Cambridge, Massachusetts, I
telephoned Dave Powers, the library's curator. He assured me the
photographs were in good hands.

The year leading up to the 1962 elections was one of declining
fortunes for the Diefenbaker government. Diefenbaker and Finance
Minister Donald Fleming had a historic clash with the Bank of Canada's
Governor, James Coyne, which ended with the unprecedented firing
of the Governor. The straw that broke the camel's back was the
devaluation of the Canadian dollar during the 1962 campaign. The
business community was gradually losing confidence in the government. Finance Minister Fleming had always said that devalua-tion of
the dollar would never be invoked. But it was and Mike Pearson's
opposition flooded the country with Diefendollars. The Diefendollar

was a replica of an ordinary dollar bill, together with an unflattering picture of Fleming and Diefenbaker, with a section that could be torn off representing the dollar's freefall. Diefenbaker knew he and his government were in deep trouble. Key sections of the population had turned against him, and his back was against the wall. When the votes were counted, he lost over a record 100 seats and was reduced to a minority position.

"Never let your dreams turn into a nightmare" was a little advice given to me at an early age. In the first weeks of 1963, I witnessed an embittered prime minister fighting for his survival. Witnessing this stage of Diefenbaker's career, I was reminded of Samuel Johnson's comment that "power and resentment are seldom strangers." Slowly but surely Diefenbaker's dream was turning into a nightmare. As prime minister of a majority government, he bore the major responsibility for our decline into a minority situation. Yet, it is my firm conviction that his tough campaigning in 1962 saved our party. While the electorate had their misgivings about Diefenbaker, they did not wish to fully entrust majority power to Pearson.

In the first days of January, 1963, I kept hoping that we could postpone the election until we had a more positive record to put before the electorate. However, the roof soon fell in after a series of confidence votes, an unbelievable fiasco on nuclear policy, a number of cabinet resignations, and finally the prime minister's unwillingness to iron out differences with Réal Caouette, when his Créditistes voted against the government on a crucial vote of confidence. January and early February was a time of high political drama. Ottawa did not seem to be functioning in the real world, and Parliament Hill was cocooned in an aura of make-believe.

On February 5th, 1963, Diefenbaker made a fighting speech in the House. He said that he had entertained the thought of an election, but felt that the people of Canada "wanted us to get our legislation through."

There are many conflicting views of what happened during the supper hour following that afternoon sitting. Here is my version. There was still hope for the government. Réal Caouette wanted to confer privately with Diefenbaker; he wished to save face and tell his troops that the prime minister had listened constructively to his views and proposals. There was only one problem: Diefenbaker would not receive Caouette and none of his colleagues could persuade him to do so. As the hour approached for the House to resume sitting, George Nowlan asked Caouette whether a conversation with *him* would suffice. "You're a good Cardinal," replied Caouette, "but I must see the Pope." Yet a stubborn prime minister had refused Caouette an audience. It was vintage Diefenbaker in one of his increasingly frequent bouts of pure bloody-mindedness. That evening the vote was taken and the government collapsed. On both the Socred sub-amendment and the Liberal amendment, the combined opposition mustered one hundred and forty-two votes. Two New Democrats, Bert Herridge and Colin Cameron, voted with the one hundred and nine conservatives. There was pandemonium as Diefenbaker moved the adjournment. The clock had been turned back thirty-seven years. At 2 a.m. on July 22, 1926, the Meighen government was defeated by one vote, only because a Progressive member had inadvertently broken his pair. (Pairing constitutes an informal tradition where, for example, government members will only absent themselves from a House vote if they are paired with an opposition member who will also refrain from voting.)

I was emotionally exhausted. We had gone down, unnecessarily, because a proud prime minister would not confer with a leading member of the opposition. Little did I realize that nearly seventeen years later, after over sixteen years in opposition, I would be sitting as a minister in yet another minority Conservative administration, only to see the government collapse again. In 1963, we went down just as we were putting the finishing touches on an excellent budget. The day after the vote, Diefenbaker announced that the Governor General had dissolved the eight-month old Parliament. An election was to be held on April 8th.

My big moment of the campaign came in its last week. The party organized a huge rally for the prime minister at the Ste-Thérèse High School in Cowansville in my riding, complete with an old fashioned French Canadian supper of tourtière, pork and beans, hot rolls, coffee, and maple sugar pie. Twelve hundred people sat down for dinner. Diefenbaker often used a train during the campaign and he arrived by train in a snowstorm with Olive on April 2nd. My wife and I rode with them from the station to the hall. We were held up for a few moments as the mayor's car got stuck in the snow in front of us. This gave Diefenbaker a little extra time to tell us just what he thought of George Hees. It was a great meeting. The meal and decorations were excellent. Diefenbaker delivered a "stem-winding" speech which brought the audience to its feet more than once. There was only one disconcerting moment. A hostile national press were sitting at tables in the front row. They did everything but heckle Diefenbaker, grimacing and groaning out loud after he had delivered some of his telling sallies. Diefenbaker, the martyr, was already acting as an opposition leader and he relished the role. The next morning in the Montreal papers, the partisan Montreal press even reported we had run out of food at the meeting. This was not the case. In fact, there was a great deal of food left over which we distributed the next day to the food bank in Cowansville.

Once back at the station, I went on board the train to say good-bye to my leader. He had already retired for the evening, but Olive asked if I would go into the bedroom to say good-bye to him and give him a little boost. When I got to the door, he had already gone to bed. He looked exhausted, but had a broad smile on his face. Stretching out his arm to give me a good handshake, he congratulated me on my speech and asked me to convey his thanks to the party workers for organizing such a splendid event. "How did we do, Heward?" he asked. My broad smile gave him his answer and he reached up and touched my shoulder. I really think he was almost asleep as I reached the door and turned around to give him a final wave. It was six days before the election and it would be the last time I would see him as prime minister. His speech had given our troops a great lift.

Election day was at hand, and, as usual after voting, I toured nearly all the polls to thank our workers. Gaétan Mireault and Louis Cournoyer had been magnificent in directing the organization. My strategy had paid off. When the results were in, I had tripled my 1962 majority, and had almost cut the Créditiste vote in half. But that was the only cause for celebration. We had elected only eight members in the province and the results elsewhere were bad. The only consolation was that, because of Diefenbaker's hard-hitting campaign, it looked as if Pearson would be held in a minority position. We won no seats in Metro Toronto. Canada had elected its third minority government in less than six years. A solid block of Prairie support for Diefenbaker stopped Pearson from winning a majority, something that would elude him to the end of his stewardship. The Liberals held one hundred and twenty-six seats, to ninety-four for the Progressive Conservatives, twenty-four for the Social Credit, and seventeen for the NDP. The Grits had taken seats from Caouette in Quebec. Speaking to the country on television from Prince Albert, Diefenbaker said: "I gave the best that was in me. I followed the course that was right."

When finally he was relegated to the left of Mr. Speaker and Leader of the Opposition, Diefenbaker's depressed mood deepened. He saw plots to remove him and he was right.

In the years between 1963 and 1967, when Diefenbaker led the official opposition, two issues came before parliament that underlined the love/hate relationship I had with my leader. They were the flag issue and the debate on capital punishment.

When Lester Pearson proposed a distinctive Canadian flag, Diefenbaker immediately labelled it the, "Pearson pennant." Diefenbaker insisted that any new flag should include the Union Jack and the fleur de lys, erroneously sensing that the inclusion of the latter symbol was important to Quebecers. The debate dragged on in the house; tempers flared and friendships were broken. Diefenbaker knew that I supported a flag that was truly distinctive, a flag that had no place for the Union Jack or fleur de lys—a flag that meant something to all Canadians. At one time, he confronted me in the House and ungraciously said, "Your father was a war hero. I'm sure the flag that was draped over his coffin as it was lowered into his grave, had the Union Jack on it." I remained silent. No flag had covered my father's coffin. Diefenbaker was in orbit and constructive dialogue with him was out of the question. As the debate dragged on, I felt national unity was being seriously damaged. Finally, I rose in the House and asked that the debate end and that members support the new flag. I pleaded with Diefenbaker to end his filibuster for the good of Canada. He was enraged. As the vote was taken on the new flag, George

Nowlan turned to me with tears in his eyes and declared, "I never felt I would walk up Parliament Hill without seeing a flag that contained the Union Jack flying atop the Peace Tower." The debate ended; we had a new flag. It was not a good day for Diefenbaker and my party. After the debate was over, Diefenbaker wrote me a letter full of sarcasm. Apparently, a picture of him and me together appeared in the newspapers in Saskatchewan. He wrote me a letter that contained the following:

> One of my friends in Saskatchewan forwarded to me the enclosed newspaper clipping which shows both of us together in public. In view of your recent opposition to my initiatives in the House, I should have thought that you would feel any association with me would be detrimental to your political future and would suggest to you that, in the future, before authorizing any such pictures of us together to appear in the press that you clear the matter with my office.

Diefenbaker's antipathy towards the two-nations gambit came as no surprise to me. In the late fall of 1964, I had made a speech at McMaster University in Hamilton. During a press interview, a reporter asked me what I thought about my leader's continued references to "one Canada." I answered that I appreciated Diefenbaker's sentiments in this regard and his firm attitude had obvious merits. I had one qualification, namely, that many French-speaking Canadians, perhaps erroneously, felt that my leader's strong "one Canada" stand possibly endangered the "French fact." Little did I realize that my gratuitous qualification would plunge me deep into hot water.

The day after my Hamilton visit, I returned to my Ottawa office. Diefenbaker had obviously read the press comments about my interview. One report read, "Grafftey assails Diefenbaker's 'one Canada' stand." Not long after my arrival, the phone rang and I was called immediately to the leader's office. Soon I was confronted by an enraged lion, out of control, shaking and waving his finger at me. "By the Gaul," he screamed. "What nonsense! I never expected such an outrage from you, Grafftey. Haven't you read your history? I stand firmly with Sir John A." Dief had lost his temper. He was in orbit. At one point, he picked up an ashtray, and I was not entirely convinced he wasn't about to throw it at me. When I attempted to reply, he merely got up, went to the door, and opened it with a loud "Get out." Mike Starr, who had served with such distinction as Labour minister, was sitting in the waiting room to see the Chief. In a later conversation, he told me he nearly entered the office during the visit, as he honestly thought violence was about to break out.

The other side of the coin involved the debate on capital punishment. Diefenbaker had defended many individuals accused of murder. He had, on many occasions, taken their cases to the Supreme Court of Canada in appeal. He, like myself, was adamantly opposed to capital punishment. While I was and still am opposed to it, I believe in life sentences in the truest sense of the word for murderers. It seemed to me that his attitude on this issue was consistent with his stand on progressive social policy. During my years as a debater in high school and at university, the capital punishment issue was debated time and time again. Statistics were used to prove both sides of the argument for abolition. Was capital punishment a deterrent or not? How often had I heard the same old arguments from both sides on this issue. Immense research efforts went into the capital punishment debate from the pro and con abolition forces. These efforts proved to be of little consequence. Minds were firmly made up long before the debate started. Emotions flared, and members of the same party exchanged blows behind the curtains in the Commons. Diefenbaker was opposed by the majority of his caucus. This was not the case in the flag debate. One member of my party grabbed me yelling, "What if your daughter was raped and murdered?" How often had I heard similar pleas. I shall never forget a scene in the House of Commons after the abolition vote was taken. Larry Pennell, the Solicitor General, sat for what seemed to be an interminable time in his seat with his head in his hands.

Some time after the vote on abolition, an inmate stabbed and killed an instructor in the woodworking room at the medium security penitentiary in Cowansville in my riding. The local press demanded that I reverse my stand on abolition. I informed them quietly that the murder victim, like myself, was unalterably opposed to capital punishment.

While Diefenbaker seemed to improvise, without much consultation, on policy matters, I worked closely with him on two questions of policy during our opposition years. They involved the Constitution and federal/provincial relations and the recognition of mainland China. In 1966, Diefenbaker asked me, once more, to represent the opposition in Canada at the General Assembly of the United Nations. In the early summer of 1958, during the visit of President Eisenhower to Ottawa, Diefenbaker had the question of the recognition of mainland China listed on the agenda for discussion. When Secretary of State Dulles became aware of this fact, he hit the roof. Ike refused to intervene and the debate on the issue never came up. Diefenbaker supported my view in 1966 that the time was right to bring up the issue of the recognition of mainland China. While at the UN, I issued a declaration calling for the admission of mainland China to the UN.

The other issue I worked on from 1962, when we were a majority government, and during our opposition years, related to constitutional renewal and federal/provincial relations. As early as March 1962, I had written the Prime Minister on the subject of federal/provincial relations, and on April 2, 1962, he replied as follows:

Dear Heward,

I am very much interested in your view of an agency for provincial affairs. I am going to have my colleagues look into it and examine its implications as there is the possibility that it might be misunderstood. Whatever the decision ultimately made thereon the thought that you have given to this important question is bound to challenge alternatives. I am grateful to you for your ideas.

As Leader of a minority government in 1963, Diefenbaker was the victim of partisan attacks from the Opposition. Because he turned thumbs down on the Opposition proposal for a bilingual and bicultural commission—the B&B Commission it was called—he was unjustly accused of being anti-French and anti-Quebec. He told me he had more fundamental changes in mind. His changes involved an "Estates General" that would consult with the people from coast to coast on constitutional changes and renewal.

After his election in June 1960, Jean Lesage, as Premier of Quebec, proposed an "opting out" formula for Quebec relating to joint federal/provincial programs such as health care and pensions. When this happened, I realized the time had come to adopt a modern constitution for modern times. Dief agreed with me and encouraged me to speak out. Since the early 60s, I have made speech after speech on the subject, both inside and outside the House of Commons relating to the necessity of scrapping the present Constitution and drafting a new one. Diefenbaker supported me in this view.

While my riding was not really typical of the rest of Quebec, my experience in representing it has largely shaped my views that with leadership and understanding, French and English can co-exist from coast to coast. A unilingual French Quebec and a unilingual "rest of Canada" is not the new Canada I envisage. Such a phenomenon would make the union mean and meaningless. The work ahead, to bring Canada together in a spirit of understanding, cooperation and unity, will not be easy. It will require time and patience, hard work and application, all carried out in a spirit of give and take. Yet if we look at the current situation, we must admit time is not on our side.

The federal/provincial constitution conference in Victoria, Trudeau's attempts at patriation (excluding Quebec), Meech Lake and finally Charlottetown were the last nails in the coffin of a constitutional framework perhaps suited to a bygone age but no longer suitable to meet the demands and realities of a new and exciting Canada. We do not know our strength if we do not know our history. Not forgetting our past, we must start anew.

How many of us have tried to keep an old car on the road, only to be told by the garage mechanic that it's not worth repairing. Scrap it and get a new one. It is thus with our present constitution. Our Fathers of Confederation met 124 years ago under conditions very different from those of the present time. They put partisan political considerations aside. The birth of Canada was a unique act of statesmanship. I am sure those who drafted our initial constitutional document would be the first to recognize that it is no longer suited to contemporary realities. MacDonald and Cartier would wish us well as we go about seeking consensus for a "new constitution."

Strong personalities such as Diefenbaker are invariably surrounded by "Yes men" and are subjected to much hypocrisy. I well remembered one MP who repeatedly damned him and said that "he must go." One evening, the member in question was visiting me in my West Block office. Diefenbaker dropped by. The member jumped to his feet and, before Diefenbaker departed, he slapped him on the shoulder exclaiming unabashedly, "We're right behind you, John."

In 1966, Gordon Churchill asked caucus members to sign a loyalty oath to Diefenbaker I felt this to be demeaning and refused to sign, saying, "My wife does not require me to sign such a pledge and neither should my political leader." In spite of my pleadings, I was thereafter not considered a loyalist and was suspect. Diefenbaker was not well served by such nonsense. Diefenbaker's final demise at the leadership convention in 1967 which selected Robert Stanfield, was a full scale tragedy. Even if he largely brought it about by his own actions, he deserved better. He surely did everything to make life miserable for the party's two subsequent leaders, Stanfield and Clark. When I was in Clark's Cabinet, Diefenbaker, when talking to me, would refer to him as "that young pup." He still occupied a front row seat in the Commons and gained quick and easy recognition from Mr. Speaker, as an ex-Prime Minister, at Question Period. His rambling partisan questions were patently out of order, but Mr. Speaker invariably turned a deaf ear. Diefenbaker's questions were mostly directed at Prime Minister Trudeau, who sat quietly in his seat with a smile on his face as Dief rambled on. I mistakenly thought the Prime Minister's smile represented a patronizing attitude towards his older predecessor. In conversation later on with Trudeau, I learned that I was wrong and that Trudeau had a healthy respect for the old lion.

After the defeat of his government in 1957, Louis St-Laurent would often be seen eating alone in the parliamentary restaurant. St-Laurent was a reluctant candidate in the 1957 elections, but the Liberal Party insisted that he should run. He was getting old and was tired and worn out after a world tour as Prime Minister in early 1957. Now in defeat, he was left alone. The same was true of Diefenbaker. He would come to the door of the parliamentary restaurant, look around for company and would invariably go to eat alone at any available table. If I saw this happening, I would often get up, sometimes with my guest, and join him. I heard the same stories more than once, but my God, he was always stimulating company.

After Olive's death, the fire went out of Diefenbaker He was lonely and despondent. A couple of weeks before he died, it was raining and I saw him standing with an aide out on the sidewalk below my West Block Cabinet offices. I rushed down to greet him. He wanted to eat at the West Block cafeteria, but it was closed. He seemed confused and walked away. It was the last time I would see him alive.

Diefenbaker was a baseball fan. On the night of his death on August 16, 1979, he was watching a Montreal Expos game on television. His body was taken to lie in state outside the Library in the Great Hall of Parliament. That his funeral was a great occasion was no surprise to me. After Lester Pearson's funeral in Ottawa, I remarked to Diefenbaker, "It certainly was an impressive service." "Wait till you see mine," he replied with a glint in his eyes. He was right. His funeral cortege moved off Parliament Hill and proceeded to the nearby Anglican Cathedral with much fanfare. This included an RCMP escort. I walked with the Cabinet behind the hearse and was accompanied by the Leader of the Opposition, Pierre Trudeau, sporting his new beard. As I approached the cathedral, I could see Brian Mulroney waiting on the sidewalk. As the coffin was being unloaded from the hearse, Mulroney approached me and glared at me without offering his hand and said, "Meet one of the Montreal generals." I had attacked Mulroney and what I termed the Montreal political generals for Clark's poor showing in the recent Quebec election, when only I and Roch Lasalle were elected.

The ecumenical service, with its resounding hymns, reminded me of Winston Churchill's funeral some years before in London. Churchill's coffin was borne on a barge along the Thames. Diefenbaker's coffin would be carried by private train to Saskatchewan where he would be buried beside his beloved Olive. On board were his admirers and loyalists. As I stood on the platform at Union Station, a 21-gun salute boomed as the train, bearing his body, pulled slowly away. I was standing beside Bunny Pound, his loyal private secretary. With tears in her eyes, she raised her hand and waved a last good-bye as the train passed out of sight. Diefenbaker was as large in death as he was in life.

CHAPTER SEVEN

Conrad Black

The year of Expo 67 will forever be clear in my memory. There was a genuine feeling of goodwill and optimism throughout the land. Canadians from coast to coast were pulling together in a meaningful spirit of unity. Understanding between the regions of Canada was at a high point—we even had our new distinctive flag. Earlier in the late winter of 1967, I visited with Joe Clark in his home town of High River, Alberta. Together with the local high school principal, we arranged an exchange visit of students between the high school in High River and one in Cowansville, Quebec, at the centre of my riding. This exchange between anglophone and francophone students was an unqualified success.

In the spring of 1967, Peter White, someone I had known since we were kids, visited me in Knowlton. Peter, the grandson of Gilbert Stairs, a well-known and respected Montreal lawyer, was accompanied by a friend, Conrad Black. Black stood over six feet tall with sandy hair and a pale complexion. I never speculated on the reason for the visit. I merely supposed that Black wanted to meet the local Member of Parliament and sought an introduction through White.

That was the beginning of scores of visits by Conrad to our house in Knowlton over the next few years. He rarely came back again with Peter White. Peter, a man of sophisticated airs, was always somewhat condescending towards me with my populist views and identification with rural people. White played the political game with the power elites.

During the summer months of 1967, I got to know Conrad pretty well. It was a hot summer and he enjoyed swimming in the pool in our back garden. I should say he enjoyed frolicking in our pool because he always shunned anything that resembled serious exercise. Frequently he arrived at our house with his lifelong friend, Brian Stewart, now of CBC fame. On occasion, each of them appeared with a girlfriend.

It was during meals at our table in the kitchen, in the summer of 1967, that I began to know Conrad. Like Pierre Trudeau, Conrad was already well-heeled and knew that eventually he would inherit great wealth. His attempt, in his recent book, to portray himself as something of an Horatio Alger character who rose from the meager beginnings of the *Knowlton Advertiser* weekly newspaper he started with Peter White never washed with me. While he was still in his early twenties, Conrad would arrive at our door in a black Cadillac sedan. He was obviously well-off, and would soon inherit millions from his father, George Black.

Conrad had the annoying habit of cross-examining me; in his gracious but persistent way he would drag information out of me I would never think of giving to others. When he had gone too far, he would laugh and change the subject. Never had I met anyone with such a detailed memory for past events.

He was a night person—staying up all night and often sleeping until noon. I could only get my own sleep when they left the house. Often, when I would go to wake him up in the early afternoon, he would be sound asleep in a little cabin, originally a bathhouse overlooking Brome Lake on the White's grounds, across the railway tracks from their main house. The Whites had purchased the cottage and grounds, originally owned by the late Hon. Jonathan Robinson, Member of the Legislative Assembly for Brome County and Minister of Mines under Duplessis.

In the summer of 1967, Conrad witnessed Charles De Gaulle making his famous Vivre le Québec Libre speech on the balcony of Montreal City Hall. He was in the crowd on the street below, and rushed back to Knowlton to report to me on the incident. The day of De Gaulle's historic declaration, I was being filmed and interviewed by a Radio-Canada crew in Cowansville. It was a steaming hot day and I invited the TV crew back to my home for sandwiches and beer. Conrad arrived from Montreal as we all sat on the lawn. I suggested we hit the pool and stripped down to the buff before diving in. As I ran across the lawn towards the pool, much to my wife's consternation, I cried out, "Don't look at the Member's member!" Black, in his recent book, took much poetic license concerning this isolated event. He claimed "that his friend, the eccentric Member of Parliament from Brome-Missisquoi, often greeted friends on the front steps of his home, totally nude, while announcing: 'Don't look at the Member's member.'" His story is amusing and I sympathize with Conrad because, like my father before me, I have the tendency to stretch and colour a good story with a few additions emanating solely from my fertile imagination.

During the summer months, and fall and early winter of 1967, Conrad and I established a good rapport. He was, and I assume still is, intensely interested in public affairs. He was a voracious reader and his knowledge of history was profound. It seemed that everything that he had either observed or read or had crossed his mind was ready for instant retrieval during conversation. We surely had some hot arguments and as we got to know one another and our respective views, it became apparent we did not share the same ideas on public policy. I shall not use the words "left" or "right," "socialist" or "conservative," or get caught up in the trap of traditional labels. On the other hand, while I believed the old New Deal days of Franklin Roosevelt and of direct government intervention were over, I still felt government existed to encourage a situation whereby the rules on the playing field were fair and even for everybody. I maintained that while direct government intervention and regulation might be over, public authority still has a creative role to play in influencing caring actions, that government has a role to play to help and encourage those who, through no fault of their own, are not getting a fair shake.

I am a strong believer, for example, in an activist government role in protecting the environment and the consumer and I tried to explain my philosophy of society and government to Conrad. His views were very conservative and he didn't pretend to want to listen to or appreciate my views. He also seemed indifferent when I told him that government must serve the general public interest and that the NDP had destroyed itself by becoming too closely and solely identified with the labour movement, just as the Progressive Conservative Party under Mulroney, among other reasons, destroyed itself by being identified solely with big business. I emphasized that I was a progressive in social policy and a conservative in economic policy, feeling I was a true Progressive Conservative. He obviously did not share my views. I had the impression that he had a Pavlovian reaction to anything that contradicted his right-wing philosophy of government, a philosophy that seemingly has not changed with the years. I sensed he considered me naive The division between us widened. While I respected his opinions, I feel he never respected mine, although there was much mutual respect left over for other things. He also found it puzzling that an anglo could hold down a seat in a riding that was 75 percent francophone.

Over the next two years, I would see more of Conrad. His editorials in the *Knowlton Advertiser* were definitely not written for the majority of rural people. He loved confrontation and was adept at burning bridges in his editorials.

In September 1967, our leadership convention was held in Toronto. This convention ultimately elected Robert Stanfield leader of the Progressive Conservative Party. Conrad was selected as a delegate from Brome-Missisquoi, although I was never sure whether he was a Liberal or a Conservative. Once the convention got underway, he was nowhere to be found. I was working hard for the Roblin forces and I believe Conrad also supported Roblin's candidacy. I knew he was writing some sort of entrance exam for the Laval Law School, but he told me he would be back to the convention to vote. As the hour for the vote approached, I telephoned his Toronto home. His mother said, "Don't worry. Conrad will be there." The problem was that he never showed up for the vote. After Roblin's defeat in a close race on the last ballot, I ran into Conrad on the convention floor. I was feeling down, knowing Stanfield would never wash in Canada in general and in Québec in particular. I blasted Conrad for not turning up. He said nothing, but it is doubtful that my outburst, justified as I believe it was, enhanced our relationship.

I have already noted that Conrad was a voracious reader. He would often leave my home late at night with an armload of books borrowed from my library. In the fall of 1967, when he left for Laval, he gave me Malcolm Muggeridge's book, *The Thirties*. He inscribed the book as follows: "To my friend, Heward Grafftey, for whose hospitality between stopping cars and electing the President of Canada, I shall always be grateful. Conrad. August 25, 1967." Often we passed each other on the highway. On these occasions, we would invariably stop our cars in the middle of the road and have intense chats about Canadian politics until an oncoming car would honk us on our way.

After he left for Laval, I believe he stayed, at first, in a hotel or motel. He often phoned us in Knowlton. He seemed lonely or bored, perhaps both. Surely the law curriculum at Laval, or at any Quebec law school, including my old Alma mater, McGill, could not begin to challenge his imagination, interest and intellect. During this period, Black and White, after establishing the *Knowlton Advertiser*, bought out a weekly newspaper, *L'Avenir de Brome-Missisquoi*.

L'Avenir de Brome-Missisquoi was published in Cowansville, in the neighbouring county of Missisquoi. Missisquoi County formed the larger part of my riding. Soon after, they would acquire the *Sherbrooke Daily Record*. Together, they would become the undisputed press lords of Brome-Missisquoi with control of one daily newspaper and two weekly newspapers.

In the late fall of 1967, I was attending a symposium on public affairs at Glendon College in Toronto. Before going out for dinner with Conrad, I drove to his house. We had a drink with his parents, who were inseparable. A teenage romance culminated in their marriage. Conrad's relationship with his father was unusual in a sense—they talked and argued as equals, more like college friends than father and son. Some visitors to the Blacks', more accustomed to the traditional father and son relationship, felt Conrad was often rude and offhand with his dad. I felt differently; his father encouraged this lively relationship with his son. On another occasion, that same year when I was in Toronto to give a political speech, Conrad invited me to lunch at the Toronto Club. Initially, I felt this was quite a stodgy atmosphere for the Conrad Black I felt I was beginning to know. Conrad was dressed in an expensive suit and looked quite unlike the informal fellow who frequently visited me in Knowlton. As we were having a drink before lunch in the lounge beside the dining room, something came about in our conversation that rather surprised me and made me a little sad. Conrad proceeded to give me quite a lecture on how to behave in the dining room. I know he felt I was a bit off-the-wall—he remembered me as a volatile and outgoing spirit back home in Knowlton. Of course, I was no stranger to the decorum required since I often visited clubs in London and Montreal with my Dad. On this particular occasion, I had no intention of letting Conrad down or embarrassing him, but he didn't seem to trust me and I received a lecture from him about my expected comportment. While Conrad saw the lighter side of my personality, I also think he had a good glimpse of my more serious side, but this time, he was taking no chances. During this lunch at the Toronto Club, I perceived a widening gap between the two of us. I was never capable of sacrificing friends over differences in religion and politics. Nevertheless, I sensed in Conrad his continuing transformation into a sort of prototype, albeit with original genius, of the right wing mogul. His carefree youth was slowly, but surely, coming to an end.

I felt the 1968 election was going to be a tough one for me and this premonition turned out to be correct. Like Louis St-Laurent before him, Pierre Trudeau became instantly popular in my part of the country. To make matters worse, as the election was well underway and I was low on funds, I appealed to my party in Montreal for financial help, after all I had gained the highest popular vote for my party in the province. By 1968, the disenchantment between me and Brian Mulroney was complete and mutual. At that time, he had already become involved in fund-raising and was somewhat in control of the political war chest for our party in Quebec. I phoned Mulroney for help from an outdoor phone booth in Bedford, Quebec while I was doing my door-to-door canvassing. Mulroney turned me down with a cool and firm "No."

In the same election I was broadsided by a caper that was hard to believe. The Liberal Party had designed an excellent newspaper supplement to be included in weekly or daily papers on the eve of the election. The supplement featured Pierre Trudeau as leader and could easily be adapted and printed for each local riding. The supplement prepared for Brome-Missisquoi was excellent. Weeklies in my riding were and are powerful forces. Low income families who could not afford or did not read dailies, read the weeklies over the weekend. Typically, the weekly would sit on the kitchen table from Friday to Monday. One such weekly in Brome-Missisquoi, as already mentioned, was *L'Avenir de Brome-Missisquoi*, owned by Conrad Black and Peter White. White, who was totally unelectable himself, was an avid Mulroney admirer and, as already stated, very patronizing towards me. While nominally a Progressive Conservative like Mulroney, White would be very happy to see me go down. The manager of *L'Avenir* was a notary in Cowansville named Raymond Boily. He also happened to be a Liberal organizer. White and Boily obtained the mailing list for every family in the riding—a list that went far beyond *L'Avenir's* normal weekly distribution. Boily and White were only too happy to have *L'Avenir* distribute the Liberal Party's excellent supplement on the weekend before the election. I knew I was in a tight race and that from my own past experience their initiative was a formidable vote-getter for the Liberals. I also knew it was like a torpedo striking me amidships. It was done with White's full knowledge. On the other hand, I have no real reason to believe Conrad Black was aware of this perfidious move against my candidacy—a move initiated with the knowledge and approval of a so-called Progressive Conservative who would eventually become Mulroney's chief-of-staff in Ottawa.

Some weeks after the campaign, Conrad visited my home in Knowlton. While I believe he was not implicated in this duplicity, he seemed sheepish when approaching me—a most uncharacteristic posture for Conrad Black. My friends feel I was naive, but when Conrad asked if I was mad at him because the *L'Avenir* distributed the Liberal supplement, I answered, "No."

After the 1968 elections when Conrad was pursuing his studies at Laval, I saw less of him than before. After his visit to south-east Asia, he came to Knowlton and reported his findings to me in conversation. His powers of observation and analysis of the situation there were truly remarkable.

Between 1968 and 1972, I was seeking reelection in my old riding. I only started in earnest to recapture my seat after January 1, 1970. The years 1968 to 1970 saw me pursuing a perfunctory law practice, writing newspaper columns and magazine articles for publications such as *Macleans* and *Weekend Magazine*. I would run into Conrad from time to time, often with his new-found business partner, David Radler, from Montreal. While the basic cement and chemistry of our friendship seemed to be intact, a certain distance had developed.

The years 1968 to 1972 should have been years for rebuilding my party in Quebec. After all, when Stanfield took over the provincial party in Nova Scotia, we held no seats. Stanfield travelled day and night to rebuild the party in his province, as Peter Loughheed started from scratch in his home province of Alberta. The national scene seemed to overwhelm Bob Stanfield and he was not alone in having difficulty understanding Quebec politics. In reading Conrad Black's *A Life in Progress*, I find it hard to come to the same conclusions as he did regarding the direct role he played in the elevation of Claude Wagner and Brian Mulroney within my party. It seems to me many men and women in high places, both in industry and public life, have difficulty judging character. Evaluating other people is not often their forté and Conrad Black was no exception to this general rule when it came to Wagner and Mulroney. In his book, Black passes very lightly over what, in fact, was his solid endorsement of Wagner for Leader and his encouragement of Mulroney's eventual winning candidacy.

From mid-1971 until the time of the federal elections in the fall of 1972, Stanfield attempted to convince me that Claude Wagner should be his Quebec lieutenant. He proceeded to send emissary after emissary to me to get me on side. Conrad Black, Peter White, Mulroney and his gang all made one attempt after another to convince me that we would pick up many seats in the Province of Quebec with Wagner as leader. I felt we had time to build from the grassroots up and that the population of Quebec would be revolted by the spectacle of the instant conversion of an old provincial liberal to the federal Progressive Conservative cause. Later, I became aware that the price to get Wagner on side with the Tories came in the form of a $300,000 trust fund. Stanfield, Mulroney, Black and many senior Tory organizers were aware of the trust fund deal. I let it be known that the party could not count on my cooperation for such a reprehensible initiative. Conrad continually pleaded with me to support the Wagner caper. He was wasting his time.

On the eve of the elections, the Quebec Progressive Conservative Association met in Québec City. Two thousand participants were expected. Only 300 or so showed up. We were to kick off our campaign. Fortunately, the hall where we met had sliding, adjustable walls. By the time the meeting was called to order, the walls were so adjusted to transform the larger hall into a smaller one. This gave the effect, for national television, of a well-attended meeting. Wagner sat in an ornate chair in the middle of the platform. Candidates were called upon one by one to come forward and shake hands with the newly-appointed *chef*. It reminded me of the Pope in Rome when his cardinals meet together in the Vatican and approach him one by one at his throne. When the name Heward Grafftey from Brome-Missisquoi was called, I remained defiantly in my place. After the meeting, the press asked me what was wrong. I said, "Nothing," but added, "Mr. Wagner must prove his worth. Right now he is just another candidate like the rest of us." When Wagner was interviewed at the same time, he volunteered, "I know I can count on the support of Heward Grafftey." He was dreaming. When I returned home to Knowlton, I got another call from Black pleading with me to come to my senses. The fat was in the fire.

I went into the elections in the early fall of 1972 with what I felt what was a comfortable lead in the polls. After a couple of weeks of intensive campaigning, I sensed something was wrong. Citizens in every corner of my rural, small-town riding were openly disgusted with Stanfield and his Wagnerian caper. Two campaigns were being waged in Canada by my party—one in Quebec and one in the rest of the country. The Quebec campaign featured Wagner as leader with the slogan, *Wagner c'est vrai*. God knows what the slogan meant, but Quebecers weren't going for it. If I seemed to be running as an independent, it was not my fault. I refused to put up the Wagner posters and propaganda in my riding, much to the chagrin of Mulroney, Black,

White and all the arm-chair generals in Montreal. They were incensed with my attitude and actions—actions designed, at least, to save my own seat. In mid-campaign, Walter Stewart of the *Toronto Star* visited me in my riding and accompanied me while campaigning. He had heard about my refusal to participate in our Quebec strategy and wanted to see what was going on. He heard the complaints about our Wagnerian strategy at the grassroots level. In the late afternoon, I invited him to my home for coffee. By coincidence, while we were talking, Jean-Jacques Bertrand, the former Premier of Quebec and Member of the National Assembly from Missisquoi, called. I picked up the phone in our living room where Stewart and I were talking. Stewart could not help but overhear the conversation. Bertrand was enraged. He said he would vote for me, but claimed Stanfield knew that when he, as Premier of Quebec, named Wagner to the bench, Wagner pledged he would never again enter active politics. He felt deceived and let me know it. Stewart mentioned the Bertrand call and described his visit to my riding in his column in the *Toronto Star*. Things were going from bad to worse.

As the campaign ended, Conrad and Brian Stewart, motored to Farnham. I was making some kind of presentation at the local hockey arena before approximately 2,500 spectators. Farnham had a total population of approximately 8,500 people and Conrad felt he could test my popularity and strength there by witnessing my presentation. While Farnham was traditionally very Liberal, I received a standing ovation when my time came to speak. As I left the arena, Conrad and Brian approached me. Stewart remained silent, but Conrad made a last-ditch stand to have me support Wagner. He didn't seem to realize my party was in the process of being virtually wiped out in Quebec.

As the campaign ended, party funds meant for individual candidates were drying up. Wagner's royal tour of the province was more than a little costly. Then there was the question of his $300,000 trust fund. His tour of the province was about to come to an abrupt end as he was told he was losing his own riding of St-Hyacinthe Bagot. His riding, a Tory stronghold, had been vacated for him by the Hon. Theo Ricard, a superb grassroots politician. The party then proceeded to pour unlimited funds into Wagner's riding. There wasn't much left

Conrad Black

for the rest of us.

Approximately two weeks before the end of the campaign, I was at the main gate of the Dominion Textile factory in Magog, shaking hands with the workers as they arrived at the plant. When the whistle finally sounded for the 7:00 a.m. shift, I crossed the street to have a morning coffee at a small cafe. Outside the cafe was notary Charlie Sanson. Sanson looked very glum. He had bad news for me. The party in Montreal had agreed to pay a certain amount to my agent, in instalments, during the campaign. Sanson had the last cheque for $25,000 in his hands. I was informed the day before that he had received it. There was only one problem—Mulroney and his boys in Montreal put a stop payment on my cheque. We had bills to pay and Sanson didn't know what to do. I gave him a personal guarantee for the bills, knowing if I lost I would be in bad shape. Four years without a parliamentary salary hadn't resulteded in a healthy financial situation for me.

On election eve, the good news came. I won with a majority of more than 5,000 votes. All the other seats in the province were lost to us and conceded early in the evening. The only seat that was held in the balance was Wagner's. At first, it was reported that he was going down with the other candidates. Eventually, he won with a 500 vote majority. He and I were the only victors in Quebec. Stanfield made much progress in the rest of Canada. He came within a hair's breadth of defeating Trudeau and forming a minority government. All he needed to do so was a couple of more seats from Quebec, seats he would never gain by following the unspeakable advice offered by Mulroney, White, Black and others.

My victory at the polls in 1972 should have constituted for me my happiest days in active politics. I had recaptured my seat under the most difficult of circumstances. I had worked hard night and day for two years and now I had my seat back again. Any joy in victory was tempered by the fact that I was isolated from my party and at war with the party organization in Montreal. My riding association was also $25,000 in debt. Stanfield never contacted me. The Montreal press speculated, "What will Stanfield and his party do with Grafftey?"

At a subsequent meeting in Montreal, a group of friends met with me in a downtown office. Present was David Angus, a Mulroney loyalist and now Senator David Angus. He said he would look into the question of my debt. I later received a call from another Mulroney loyalist, Guy Charbonneau, now Senator Guy Charbonneau. He was our chief fundraiser in the province. My meetings with Angus and Charbonneau were cool to say the least. At the meeting with Charbonneau, I insisted that the funds be sent to my agent and not handed over to me. This was agreed to and that was the end of this specific confrontation. Our constituency debts were paid.

Conrad Black, in his book, *A Life in Progress*, wrote that his brother Monty reported to him, in effect, that "your friend Heward Grafftey recently became apoplectic at a service club meeting in Montreal, addressed by Stanfield just about a couple of weeks after the elections of 1972."

On the morning of the meeting in question, I drove to Montreal. The euphoria of victory had worn off. I was deeply depressed about my role in and relationship with my party. Little did I know I would soon be plunged into an even deeper depression. Monty Black had reason to report my displeasure to his brother Conrad. Here is what happened.... As I entered the meeting hall for the service club luncheon at the Sheraton Mount Royal Hotel in mid-town Montreal, it was easy to see there was an overflow crowd in attendance. I was immediately ushered into a reception room beside the hall. The organizers of the meeting greeted me warmly. This was not the case with the score or so of my party's senior organizers present for the occasion. They studiously avoided me. When I came face-to-face with Brian Mulroney, he lashed out at me. Under the circumstances, it was, at best, a vulgar performance. In effect, his outburst was a bridge burner. Stanfield himself, glanced furtively at me, but kept his distance. When the meal got underway, Stanfield sat at the centre of the head table beside the host. To the right of Stanfield was Claude Wagner and to the left of the host sat Senator Jacques Flynn. I was relegated to a seat at the end of the head table in no-man's land.

When it came time to speak, Stanfield, in his introductory remarks, said, "It is a great pleasure for me to be here, accompanied by two outstanding members of my Quebec caucus, Claude Wagner, MP, and the Hon. Senator Jacques Flynn." Someone from the back of the hall yelled out, "What about Heward Grafftey?" Stanfield, with no reaction to the interruption, merely carried on. Later on, some party members said Stanfield simply forgot about me. I disagreed. He was playing hard-ball with me. When Stanfield finished his speech and the meeting came to an end, the press gathered around him and one reporter asked, "Why didn't you mention Heward Grafftey in your remarks? After all, he's half of your elected caucus from Quebec." Stanfield remained uncommitted and shrugged off the question with a smile. Somewhat to my embarrassment, many people at the meeting had gathered around me at the end of the head table to express their astonishment at Stanfield's omission and ask for my reaction. Peter White approached me and offered his congratulations on my victory and relayed best wishes from our mutual friend, Conrad Black.

After the luncheon, I took a taxi to the Queen Elizabeth Hotel, where Stanfield presided over a meeting of senior Quebec organizers. Once in the meeting room, he asked me to sit on one side of him at the end of the table where he presided. Claude Wagner sat on his other side. We were hardly into the meeting when it became apparent to me that Peter White was taking over. Thick-skinned as ever, White had conveniently forgotten his central role in the recent electoral debacle. He had suggestion after suggestion about future organizational initiatives for the party in Quebec. Humility was not his strong point. It often seems to me that the *unelectable* are full of great ideas about how the *electable* should get elected. To compound their arrogance, they often look upon those in elected office with haughty disdain. White was a prime example of this phenomenon. Stanfield knew that, at times, I had a short fuse. I suggested to White at the meeting that in view of his track record during the recent campaign he should attempt to listen more and speak less. Silence fell around the room. My abrupt intervention was somewhat of a meeting stopper. Stanfield was visibly ill at ease. He said nothing to me or to the others at the meeting after my comment to White, but gave me a gentle kick on the ankle under the table, together with a pleading glance as if to say, "Please, Heward." The meeting, which was half postmortem and half the usual exercise of individual self-justification and platitudinous exhortations for the future, came to a quick end.

The next day in Knowlton, my phone rang off the hook. John Diefenbaker called. He suggested I sit as an independent. This suggestion was entirely out of the question for me. It would take eight years of Mulroney rule to ultimately drive me and millions of good Progressive Conservatives out of the party.

I had been re-elected in Brome-Missisquoi with a comfortable majority. I knew deep down that my 1972 win was and would be my biggest electoral achievement ever. Yet, my sense of sadness and isolation was complete. I never let these sentiments slip into anything resembling self-pity. For me, self-pity has always been an unbecoming and destructive characteristic. It only further alienates us from others and from constructive thinking and reality. Nevertheless, at a time that should have been one of real happiness and a celebration of victory, I was plunged into a deep melancholy.

Before Parliament was convened in early 1973, Conrad visited me in Knowlton. He was accompanied by a very attractive woman. She sat in silence as Conrad and I conversed. Our conversation really wasn't pleasant. Admittedly, I wasn't always temperate in reacting to his jovial acceptance of the whole Wagner debacle and of his whitewashing of the role he played in the whole matter. He continued to extol Wagner's qualities as a potential leader of the party. When I asked him how his opinion squared with Wagner's inability to deliver the goods in the recent election, he remained noncommittal and silent. Tension was in the air. I felt sorry for his lady friend. I rather think his visit, more than just social, was sort of a last attempt to gain my support of the party's Quebec strategy, with Wagner as Stanfield's lieutenant. Conrad knew I wasn't buying it, and as the afternoon wore on, the atmosphere in my living room became decidedly cool. Things, I guessed, would never be quite the same between us. Gone were the carefree days and conversation of the summer of 1967 and afterwards. When we shook hands at my front door and said good-bye, I remembered those happier times and couldn't help wishing that things were better between us.

During our afternoon conversation, we hadn't burned bridges, but neither had we enhanced the positive elements of a long-term relationship. It wasn't the most pleasant of times. I believe Conrad is thicker skinned. Perhaps he doesn't agree with my recollection of this incident.

Between 1972 and 1974, I saw Conrad from time to time, both in Toronto and Montreal. In Montreal, he had started writing his long tome on Maurice Duplessis and was working on his MA at McGill. Conrad was a great student of Napoleon. As with his attitude towards Napoleon and Lyndon Johnson, Conrad had what seemed to me an unreserved admiration for Le Chef. His knowledge of Napoleon was astounding. Unlike Ludwig von Beethoven and many European intellectuals who originally admired Napoleon but became decidedly disenchanted with him at the end of his career, Conrad, I felt, saw few, if any, warts on the emperor. When it came to Duplessis, he shared my conviction that Le Chef was not evil personified and that the legendary *Quiet Revolution* introduced by Premier Jean Lasage in 1960 did not constitute the end of the dark ages for my province and the beginning of a new millennium of unqualified perfection. Yes, Duplessis practiced patronage politics. Yes, he paved churchyards on the eve of elections. He exercised power with authority and a strong hand. Was he any worse than Joey Smallwood in Newfoundland or countless other premiers in the rest of Canada? Many of the accusations against Duplessis were justified, but I always sensed a slight anti-Quebec bias in certain Anglo newspaper columns when it came to Maurice Duplessis. I often asked myself, "Why do these scribes not submit Joey Smallwood, for example, to the same test?"

After the 1972 elections, Stanfield gave Wagner a suite of offices in the Centre Block. For a freshman MP, he was being treated with kid gloves. He also had extra staff paid for out of party funds. As time wore on, Stanfield and many other caucus members tired of Wagner's prima donna attitude. He had over two years to build up the party in Quebec but, after the votes were counted in the elections of 1974, only Wagner, Roch Lasalle and myself were elected. Stanfield campaigned on wage and price controls. This opposition policy didn't fly and the Liberals under Trudeau returned with a majority government. Little did it matter that the Liberals, in a very short time, would themselves impose wage and price controls; just as, after the 1980 vote, they would tax at the pumps after defeating the Clark government on a budget measure of taxing eighteen cents per gallon.

After the 1974 vote, it was clear that Stanfield was finished. He had gone to bat three times and struck out three times. The day after the 1974 elections, I received a congratulatory telephone call from Wagner. He suggested to me, at least indirectly, that he was preparing himself for the next leadership campaign.

When I decided, a few months later, to throw my own hat into the ring, I knew money had to be raised before I announced my intentions to the press. Initially, I decided to solicit funds myself by contacting prospective donors. Perhaps this was a mistake. I thought senior businessmen would not ignore my track record over a period of about twenty years as a Member of Parliament. Conrad Black writes in his book that the late Steve Roman, the Toronto businessman and financier, had met with me. This was true. Steve Roman, like Black, had extreme right-wing views, and I did not begin, after Roman's questioning, to pass his litmus test. I ended up without a cent. Roman recounted the meeting to Black with much amusement.

During my years in a rural and small-town area, I had lost touch with the movers and shakers in business in the larger metropolitan areas. This was unfortunate negligence on my part. I paid the price and was only able, in the end, to raise around $50,000—not enough to mount a credible campaign. One Montreal businessman and prospective donor whom I contacted said, "Heward, why didn't you get elected in a riding like Westmount or some other important riding where you could have some clout?"

Before I announced my intention of running, I met Conrad in his condominium in mid-town Montreal and told him about my leadership intentions. He didn't seem impressed and offered little encouragement. Another wealthy friend said, "Heward, in all honesty, you're too short to become a leader or a prime minister." When I told him I was taller than Winston Churchill, he remained silent, but perhaps when it came to the television age he was right. One of my fundraising initiatives rather puzzled me. I met with Paul Desmarais, the Chairman of Power Corporation, to plead my case. Desmarais remained noncommittal, but about three weeks after the visit, I received a call from Brian Mulroney, saying that he had $1,000 for me from Desmarais. Desmarais later turned out to be one of Mulroney's major backers. I could sense during my personal fundraising efforts that my moderate views on social and economic policy and my stance on environmental and consumer protection ruled me out with the business elite.

On the eve of the leadership vote, I met Conrad on the convention floor and he greeted me warmly. By that time, he had become disillusioned with Wagner over the latter's disavowal of any trust fund. Like Stanfield, he had become uneasy with Wagner's instability. I was later to learn that Conrad then encouraged Mulroney to go for the brass ring. After the final vote that gave the leadership to Joe Clark, Conrad and I met once more on the convention floor. "Heward," he said putting his hand on my shoulder, "everybody said you easily made the best speech. You've surely earned yourself a seat in a future cabinet." I was tired and unimpressed.

Over the next couple of years, I would see Conrad from time to time. Our conversations were very brief. He was usually preoccupied with some associate or another. We were living in different worlds. During this period in the mid-seventies, Conrad's friend, Brian Stewart, was assigned by the CBC to cover Parliament Hill. Brian would often convey messages from Conrad to me. I remember standing outside the West Block, where my offices were situated, when Brian informed me of the death of Conrad's parents within days of one another. I knew how terribly this must have affected Conrad, especially the tragic ending of his dear father as he plunged to his end down a stairwell at home. When, finally, I was named by Joe Clark to his Cabinet, Conrad sent me a fine letter of congratulations. I was glad to receive it and told him so in my acknowledgement.

After my public life came to an abrupt end, it was two years or so before I saw Conrad again. Conrad and his wife and son were visiting Peter White in Knowlton. The Whites had bought Meadowlands, our old farm. I went over to the farm with my wife and two sons, Clement and Arthur, and had a drink with them. Conrad left his son at the Whites as I drove his wife and him with my boys to the nearby airport at Bromont, where his corporate jet awaited him. After my boys inspected the inside of the jet, Conrad and his wife flew off to the lower St. Lawrence. He had a meeting with Paul Desmarais.

The last time I saw Conrad was a couple of years ago in his ornate offices in Toronto. As we talked, he called his wife to make plans for dinner. When he hung up, he mentioned that his wife reminded him to tell me they had my 1968 election posters hanging up in their basement. When our meeting came to an end, I walked down the street away from his offices. He passed me and waved from his chauffeur-driven Rolls Royce. Our pleasant times and conversations in the summer of 1967 seemed so long ago to me. He was no longer a young man; I was no longer a young man. I could not avoid a sense of nostalgia as his car disappeared around the corner after pausing for a few seconds at a red light.

CHAPTER EIGHT

Ralph Nader

When I first met Ralph Nader in Toronto in November of 1965, his name was not a household word—his book, *Unsafe At Any Speed*, had not yet hit the market. At first meeting, it was easy to see that Nader was no ordinary mortal. His dark complexion, sombre black suit and plain, worn black shoes, conveyed a monastic impression. He appeared to be an intensely private man, sincerely focused, driven and dedicated to the cause of consumer protection.

A number of events occurred and some time passed during my battle against the world-wide epidemic of highway deaths and injuries before I actually met Ralph.

It was a sunny day on Friday, August 21, 1964, when I left my Ottawa apartment around 7 a.m., to board an eastbound Canadian Pacific Railway train for Montreal. About the same time as the train pulled out of Ottawa's Union Station, Basil Czopyk was driving his truck full of rocks towards Leonard, Ontario, a small village on the C.P. rail line between Ottawa and Montreal. Czopyk usually stopped for coffee at Leonard. From time to time he boasted how he raced to beat the early morning train over the rail intersection in the middle of this quiet hamlet. This particular Friday morning he wasn't going to make it. My train picked up speed as it left the outskirts of Ottawa. Twenty minutes after departure we were hitting around seventy miles per hour. I had taken a chair in the dining car to eat breakfast and read the newspaper. Then it happened!

The rail car began to pitch and lunge and people and furniture were thrown everywhere. Orange and yellow flames enveloped the windows. I was thrown the length of the car with piles of other diners. Finally the rail car came to a crashing halt at an acute angle. I scrambled out and jumped on to the gravel rail bed. It was difficult, at first, to understand just what had happened. In front of me was the wreckage of a truck amidst a pile of stones. Czopyk had driven into the middle of the train. He was killed instantly. The engine and front cars continued on. The rail car he hit left the tracks tumbling end over end like a football before coming to a rest on its side in a nearby field. Those in the dining car, including myself, and in one other car at the rear of the train, were fortunate. The automatic brakes were activiated, and while many passengers were shaken up as these two cars ripped up a hundred yards of track, many injuries were prevented and lives saved. But I could hear the screams and moans that issued from the car that was hit, as it lay on its side near an old farm shed.

Sliding down the embankment to the scene, I could see what had happened. As the railcar spun in mid-air, many were tossed through broken windows, then the car rolled over and crushed them. It was difficult to tell who was dead and who was injured. A stunned trainman attempted to set up communications with some equipment which he attached to the tracks. I ran to a nearby farmhouse and on an old crank phone told the operator of the accident, asking for ambulances. Forty minutes later, a country doctor arrived. Helicopters from the news media hovered over the scene of the tragedy. Finally, more than an hour after the accident, one privately-owned ambulance appeared.

I don't know when the last victim was removed, but many seriously injured passengers still lay in the field more than two hours after the crash. And we were not miles away from civilization in some isolated wilderness, but only twenty minutes from our nation's capital. The final toll: eight dead and more than twenty seriously injured.

In mid-winter 1970, Arnold Deacon and his twenty-year-old daughter, Monica, heard a loud boom. Monica looked out the window of her kitchen in Waterville, Quebec, near the Quebec/Vermont border. A bus had crashed off a nearby bridge. After spotting the mangled wreckage of the bus and people strewn in the snow on the river bed, the Deacons called the police, then immediately took several blankets to comfort the injured while awaiting the ambulances. Arnold Deacon later said that he and his daughter called the police three times before ambulances arrived on the scene. The police told him they couldn't help because it wasn't in their area of coverage. Twenty-two of the passengers had been injured, several critically. When help finally arrived, it was too late for seventeen-year-old Carol Dupuis of Beebe. She was already dead.

In a rural area of Quebec, a traffic victim lay in the snow in mid-winter. The investigating police officer wasn't certain in which ambulance region the accident had taken place, so he called two ambulances to make sure—one from each adjacent area. Forty minutes later, one ambulance arrived; but before the operator could load the victim aboard, the second was at the scene. The police officer soon had to rule over the ugly argument which arose between the operators, both of whom claimed a right to the victim.

These are only three examples, but such tragedies occur with horrifying frequency. Somewhere along the line we have mixed up our priorities. Generally speaking, proper emergency services are a community responsibility which, admittedly, require the assistance and understanding of senior governments. When we are faced with property damage, police are at the scene of a crime in no time at all. Alarms bring fire engines, trained personnel and expensive equipment speeding to a fire. Yet when it comes to the question of physical injury or illness, we allow human beings to suffer and sometimes to die, after lying exposed to the elements under the morbid gaze of the curious. Why? The answer to this reveals the disgraceful deficiencies in our society.

Let us ask ourselves a few basic questions:

If I am seriously injured or fall seriously ill, would my transportation to hospital be organized in a manner most conducive to my recovery?

If I arrived at hospital, unconscious and unidentified, would I receive the best possible life-saving treatment? Would there be properly trained personnel available to treat me?

Are there the necessary facilities in my hospital to admit me to a resuscitation room immediately, or would "red tape" kill me?

Would there be sufficient blood and plasma substitutes available, and would experienced personnel be on duty to conduct the necessary resuscitation and investigations required?

Would emergency staff realize that perhaps I shouldn't be moved from my stretcher or be given an anesthetic which might cause death as a result of my degree of shock?

Would someone be on hand immediately to take the necessary x-rays and do the proper tests, and could the stretcher be placed on the x-ray table without moving me off it?

Would the operating room staff personnel be ready to go into immediate action within ten minutes, or would I die as they got ready?

Generally speaking there's only one answer to most of these questions. It is "No."

We may ask why the above state of affairs exists. The answers are many. The world-wide epidemic of death- and injury-producing incidents, is the third biggest killer in North America, after heart disease and cancer. Today, more people under the age of forty are killed in or by motor vehicles than by any other illness or epidemic. When we realize that very often burns from fires are a cause of home injuries and that in 75 percent of the cases that result in death and injury on the road, the head is involved, we can con-clude that the costs to the health care system are astronomical.

I use the word *incident* rather than *accident*. Many death- and injury-producing incidents are loosely called *accidents*. They are not accidents at all, but are more often the result of human error. Human error sometimes results in probabilities that cause death and injury. A pure accident can be defined as "an act of God—an unforeseen or fortuitous event."

If I drive my car at 80 mph along a secondary highway after consuming seven beers and crash into a tree, seriously injuring myself, this is no accident—it is a probability. Unfortunately, my lack of judgement, in all likelihood, will be reported by the media as an accident. More seriously, it will be entered into official statistics as an *accident*. The train wreck I was involved in was reported as an *accident*. For months, Basil Czopyk had been playing games of chance at the railway crossing. What, in this case, was reported as an *accident* was surely a probability that eventually turned into a full-scale disaster.

I truly believe that if we are to make real and meaningful progress in combating the world-wide epidemic of death- and injury-producing incidents, we shall have to understand a lot more about human behaviour and ask ourselves, "Why do people get into death- and injury-producing situations and what can we reasonably do to bring this epidemic under control?" One thing, among many, we can surely do to reduce this toll of death and injury is to direct and communicate sound information to individuals and their families in the best possible way at the community level. This means using the very best of modern communication technology.

Many things stand in the way of our attempts to combat the epidemic. The struggle for survival is so central to our make-up we might say that this struggle and drive supersedes the sex, thirst and hunger drives all put together. It is so great that often otherwise intelligent people don't believe death- and injury-producing incidents or accidents can happen to them. They feel it only happens to others. The result is that it is often hard to motivate individuals to take action against an epidemic they do not feel affects themselves or their families. In my work, how often have I heard the words, "Good God, not me!" from the lips of the dying or injured as they lay on the sidewalk or road under the impersonal stare of onlookers. They never believed it could happen to them and their loved ones until the terrible event took place. We must convince everybody at the community level that this epidemic does, in fact, involve everyone. Most of us must seriously admit that when we shut the door of our car and get behind the wheel, our attitude changes. Too often, we become aggressive and forget the basic norms of decency and courtesy on the road.

Another obstacle to action involves young people and their sense of invulnerability as they test the outer limits of risk.

During the past thirty years as I have worked in the areas of safety at work, play, on the road, and in the home, I have noted that most of the things that kill and injure, in relation to the epidemic, have only been around since the turn of the century. Examples of this are the motor vehicle itself, chemicals and toxins, and electrical appliances and tools. In terms of research, this can make investigative procedures somewhat difficult in collecting relevant and significant data.

One result of death- and injury-producing incidents is rarely addressed—it involves survivors and their families who lose a loved one or friend or have to cope with a serious injury of a family member. I can never forget the train wreck that I experienced. As I tried to help comfort the dying and injured, I was aware of scores of surviving family members and friends of the victims standing by in stunned horror. Some wept openly, others wiped tears from their eyes and some stood silently by with grief etched in their faces. The long-term negative effects on survivors of these incidents are incalculable. Many years ago, a number of inner-city children from Montreal were taken outside the city on a swimming excursion. Twelve of the children died when their boat overturned. On the fortieth anniversary of this tragedy, a *Gazette* reported interviewed family members of the victims. Edgar Fonseca told the *Gazette* that he lost two sisters in the tragedy and said, "My sisters played the piano and my mother is still lugging it around today. My mother kept asking why did God take them and what was he going to do with them. One of the reasons my parents divorced is because they blamed each other for this."

Employers know that when a worker loses a child, wife or husband from a death- or injury-producing incident, they lose the worker's productivity for a long period of time.

Two years before the train crash of 1964, I became involved in the question of emergency response measures in my constituency of Brome-Missisiquoi. The greater proportion of motor vehicle and highway deaths and injuries takes place in rural areas. In my part of the world, traffic victims would lie on the road, sometimes for almost an hour before help of any kind would arrive. I say help of any kind because, more often than not, badly designed and ill-equipped ambulances arrive on the scene of the accident with personnel who had little or no training to care for the injured. This was and is a most serious matter because it is already recognized by trauma experts that the chances for survival are greatly enhanced when the rule of the *Golden Half-Hour* is respected. This means, at least, that within half an hour of an accident, the victim must be treated for shock, airways must be opened, bleeding stopped and proper splinting procedures must be carried out if required. In the early 1960s, traffic victims all over North America were arriving at community hospitals *dead on arrival*. The loss of life was a needless and senseless sacrifice.

I decided to take action in many municipalities in my riding. This included my own home town of Brome Lake and involved converting police cruisers to station wagon-like ambulances as the police are normally the first on the scene of an accident. My initiatives also involved training police officers in emergency paramedical techniques, encouraging local organizations, such as the Lions Club, to donate money to purchase up-to-date emergency equipment for the police ambulances and cooperating with Bell Canada to install proper communications equipment between the police, the ambulance and local hospitals. These improvements were greeted with much enthusiasm and support.

On July 1, 1965, together with Alexander Brown and Réal Casavant, both researchers for Radio-Canada, I published what later became an all-party brief on motor vehicle and highway deaths and injuries in Canada. The brief was supported and signed by leaders of all parties, including Prime Minister Lester Pearson who applauded and encouraged my efforts. The July 1 holiday weekend normally involves a horrendous toll of carnage on North American highways, and our brief received national publicity. It recommended a number of legislative changes, especially involving federal jurisdiction. One such suggested change was the building of better and safer cars. Since the turn of the century, in the area of safety standards, aircraft, ships and rolling stock on railways had been built and inspected under the strictest rule of law. For example, it was because of federal standards that the braking system was activated during the 1964 train crash. This single standard saved lives and reduced injuries. In the transportation field, only the automobile and other motor vehicles fell largely outside the rule of law when it came to the mandating of safety standards. Our brief called for, among other things, the building of a publicly-funded prototype safety car where safety standards would be mandated. I say *safety standards* as opposed to *safety features* because safety features were and are invariably added to intrinsically unsafe engineering procedures in the building of motor vehicles. The auto industry's engineering procedures were more often directed towards marketing and sales considerations than to questions of safety.

Safety standards are designed to prevent accidents and to reduce the chances of death and injury once an accident takes place. A few standards in the area of prevention involve lighting, brakes and the manoeuvrability of the vehicle. Standards to reduce death and injury once an accident takes place involve seat belts and air bags, and delethalizing the interior of motor vehicles by, for example, padding and recessing the dashboard. Our brief referred to the world-wide epidemic of death and injury on the highway using epidemiological terms, calling the driver *the agent*, the car *the microbe*, and the roads and surrounding *the environment*. We then called for an attack on the epidemic on all three levels by policing and educating better and safer drivers, by building better and safer roads and by building better and safer cars. The anatomy of most motor vehicle crashes involves all three factors.

I first met Ralph Nader in Toronto in November 1965, a short time after I was re-elected in the 1965 federal campaign. I was accompanied by Alex Brown, who was by then a researcher for the famous and legendary weekly television series, "This Hour Has Seven Days," which appeared each Sunday night. Nader, a guest on the show, told me he had just completed a new book, *Unsafe At Any Speed*, which was to be published in early 1966. I would subsequently pick it up and read it in January 1966 on a visit to San Francisco. At the television studio, I was interviewed by Warner Troyer on car safety. Troyer also interviewed Nader and a representative from American Motors. General Motors, Ford and Chrysler had refused the invitation to send representatives to be interviewed. The representative from American Motors and their senior executives must have regretted their acceptance. Nader tore the American Motors official to shreds, accusing the auto industry of dragging its feet on the implementation of safety standards. The American Motors official was obviously ill-prepared for such a confrontation. It was truly a memorable television interview, still talked about in the corridors of Radio-Canada and elsewhere. At that time, it would have been possible to install air bags in motor vehicles, thereby reducing the loss of life by 5,000 per year on North American highways. Tragically, this initiative took almost thirty years to get underway.

Watching Nader in action it was easy to see he knew his facts and had done his research homework with impeccable accuracy. And so it was with *Unsafe at Any Speed*. Nader's dedication and thorough research methods have made a lasting impression on me, and for the better.

Early in 1966, Nader contacted me. U.S. Senate hearings on car safety were soon to get underway and he wanted to know if I would testify before the relevant committee. I accepted his invitation and prepared a brief to be presented before the Commerce Committee of the U.S. Senate. Before I knew it, I had become the opposition spokesman for car safety in Canada. The press jokingly referred to me as Canada's Ralph Nader. My questions on the subject directed to various government Ministers in the House often fell on deaf ears. Bud Drury, the then-Minister of Industry, was visibly nervous and ill at ease when I questioned him on the subject. At one time, he even went so far as to say that nothing much could be done in Canada since most motor vehicles were manufactured in the United States where safety standards were set. I disagreed. This attitude on the part of the Minister had, for me, serious and broad implications for Canadians in the whole field of consumer protection.

Ron Todgham, President of Chrysler Canada, invited me for lunch with his senior officials at Ottawa's prestigious Rideau Club. Todgham was brash and insensitive, even suggesting to one of his aides that I should be "fixed up with one of their cars." I brushed him aside and was well aware that the auto industry arranged to put next-to-new vehicles into the hands of state and federal legislators at ridiculously low prices. The aide who worked in the area of government affairs and public relations for Chrysler Canada and who attended the lunch was visibly embarrassed and the subject was dropped.

The North American car industry was very concerned and prepared to excercise its considerable influence. As already mentioned, for years cars had been manufactured without a great deal of regulation and industry officials were not about to see a change in the status quo. General Motors in the United States decided to harass Nader. Even his sexual preferences were a subject for their investigation. They put a private detective on his trail. Ralph was followed and harassed with numerous telephone calls. He fought back and General Motors was caught red-handed. Their Chairman was subpoenaed and reprimanded before the U.S. Senate by Senator Robert Kennedy.

My trip to Washington and subsequent appearance before the U.S. Senate could not have been more successful. Ralph met me outside the committee room and made all the detailed arrangements for my appearance and testimony before the Senators. I was given twelve minutes to present my brief, but was allowed to file supplementary material with the clerk of the committee at the end of my presentation. Both my testimony and supplementary material went on the Senate record. During the hearings, I sat beside Jimmy Hoffa of the Teamsters Union. Hoffa showed the committee results of research carried out by his union. The research resulted in the invention of a device to prevent trucks from jack-knifing and causing serious accidents. My Senate appearance received national television coverage, both in Canada and the United States, where my intervention was featured on the NBC Evening News. After my Senate appearance, Robert Kennedy sent me a most gracious congratulatory letter. Kennedy's tragic assassination meant that Ralph and I had lost a dedicated ally. I cannot help but think about what would have happened had he reached the presidency. We surely would have had an exalted friend at court.

Later that winter, I testified before the House of Representatives in Washington. Once more, Ralph Nader made the detailed plans and greeted me. At that time, I met Republican Senator Ed Speno, of the New York State Senate. Ed came to testify and subsequently invited me to appear before the New York State Senate committee relating to car safety. It was here that I learned that the auto industry argued on the state level that the jurisdiction for safety standards fell within the federal authority, while they claimed the very opposite while testifying on the federal level. Ed was a dedicated crusader for car safety. He had also proposed the building of a publicly-funded prototype safety car. I invited him to Ottawa to confer with officials in the Department of Industry in order to get joint cooperation between Canada and the State of New York in the building of such a publicly-funded car. Hard as we tried, the whole idea boggled the imagination of officials, both in New York State and in Ottawa. The auto industry lobbied hard against this initiative. Thirty years later, the need for such a car still exists.

Some months after the publication of our brief, the question of the building of safer cars under the rule of the federal authority went before the Commons Justice Committee. The National Film Board had produced an excellent film on the subject. I arranged to have the film shown before the committee. At that time, Pierre Trudeau was Lester Pearson's parliamentary secretary. He was a member of the committee and was very supportive of my efforts. One of the results of our committee efforts was the strengthening of the mandate of the Motor Vehicle Branch of the Department of Transport. Its director, Jim Bancroft, most fortunately turned out to be a dedicated and imaginative public servant. He followed my work with interest and was supportive in every way.

In the fall of 1966, John Diefenbaker, as leader of the opposition, named me to be a delegate to the United Nations Assembly. While there, I arranged what was for me a very historic meeting. On the 13th of September 1899, H.H. Bliss, a real estate agent, was stepping down from a horse-driven trolley at the corner of Central Park and 74th Street in New York City. He was struck down and killed by a horseless carriage; thus, becoming the first recorded victim of the automobile age. I invited Ralph Nader to meet me at the corner of Central Park West and 74th Streets where we laid a wreath on the spot where Bliss met his fate. Two factors worked against a large media turnout. It was raining very hard and Bobby Kennedy was in town campaigning for his New York Senate seat. In spite of this, a good contingent of the press corps was on hand. Apart from the fact that I had read about the Bliss incident in the literature on deaths and injuries on the highways, I had the distinct impression that nobody really knew about the significance of this corner in the heart of Manhattan. By this time, it was easy to see that the media considered Nader a national figure.

Twenty-three years later, I organized a much larger gathering at the same corner on September 13, 1989, the ninetieth anniversary of the event. Safety directors from various North American corporations were invited and attended, as did officials from the Canadian Consulate in New York City. One factor reduced the attendance somewhat—Mayor Koch had been knocked out of political life in a vote the day before and officials of the city transportation department, who had accepted my invitation, did not turn up. Instead, they flocked to attend a meeting of the winning candidate, as they owed their positions to patronage considerations and hastened to City Hall to show their allegiance to the victor.

Officials from the New York City Parks Commission showed up. They had been most helpful in getting permission to install microphones and seats by a small stand erected for the occasion at the historic corner. I was able to make arrangements to have a vintage car at the corner for the ceremony. This model was as close as possible to the car that actually killed Bliss, and attracted much curiosity and attention. On the arrival of the car at the scene, my imagination was stirred and it was easy for me to visualize the tragedy ninety years before. My staff insisted on one other matter. They said it would not be correct to proceed with the ceremony without contacting and inviting some descendants of Mr. Bliss. This was easier said than done—how to proceed! There were not all that many Bliss's in the New York telephone book and only one, a New York attorney, gave me a clue. It turned out to be a good one, and I invited two of the Bliss great-granddaughters who lived in Connecticut. One of them came with a teenage son who, ironically, totalled a car the next day. Each had a red rose in their hand which they placed on the wall at the corner in memory of their great-grandfather. The ceremony went off without a hitch. Of all the press reports across North America, none pleased me more than the one that appeared in the *Toronto Star* with the head-line, "Ex-MP Heward Grafftey Crusades for Auto Safety."

I intend to arrange another gathering, God willing, at the same corner on the 100th anniversary of this event, September 13, 1999. It is my fervent hope and prayer that, at this future date, we shall have made major inroads in our fight against the senseless slaughter on our highways.

In early May of 1967, I arranged for the Liberty Mutual safety car

With Ralph Nader and members of the New York press,
November, 1966, at Central Park West and 74th Street,
commemorating H.H. Bliss who was killed by a horseless carriage,
September 13, 1899—the first recorded victim of the Automobile Age.

to come to Montreal and Ottawa. Frank Crandall, the legendary safety engineer at Liberty Mutual, had built many safety features into an ordinary model car. The result was not the one hoped for from the building of a publicly-funded prototype safety car. Nevertheless, it was a great improvement over the status quo. Frank called the steering column in most conventional North American motor vehicles "the bayonet in the front seat." Frank's car had no such column and the so-called bayonet was removed.

It is hard for me to forget the visit of Frank and his car. One Saturday morning I was receiving constituents in my office at Knowlton. The phone rang. It was an urgent call from Frank. He and the car had arrived at the U.S./Canadian border point on their way to Ottawa. Canadian customs officials had never seen anything like the car before. They hesitated to clear it and Frank at the border. After a long and frustrating conversation with me they consented to let Frank into Canada with the car. All was well. In Ottawa, the car was shown off in the lobby of the Chateau Laurier Hotel. It drew much interest from the public at large, the media, public officials and politicians. It then proceeded to Montreal to the Montreal Neurological Institute. Head injuries are too frequently involved in the epidemic on our highways. Surgeons at the Montreal Neurological Institute work around the clock treating the heads of traffic victims. One victim in a wheel chair was wheeled into the parking lot behind the Institute. He had fallen asleep while driving. Frank's car was equipped with an alarm-type device in order to prevent such an occurence when the driver falls asleep. Apart from the border incident, the visit with Frank came off without complications and was a great success.

In the spring of 1967, I invited Ralph Nader to Ottawa and hosted a lunch for him at the Parliamentary Restaurant. Journalists, Members of Parliament and government officials were in attendance. The same day, we had a meeting with the Consumer Affairs Minister, John Turner. Nader was not impressed and felt Turner was not really briefed on the matter. After the meeting with the Minister, Ralph did a number of television interviews before going on to Montreal to attend Expo 67. Ralph stayed with relatives on the South shore of Montreal. It was hard for me to imagine him relaxing at Expo.

Later in the year he returned to Canada. I invited him to Montreal. The francophone media were extremely interested in my car safety efforts and I acted as an interpreter for Ralph on a French television interview he gave. That same night, he stayed at my Montreal apartment. The next morning at breakfast, I remarked I could hear the radio playing in his room most of the night. He told me it was his habit to go to sleep with the radio on. As we were waiting for the elevator after leaving my apartment, I asked Ralph if he ever considered entering active politics in order to reach his consumer protection goals. His answer was a firm "no." He told me he had seen "machine politics" in action in his home state of Connecticut and had been disgusted. His attitude in this regard has changed with the passage of time. It seems his name will be on the ballot for the Green Party in California for the 1996 presidential race.

He could, at times, be "prickly" and very distant. Occasionally he might smile and joke. He never hesitated to tell me to "lighten up and relax." More often, he himself was deadly serious and intense. Eventually he would, with Nader's Raiders, have a loyal and dedicated following, yet he gave me the impression of being a "loner" fiercely dedicated to a cause. He had little time, or desire it seemed, to socialize. The next morning a taxi arrived to take us to Dorval airport. The doors of this ramshackle cab seemed about to fall off. It was a very poor example of a safe car. The seat belts in the back of the car, as is too often the case, were wedged between the seats. They were broken and couldn't be used. To make matters worse, the sullen cabby raced towards Dorval at breakneck speed. As Ralph winced, I asked the cabby to slow down.

I talked with Ralph in the spring of 1968 on a parliamentary visit to Washington. I would not see him again until the spring of 1972 when we addressed a gathering on the subject of consumer protection in the auditorium of the High School of Montreal. I was in the middle of my bid for re-election in the 1972 federal vote later that year and I was the last speaker on the program. By the time I spoke, the crowd had had enough. It was not the sort of crowd accustomed to hearing my kind of speech—more designed for the rural stump than for them. In short, I bombed. I don't think Ralph was impressed either. By this time, he was the complete public figure, surrounded by the press and admirers. I really had little or no opportunity to have a private word with him.

Since the mid-seventies, Ralph and I have kept in touch through correspondence and telephone. I sent him copies of my family reference books entitled, *Safety Sense on the Road*, *Safety Sense in the Home* and *Safety Sense at Play*, and he has been most supportive of these initiatives. In the meantime, we both soldier on.

In the last thirty years, there has been progress in the attack on the epidemic of motor vehicle highway deaths and injuries, but not nearly enough. We shall have to mobilize the conscience of our people and the technology of our times. We shall have to understand more about the relations between the brain and human behaviour as we continue to ask the question, "Why do people get into death- and injury-producing situations and what can we realistically do to change behaviour patterns?"

My career in public life ended in early 1980 with the collapse of the Clark government when Pierre Elliott Trudeau and his Liberals were swept into power.

After serving eighteen years as an MP, I opened an office in Ottawa specializing in research and development and technology innovation, to work with governments, universities and the private sector. I also began to focus on safety issues. As Science Minister, my dream had come true. Working from this Ministry, apart from other things, I could effect major changes in the battle against the epidemic of death- and injury-producing incidents. Once in the private sector, my government affairs office and business bloomed. Over the past twenty-five years in public life, I had gathered much research in the whole area of safety issues. In 1980 I organized this research into four main areas: road, home, play, and work.

After looking at material from all over the world, I came to the conclusion that there were no properly designed family reference books in the field. The Disease Control Centre in Atlanta, Georgia was very influential in helping me come to this conclusion. While there was much material for the experts, there was little readable material for the public at large. What existed for the public was fragmented and often impossible to decipher. I was persuaded to edit, publish and distribute family reference books. This meant the diversion of monies and my energies from government relations work into my newly-founded company, Safety Sense Enterprises, incorporated in 1988 for the purposes of the production and marketing of my four books.

Since 1980 I have had literally hundreds of personal encounters all over North America and Europe with experts in the safety field. These included meetings with human resource and safety officials in private sector companies, government officials, safety directors at the state and provincial levels in North America, driver education officials and loss control and marketing officials in the casualty insurance sector. It has been a memorable experience. I intend to dedicate the rest of my life to battling this world-wide epidemic. I hope I shall have enough time to make a difference.

The twentieth century (a century where we have a virtually doubled life span in the western world) has seen tremendous improvements in the field of the delivery of medical and health care services. Meanwhile, the epidemic of death- and injury-producing incidents continues on its relentless course. The noted medical missionary, Albert Schweitzer, talked about the reverence of life. Our greatest gift is the gift of life. We are all unique, and we have unique roles to play. Death- and injury-producing incidents are not inevitable. It is our responsibility to do everything possible to avoid them so we can fulfil the purpose of our life. Abraham Lincoln once said, "There are no accidents in my philosophy; every effect must have its cause." Whether or not we agree with the late President Lincoln, most of what we choose to call accidents is a result of human error and circumstances which often lead to death and injury. Is it too much to hope that we can enter the twenty-first century having made great progress in ending the senseless slaughter brought about by this recent and modern epidemic? I think not. Ralph Nader thinks not.

CHAPTER NINE

Pierre Elliott Trudeau

It was early on a lovely sunny afternoon, June 4, 1979. I had parked my car on the grounds of the Governor General's residence, and accompanied by my sister, Ann, my constituency secretary, Margaret Macey, and my House of Commons secretary, Denyse Bergeron, walked up the road towards Rideau Hall. This was to be a great day for me and I was profoundly happy. Since 1957, I had run in nine federal elections. After 1963 I spent twelve years to the left of Mr. Speaker on the Opposition benches. Some days before, I had conferred with Prime Minister-elect Joe Clark and was about to be sworn in as Minister of Social Programs. New horizons were opening up for me. I was to have a greater opportunity to serve Canada and her people.

As we approached the circular driveway leading up to the entrance of Rideau Hall, my constituency secretary, Margaret Macey, cried out, "Oh, there's Pierre Trudeau." In addition to being an avid Elvis Presley fan, Margaret had always suffered from an acute case of *Trudeaumania*. Pierre had just paid his last official visit to Governor General Ed Schryer before a new Cabinet was to be sworn in. The sight of him with a yellow, silk handkerchief jauntily tucked into the pocket of his sports jacket, as he drove his silver Mercedes convertible, top down, reminded me of his early carefree days in Ottawa. At that time, during the mid-sixties, I would see the same car parked behind the Commons. Now it was out of mothballs and the new Leader of the Opposition had a smile on his face and a renewed light-hearted look about him.

My future Cabinet colleagues, walking together with Joe Clark up the driveway beside me, had a puzzled look on their faces as I went directly up to Pierre Trudeau in his car and shook hands with him. After a short exchange, I said, "God bless you, Pierre." He put his hand on my shoulder and replied, "God bless you, too, Heward, and all kinds of good luck." I knew and could sense that he meant every word. My future Cabinet colleagues, perhaps, had reason to be a little bewildered at this friendly exchange, and Joe Clark had a slight frown on his face. After all, I had been one of two Tory opposition members in the Commons for the past seven years. At one time, I was the only Tory opposition member. My friends in Parliament from Quebec were mostly Liberals. To add to this, since 1953, I had had a happy, long and healthy acquaintance with Pierre Trudeau. While we did not agree on political issues, I always respected, admired and liked him, and felt he was a gentleman in the finest sense.

To say the least, he was *his own man*. I don't think I am being too presumptuous when I say the feeling of respect was mutual. Pierre always expressed his admiration for me as an anglo. He lauded me, an anglo, getting elected in a largely French-speaking riding. The chemistry between us was, and still is, good, and we enjoy each other's company.

Pierre Trudeau's political career has been analyzed time and time again. The same can be said for his character and personality. Pundits, academics and commentators have probed ceaselessly, in a relatively futile pursuit, to find out what makes Pierre Trudeau tick. I do not propose to analyze the private or public Pierre Trudeau. I wish to write about some very happy occasions I had with someone whom I like very much. If anyone had told me in 1953, when I first met Pierre Trudeau, that I was meeting with the future prime minister of Canada, I would have been more than a little surprised.

Pierre Trudeau's religious faith was and is obvious to me. It is not worn on his sleeve, but his family upbringing and strict Jesuit training at Brébeuf School and College and his teachers there surely left their mark on him. His Jesuit teachers reinforced his belief in God and helped an already independent soul to really think for himself and be his own man. I cannot and do not want to write on this subject at length, but the good chemistry between Pierre and myself is largely based on our solid faith. While he is a Roman Catholic with his belief in the apostolic succession and acknowledgement of His Holiness the Pope as the Vicar of Christ, I, am an anglo Catholic in the High Anglican Church and centre my life, as Trudeau does, on the Blessed Sacrament of Holy Communion. I believe Pierre shares my religious convictions. We have never discussed it over the years, but I feel we sense in each other this shared conviction, and it is the solid basis of our good fellowship and outlook on life. In a recent conversation with him, I asked him if he had only one author to read who would it be? He answered without hesitation, "Cardinal Newman."

Mr. and Mrs. Tom Guérin lived in the baronial Chateau Apartments on Sherbrooke Street West at the corner of Mountain Street, diagonally across from the Ritz-Carlton Hotel. Tom had been a Liberal member of the National Assembly in Quebec. His father had been the mayor of Montreal. Mrs. Guérin was a wealthy New Yorker and the family lived well. The Guérins also had a magnificent stone chateau-like residence high on the slopes of Mont St-Hilaire, on the south shore across the river from Montreal.

It was at the Guérins' Chateau Apartment in 1953 that I first remember meeting Pierre Trudeau. Tom and his wife had two charming and intelligent daughters, Alice and Carol. I often went out with the older daughter, Alice, and Pierre and Carol were frequently together. About every two weeks, the Guérins had blacktie dinners. Apart from Pierre and me who were permanent fixtures, they normally invited a few other guests. The conversation was always lively. Politics and the arts were always on the conversational agenda and a sense of fun and much laughter prevailed. Pierre was teaching at the University of Montreal where Carol was a student. Carol was about seventeen or eighteen and Pierre would have been in his early thirties. I remember him well, especially his highly informative and intelligent conversation, his self-assurance and original ideas. He spoke in a low voice, as he does today, and I always felt he was somewhat shy but that is not to say that he did not have a high sense of self-appreciation and awareness. As the expression goes in French, *he was happy in his skin*.

When we first met, very few English-speaking Quebecers of my generation in Montreal spoke or attempted to speak French. I sensed that Pierre always appreciated that I insisted that we speak together in

French at least fifty percent of the time. He was not only completely bilingual, with a French-speaking father and an English-speaking mother, but like Louis St-Laurent before him, he was totally bicultural. While my parents originally sent me to French school and I eventually became bilingual, I never felt I had a sense of being really bicultural until I had run in six or seven elections in my largely French-speaking riding.

When Pierre became Prime Minister, Mrs. Guérin, after the death of her husband, Tom, would sometimes visit him at 24 Sussex Drive. On these occasions, Pierre would send me a note in the House informing me of her visit. In the late 1960s, Carol had fallen seriously ill and just a few years ago, my dear friend Alice died of breast cancer. I believe Pierre will always have a special place in his heart for the kind and delightful Carol.

About 25 km northwest of Montreal, Ezio Felli lives in a brown brick bungalow in St-Eustache. Although officially retired, he still carries on his work for a few select customers. A tailor by trade, a part of the basement of his home is reserved for his workshop. Over his sewing machine on the wall is a board on which are tacked various pictures of Ezio's well-known clients in their sartorial splendor. One picture shows a smiling Pierre Trudeau on Parliament Hill, decked out in one of Ezio's sports coats.

Ezio operated under the name of Tobia Felli Reg'd. His father, Tobia, started the business in Montreal some seventy-five years ago. Their shop was situated near the University of Montreal on what was once known as Albani Avenue. (During the Lévesque years the street was renamed Jean-Brillant.) Tobia and his son, Ezio, were a superb team, often working with relatives recently arrived from Italy in the back of the shop. They called themselves British Custom Tailors and had a fine selection of cloth bolts in the front of the store. Classical music, usually opera, played on the radio in the workshop. During the Depression years and during the war, it was necessary to put down a deposit, permitting the Fellis to order the necessary cloth. Usually after at least two or three fittings, their beautifully hand-sewn suits were ready. They were unsurpassed in quality and workmanship, and reasonably priced. Tobia, the father, was a man of great girth who would sit by the wall in the fitting room behind a drawn curtain with his hands clasped over his stomach giving direction to his son, Ezio, who, with a handful of pins, would prepare the suits for further tailoring. I remember going to their shop as a boy with my mother or father. The close quarters in the fitting room left little space for Ezio, his father, me and whatever parent I was with to budge. It would be more than fair to say that the Fellis had what could be termed the carriage trade among Montreal's English-speaking population. Among other things, they tailored riding habits for members of the Montreal Hunt. When Tobia died, his son carried on the business.

Ezio told me he remembered Pierre as a young man with a beard arriving at the shop on Albani Avenue on a motorcycle—the shop was not far away from Brébeuf College where Pierre attended classes. When he was Prime Minister, the visits were not so tranquil since Pierre arrived with his RCMP escort, causing quite a stir and commotion on the street. In the early 1970s, as Prime Minister, he invited Ezio and his family to visit Ottawa and tour Parliament and Ezio has never forgotten this kindness.

In 1952, I was President of the McGill Liberal Club and Vice-President of the Young Liberals for St-Antoine Westmount. One day, a few years later, Prime Minister Diefenbaker called for me in the House of Commons to discuss some business with him. While I was sitting beside the Prime Minister, Paul Martin, Sr. sent a note accompanied by a picture to Dief. The picture showed me standing beside the Liberal Fisheries Minister, Jimmy Sinclair, at the Liberal Reform Club in Montreal. The accompanying note read, "John, is Grafftey explaining his conversion?" When Sinclair visited Montreal in 1952, Prime Minister Louis St-Laurent had recently appointed him Minister of Fisheries. Before that, he was Finance Minister Douglas Abbott's parliamentary secretary. Prime Minister MacKenzie King refused to name the brilliant Sinclair to his Cabinet because of the latter's refusal to go along with King on the conscription issue. Sinclair insisted that reinforcements were badly needed in Europe and would not tolerate King's "conscription if necessary, but not necessarily conscription," stance. On his visit to Montreal in 1952, Sinclair was in high spirits.

He was accompanied by his executive assistant, my good friend, Al Fraser, who subsequently became Clerk of the Commons. While I hosted the Minister at a joint meeting of the McGill and Westmount Liberal Clubs, there was time left over for kicking up our heels. This included a visit to Montreal's Bellevue Casino. The Bellevue Casino in mid-town Montreal had a world-class floor show, attracting international stars in the pre-TV age. The tall, high-kicking girls in the chorus line were unsurpassed. They were on a par with the Rockettes of New York's Radio City Music Hall. We had front row seats in the first balcony and Jimmy more than enjoyed himself. His Montreal trip also included a visit to Tom Guérin's at the Chateau Apartments. Tom wanted an ambassadorial post in South America and insisted I arrange a visit with the Minister. When we arrived at the Guérin apartment, Pierre Trudeau, Alice and Carol were chatting in a small living room study. Jimmy Sinclair and I went into the main living room to talk with Tom and left after about half an hour, the time it took to down a scotch and water. Trudeau never emerged from the living room study. Had he done so, undoubtedly I would have introduced him to his future father-in-law.

In the early 1950s, I was completing my law studies at McGill before being admitted to the Quebec Bar. Around this time, Pierre was writing for *Cité Libre* and teaching at the University of Montreal Law School. With Jean Marchand, he would become known for his involvement in the asbestos labour dispute, when Premier Duplessis was using the provincial police as strike breakers against the asbestos miners. Duplessis would make life miserable for Trudeau, interfering with his teaching at the University of Montreal. Such was the power of *le chef* in those days. Trudeau was always physically fit and, among other things, loved judo. Even as Prime Minister, he continued his judo lessons in Ottawa and eventually earned a black belt.

During this period when I got to know him, Trudeau was only one of many whom I knew were to inherit substantial wealth. Most of my friends, affected by what might have been good fortune, were, in effect, adversely influenced by this unearned windfall caused by an accident of birth. The effects were varied. Some of my friends went to absurd lengths to hide their good fortune. One even walked to work, not because he liked the exercise, but he did not want his office colleagues to see his expensive car. The conservative Montreal establishment, both French and English, frowned on any extravagant display of material wealth. It was said they were "ostentatiously unostentatious." I suppose this phenomenon knows no limits. I once met a woman in Prout's Neck, Maine who was riding an old bicycle and wearing shabby blue jeans and an old flannel workshirt. The only give-away was a huge, beautiful diamond broach on her shirt. She introduced herself as Mrs. Rockefeller.

Many of my well-to-do friends, freed by wealth from normal nine to five jobs, just didn't know what to do with themselves or their lives. Their conservative attitudes did not permit their minds to leap forward to have "sea room" to create constructive activities. While they were liberated from the normal economic constraints which plague most ordinary mortals, they lacked the imagination to profit from their inherited freedom. They were often lost and bored. This resulted in frenzied travel, endless cocktail parties, entertainment and membership in countless clubs.

Of course, there are exceptions to every rule. I met two of these exceptions in their early years, but must confess, at that time, I did not perceive the exceptional qualities that separated these men from the general rule. One was Pierre Trudeau, the other was Conrad Black.

During the early fifties Trudeau was involved with his magazine, *Cité Libre*. His writings were imaginative and his logical and cerebral approach to public issues was unique. It was not difficult to detect his hatred for Premier Maurice Duplessis. Trudeau came to detest *le chef*'s authoritarian methods and patronage practices. Trudeau, himself, as a university teacher, had already fallen prey to Duplessis' ruthless scorn. There were, in my view, added reasons for Trudeau's opposition to Duplessis. Duplessis and his Union Nationale government continually demanded more powers for Quebec. The logical result of such a power grab would, in Trudeau's view, leave the federal authority in a weakened state. This ran contrary to Trudeau's socialist views at the time—views that called for strong, centralized power in Ottawa.

In 1962 and 1963, Trudeau assailed Prime Minister Pearson in *Cité Libre* over the latter's stand allowing nuclear warheads on Bomarc missiles in Canada. Pearson did a flip-flop on this issue, reversing his original position and committing what the French choose to call a *volte face*. Trudeau was so indignant and vociferous on the issue that I originally wondered why Lester Pearson seemed to embrace him so warmly once he reached Ottawa. Pearson paved the way for Trudeau's nomination as a candidate in Mont Royal riding, then made him his parliamentary secretary before giving him the Justice portfolio and ultimately helping him to become Liberal Leader and Prime Minister. In retrospect, the answer is clear to me. Pearson and Trudeau shared, in the early sixties, left-of-centre views on most public issues. The second reason for Pearson's spirit of forgiveness for Trudeau's attacks in *Cité Libre* is equally clear to me. Pearson, himself, as Opposition Leader, originally opposed placing nuclear warheads on Bomarc missiles in Canada. The Liberal caucus forced him to change his stance for purely political advantage. This cynical political move gained for him and his party much support from south of the border, especially from the Kennedy administration. Because Pearson was really no more than lukewarm on supporting nuclear weapons in Canada he easily forgave Trudeau for his attacks.

In the election of 1963, Trudeau supported and worked for Charles Taylor, the NDP candidate in Mont Royal although I cannot say whether or not Trudeau was ever a member of the NDP. Taylor, an old friend and neighbour of Trudeau's in Outremont, came from a well-to-do Montreal family. I attended McGill University with him and we debated together as a team. He is now a professor of philosophy at McGill and a respected commentator on Quebec politics. In 1963, Taylor was soundly defeated at the polls by Allan MacNaughton. MacNaughton had held this Liberal stronghold even during the 1958 elections. When Trudeau eventually got the call from Pearson before the 1965 elections, I never believed he would embrace the Liberal cause. Pearson had to strengthen the Quebec wing of his party and government, which had been rocked by ministerial scandals. Pearson mostly wanted Marchand in Ottawa, but, as the story has often been told, the latter would not go without Pelletier and Trudeau. Trudeau must have felt that the NDP was going nowhere in Quebec. He swallowed some principles and became one of the three wise men from my province. Perhaps he was more realistic than I was when, in 1968, I stuck to my guns and ran as a Tory feeling we could eventually build my party of choice in Quebec from the grassroots up. Who could blame me for not foreseeing the corruption and disgrace of the elitist Mulroney years, which not only destroyed my party in Quebec, but destroyed it across Canada as well. Trudeau realized he had a chance of influencing the Liberal Party and government and of transforming it to his left-of-centre views. In this, Lester Pearson would prove to be his greatest ally and mentor.

In 1965, Allan MacNaughton vacated his seat in the Town of Mont Royal. He was on his way to the Senate. Some call it a reward. I still persist in calling it a punishment in spite of the handsome remuneration. Trudeau was parachuted into the seat as the official Liberal candidate, pushing aside other deserving prospects, such as Victor Goldbloom, who had served as a member of the Legislative Assembly in Quebec City. Allan MacNaughton later confided to me in conversation how outraged he was at what he termed Trudeau's intrusion into his old riding.

Nineteen hundred and sixty-five was still the age of black and white television. During the elections, CBC and Radio-Canada provided free television time to each of the parties. The studios were situated in the old Ford Hotel on Dorchester Street (now René-Lévesque Blvd.) in downtown Montreal. The Ford Hotel's rates were pretty low and many of my university friends used to take a room at the Ford from time to time in order to entertain lady friends. They nicknamed the hotel the *Riding Academy*.

It was in the old CBC building that I met Pierre Trudeau during the 1965 elections. Radio-Canada had organized a television debate between the parties. Pierre was informally dressed in sports clothes and the only prop on the set was the customary potted palm amidst the studio equipment. I needled Pierre a little, feigning surprise at his latter day conversion to liberalism. He took it all in his stride. I would not get used to the fact that he had made the plunge into public life, and I had the feeling he would never be comfortable with the cut and thrust of partisan politics. Again, I was proved to be wrong.

Even after his arrival in Ottawa, Trudeau continued to march to his own drummer. When he appeared in the Commons attired in sandals, sports clothes and ascot, Diefenbaker would rise from his seat on a point of order asking Mr. Speaker to discipline the rookie member who, in Diefenbaker's view, was an unacceptable spectacle. Mr. Speaker merely smiled and did nothing about it. Trudeau was enjoying his new role to the hilt. When I parked my car in the Commons parking lot behind the House, I often saw his Mercedes. Just as often, I would see him at the House restaurant dining, from time to time, with one or another of a number of gorgeous young ladies. Soon he was named parliamentary secretary to Prime Minister Lester Pearson. Trudeau had gained Pearson's ear and was on his way.

My relationship with Trudeau was always pleasant and cordial, even if we were members of different parties sitting on opposite sides of the House.

In the fall of 1966, I showed a film entitled, *Every Second Car*, to the Commons Justice Committee. The film had to do with the manufacturing of safer cars and the federal role in enforcing safety standards. When the showing was completed, Pierre approached me and encouraged me in my efforts. He said I had embraced a most worthy cause. To this day, in conversation, he well remembers my efforts in trying to reduce the carnage on our highways. It was at the United Nations in 1966 that I had one of my most amusing encounters with Pierre Trudeau. Dief had named me a delegate to the United Nations in 1958 and again in 1966. During my 1966 stewardship at the UN, I was guilty of what could be easily termed an act of mischief.

In the early summer of 1958, during the visit of President Eisenhower to Ottawa, Diefenbaker had the question of the recognition of mainland China listed on the agenda for discussion, but the debate on the issue never came up. Diefenbaker, in conversation, supported my view in 1966 that the time was right to bring up the issue again. Pierre Trudeau was also a delegate to the UN in 1966. He represented the government as Pearson's parliamentary secretary. I conferred on many occasions with Pierre, who seemed quite sympathetic to my views on the subject of China's recognition. As well, many United States diplomats, who spoke with me off the record at the UN, suggested that a middle power like Canada was in a good position to break the ice on the question. I must confess that my subsequent actions were not, in retrospect, all together praise-worthy.

I obtained a good quantity of stationery with the Canadian/UN letterhead at the top and released a firm statement calling for recognition of mainland China and delivered it to the press offices in the lounge of the UN building. I fully realized what the consequences might be. A number of UN-member countries were not burdened with opposition parties. Representatives of many countries called our Canadian office in New York asking for clarification. George Ignatieff, our Ambassador to the UN at the time, was furious with me. His telephone was ringing off the hook. The morning after I had issued my release, we had our usual briefing meeting in our New York offices. Paul Martin, our Minister for External Affairs, had flown down to New York from Ottawa and was in attendance. He was enraged at hearing the news of my press release and, at that time, he seemed confused and was not sure that I was involved. Pierre Trudeau sat beside me at the meeting with his head inclined downward and a look of slight bemusement on his face. Relations between Pearson and Martin were not all that good and Martin could easily have thought that Trudeau had perpetrated this mischief with the Prime Minister's encouragement. Such was not the case. I confessed and got quite a lecture from my old friend Paul. All across Canada, daily newspapers reported "Grafftey calls for recognition of mainland China at UN." Many US diplomats quietly thanked me outside the UN General Assembly chamber. A few months ago, I was reminded of this issue. I was in the office of the Deputy Minister of Health Canada discussing measures to reduce death and injury from trauma. She told me that in the fall of 1966 she was an official in External (and was assigned to the UN office in New York). She remembered my being there. I asked her if she recalled the China affair. "How could I forget!" she replied. "That's really why I remembered you." I can only hope my initiative was, to some extent, constructive.

The summer months during Expo 67 are unforgettable to me. Jean Drapeau, Montreal's colourful mayor, hosted international visitors with great taste and imagination. The Hélène de Champlain Restaurant, situated in a beautifully restored old stone house on Ste-Hélène's Island was the principal reception centre for visitors from every corner of the globe. In the relaxed atmosphere of these receptions, I often met with Trudeau. The last thing I had in mind was that, in less than a year, he would be Prime Minister of Canada.

Over the next year, events moved quickly for Trudeau. As Justice Minister, he would put his progressive imprint on many laws.

It was his chairmanship of the federal/provincial conference in Ottawa in the winter of 1968 that marked him as a potential Liberal leadership candidate and Prime Minister of Canada. His showdown with Premier Daniel Johnson of Quebec in the new Confederation Hall in the West Block of the Parliament Buildings is now legendary. Robert Stanfield named me as an Opposition observer to the conference and I left the meeting convinced Trudeau had almost made up his mind to throw his hat in the ring. Paul Martin, Sr. had come to the same conclusion. I remember Martin, who badly wanted the Liberal leadership for himself, storming out of the conference hall. He was enraged at the national publicity that boosted the image of his younger Cabinet colleague. Martin made no attempt to hide his displeasure.

About this time, I went to have breakfast early one morning in the Parliamentary Restaurant. Jean Marchand was sitting alone and I joined him. During our conversation, the subject of the Liberal leadership came up. I asked him if he intended to run and he allowed that his English wasn't good enough and that the answer was a definite "No." The candidacy of Pelletier was out of the question. By 1968, his distaste for the political arena was more than apparent. Pearson wanted a Francophone successor and the way was opening up for Pierre Trudeau. In a recent conversation, Trudeau told me that Marchand advised him that capturing the Liberal leadership would be much harder than winning the next federal election. This proved to be true. Trudeau had much opposition within the Cabinet, and Bob Winters would mount a formidable campaign against him. On April 6, 1968, Pierre Trudeau was named Liberal leader and automatically became Prime Minister of Canada. I knew I would have a huge battle on my hands in Brome-Mississquoi and deep down I wanted the Grits to name anyone but Trudeau. When the results of the last ballot were announced, my heart sank. Within a few days of gaining the Liberal leadership and being sworn in as Prime Minister, Trudeau was back in the House of Commons. He had the wind in his sails and, sitting almost directly in front of him across the floor of the House, it was not hard for me to sense his fighting mood and self-confidence. Within hours, he went to the Governor General and Parliament was dissolved. Once more, we were going to the people.

Since 1957, in a little over ten years, I had fought five general elections and was now going into my sixth. Four of the five elections in which I was involved resulted in minority Parliaments. It seemed we had never stopped campaigning, and here were the Liberals with a fresh, new leader from my province. Just as Beatlemania had hit England and North America in the early sixties, Trudeaumania was hitting Canada in the late sixties. Pierre Trudeau liked a good time and had his own peculiar sense of fun. Having said that, I always thought that with his cool, logical and cerebral approach to public issues, he must have inwardly laughed at this manic phenomenon that could only increase his cynicism about the Canadian voter. On the other hand, he did little or nothing to discourage the public love affair with the new-found image. While Robert Stanfield was pictured fumbling a football, Pierre Trudeau was shown doing backflips off diving boards. In terms of image, there was no contest. Trudeau fought a brilliant campaign. Who can ever forget the showdown with rock-throwing Separatists in Montreal during the St-Jean Baptiste parade on the eve of the federal vote in June. Trudeau stood his ground while other public leaders fled.

While Trudeau made few, if any, major mistakes on the campaign trail during May and June of 1968, he was aided and abetted by Robert Stanfield. Stanfield committed the first in a series of major policy gaffes during his career in public life as Opposition Leader. It was said time and time again that Robert Stanfield was the best Prime Minister Canada never had. How often did I hear that assertion? The only trouble was that I knew from the very start that it would be impossible to form a government and gain power with Stanfield as leader. Admittedly he was plagued with poor advice from those he listened to in Quebec. The Progressive Conservative Party held a national policy forum in Montmorency, just outside Quebec City, in

August 1967, a few weeks before the leadership convention that elected Stanfield as Leader. Marcel Faribeault, a distinguished Quebec notary and head of the *Trust Général*, pleaded for the adoption of the two-nation policy. Faribeault locked horns with Peter Lougheed, who was on the way to reviving the party in his own province of Alberta. Lougheed was unalterably opposed to the nonsensical two-nations gambit that was being embraced by Brian Mulroney and a coterie of Montreal backroom artists. Mulroney and his gang gloried, or so it seemed to me, in giving a succession of Tory leaders poor advice between elections. As long as Mulroney wasn't leader himself, his efforts at getting people elected in Quebec were half-hearted and lacklustre to say the least.

Stanfield took the two-nations theory hook, line and sinker, and during the elections of 1968, Trudeau reeled him in. *Nation* means one thing in French and another in English. While it has a social connotation in French, it has a purely political connotation in English. In the 1968 campaign, Stanfield adopted the two-nations theory and the unelectable Marcel Faribeault as his Quebec lieutenant. Ernest Lapointe was MacKenzie King's lieutenant in Quebec. After Lapointe's death, the validity of the lieutenancy principle died with him. This fact escaped Stanfield and his Quebec advisors, and on election day, we were soundly whipped.

This was not the end of Trudeau's good luck. In the elections of 1968, 1972 and 1974, he always proved to be a formidable campaigner. Who could have ever believed or guessed that he would profit from what I call the "three strikes and you're out" scenario. In three successive elections, Robert Stanfield struck out each time by committing at least one major blunder, thus assuring Pierre Trudeau's occupancy of 24 Sussex Drive. Strike One was the two-nations policy in 1968; Strike Two was the naming of Claude Wagner his Quebec lieutenant in the 1972 elections. Again, Brian Mulroney and his circle of friends advised Stanfield to embrace Wagner. Mulroney and others were dispatched with $300,000 to convert the "hanging judge" to the Tory cause. Not long before, Wagner had been a provincial Liberal. While Stanfield nearly formed a minority government after the 1972 elections, we were decimated in Quebec. Wagner and I were the only two members elected. While we made significant gains in the other provinces, Quebec punished Stanfield and his party for insulting their intelligence with the Wagner initiative.

In the 1974 elections, it seemed we had a good chance to win. Public support and opinion were on our side. Just as a tennis player often takes his or her eye off the ball, and hits it out or into the net thinking the point is already won, so Stanfield took his eye off the ball and acted as if he and his party were already in power. With little or no caucus consultation, he adopted a policy of wage and price controls—Strike Three. Once more, Trudeau had a renewed lease on Sussex Drive.

Academics forever want opposition parties to show off and announce their policies. While it is true that responsible opposition parties must prepare policies for the hoped-for transition to power, the public rarely, if ever, votes for their policies. In modern times, they have, more often than not, voted governments out. This nicety escaped Stanfield's notice and Trudeau whipped him with glee.

Pierre Trudeau came to Cowansville, in my riding, during the 1974 campaign and addressed about 1,000 workers at a noon-hour rally in front of the Town Hall. I parked behind the Town Hall building and could hear him roar over the loudspeaker, "I admit Heward Grafftey has been a good Member of Parliament, but this time enough is enough—a vote for Heward means your wages will be frozen at the gate." I increased my majority in the 1974 vote, but Trudeau took Stanfield down for his third successive fall and formed another majority government.

While Stanfield was perceived as being decent and honest, such fundamental errors of leadership on his part guaranteed him permanency and virtual tenure in his role as Leader of the Opposition. Trudeau would exploit these God-given gaffes handed to him on a silver platter. While the lustre wore off Pierre Trudeau's crown, gifts from heaven would not end with Stanfield. Trudeau could count on Joe Clark outdoing Stanfield. After losing to Clark in the 1979 elections, Trudeau had no stomach for the role of Leader of the Opposition. He sat haplessly in his chair in the House with a newly-grown beard.

Late in November 1979, the Liberal House Leader, Allan

MacEachen, whipped up the troops and down went Joe's minority government. Clark literally handed power back to the Grits in what history will record as one of the greatest acts of leadership stupidity in the history of Canadian politics. The budget measure that taxed gasoline by eighteen cents at the pump was what did it. Soon, Trudeau was back at Sussex Drive with a majority government.

While both Stanfield and Clark were and are honourable men, and while Trudeau was a good campaigner, I've never felt that the media has truly pointed out how the charismatic Trudeau, with all his campaigning skills, could have succeeded without counting on two-nations, Claude Wagner, wage and price controls, and Clark's unbelievable performance in the House on that evening late in November 1979. It is fair to say Pierre had luck on his side. I remember a sports writer saying to a pro golfer after he had won a championship, "Weren't you lucky today?" The golfer replied, "Maybe, but it seems the harder I work and practice, the luckier I get." I know, in playing tennis, an aggressive opponent who plays well will push me into making horrendous fundamental errors. I have what is called an *off day*. One day I got beaten and said to my opponent, "I was playing badly." "No, you weren't," my opponent retorted, "I was playing well." Is it the same in politics? Was Trudeau playing so well that he pushed Stanfield and Clark into their off days? Somehow I feel my analogy is not all that solid. Stanfield and Clark could have conceivably courted defeat all by themselves.

I spent the years between 1968 and 1972 preparing to recapture my seat in the townships. From time to time, whenever I encountered Carol Guérin, she would pass on a message of greeting from Pierre Trudeau. Apart from that, I saw nothing of him except on television. By the time of the 1972 elections, Trudeau was still riding high in Quebec.

I recently told Trudeau an amusing incident that occurred during the 1972 election. We both laughed heartily. I was canvassing the home of a constituency high school principal. In 1972, our party was at an extremely low ebb in my province and while I didn't entirely disassociate myself from it, it was pointed out to me by some constituents that it seemed I was running as an Independent. As I left the high school principal's home and was turning to go down the pathway in front of his house, he yelled at me, "You've got my vote, Heward. I'm right behind you and Trudeau. You make a fine team together. Say hello to him when you get to Ottawa."

The two years I spent in the House after my re-election in 1972 and before the 1974 elections were not truly memorable for me. Trudeau continued to be a charismatic leader, but his speeches in the Commons rarely made for great occasions. The rule forbidding speeches being delivered from prepared text had long been abandoned. The House was no longer a debating chamber. This suited Trudeau, who read his dull speeches from a prepared text in a low voice. This was hardly the stuff of inspirational oratory.

Soon after the 1974 elections, my friend and colleague in the house, Perrin Beatty, got married. During his student days, his new wife, Julie, had shared lodgings with Margaret Sinclair, soon to be Margaret Trudeau. Some days after the wedding, the Beattys held a lovely buffet dinner reception at the old Rideau Club on Ottawa's Wellington Street. I sat near Pierre and Margaret and they seemed so very happy together. When I left the club, there was a light snowfall. Pierre lifted Margaret from her feet and carried her over the snowbank and into the waiting limousine.

Around the same time, my wife and I shared the same table with Margaret Trudeau and Mitchell Sharp at a dinner reception at the Governor General's at Rideau Hall. Margaret and my wife engaged in good and lively conversation, and seemed very happy. Yet, the saying goes that "things are not always what they seem." For a sensitive and very private man the separation and divorce must have been extremely hard for him to endure. In recent years, whenever I have met with him, he has mentioned Margaret in a kind and gentle way.

While many writers have written about Trudeau's Jesuit schooling at Brébeuf School and College, few, if any, have understood the importance of this training in shaping his thinking and outlook. Private conversation with Trudeau is never rushed. He speaks deliberately in a very low voice, and you can almost see his brain at work, cool and deliberate. He often shows his impatience in conversation with those who have not thought out their positions or arguments. He prefers healthy confrontation to endless "think-ins" with those who are exploring a subject but have no firm views or opinions of their own. Once I ventured to discuss constitutional change with him, but had not come to any firm conclusions of my own on some specific points. He became somewhat testy and the conversation ended when my rejoinders were met with a long period of silence on his part. In short, most of the time Pierre Trudeau is sure of himself, says what he means, and means what he says. This characteristic spells trouble for him at times, especially in the political field where double-talk is often at a premium. At the opening of the last Parliament, I was sitting beside Mitchell Sharp during the inaugural ceremonies in the Senate. Sharp brought up a case in point regarding Trudeau's self-confidence. Sharp, an ardent Trudeau admirer, stated that the former Prime Minister often expected others to have the same degree of self-confidence as he has himself. He described a problem with John Turner. When Turner offered his resignation as Finance Minister, Sharp felt Turner just needed some prime ministerial stroking and massaging. Instead, Trudeau accepted his Minister's resignation on the spot and offered him a senate seat. Turner's nose was out-of-joint. He was so enraged that he immediately announced his resignation to the press. Sharp felt the whole incident was unnecessary.

After the 1974 elections, I was destined to stay in opposition for another five years. They were a long five years. They say that governments too long in power become stale and arrogant. What is less apparent, but equally important and rarely understood or noticed, is that oppositions too long in opposition become dispirited and oppose badly. Democracy is not well served. That was the case with me and my party during the years between 1974 and 1979.

After the 1976 Progressive Conservative Leadership Convention, when Claude Wagner went down to defeat on the last ballot at the hands of Joe Clark, Wagner went into a long sulk. He was ripe for the picking and Trudeau put him in the Senate. That left me and Roch Lasalle alone in Quebec.

Whether or not it was done with Trudeau's knowledge, Jean Marchand visited my West Block office on at least two occasions. He mentioned how tired I must have been after so many hard grassroots battles in Quebec and he alluded to the desirability of my going to the Senate. I told him directly that I would rather accept welfare than sit in the Senate—a body I have no use for and feel should be abolished, if not immediately, then when we write a new Constitution. Occasionally in Ottawa or elsewhere, people insist on addressing me as Senator Grafftey. I honestly feel insulted as those involved surely don't know me very well. With difficulty, I try to be polite, but am forced to correct their error.

Around this same time, Trudeau felt Jack Horner was ripe for the picking. Horner, another defeated Progressive Conservative leadership candidate bristled at the thought of serving under Clark. He crossed the floor to serve as Trudeau's Agriculture Minister. Maybe Pierre felt I was ripe for the Senate, too. I rather think that is the case and, at least, he secretly admires me for turning Marchand down flat.

After the defeat of his government in the spring of 1979, Trudeau never really attempted to adapt to the role of Leader of the Opposition. He sat in his chair opposite me in the House in a sullen mood. He had grown a beard and seemed totally dispirited. When I walked with him in the procession at John Diefenbaker's funeral, while he was as friendly as ever with me, his mood seemed dark. I wasn't surprised.

The Clark government received a lot of criticism for postponing the new Parliament until the fall of 1974. Few remembered that Diefenbaker had done the very same thing when he had been in a minority situation in 1957. The difference was that the 1957-58 Parliament passed a fair amount of popular legislation, and Diefenbaker went to the Governor General to call a snap election when we were far ahead in the polls. For one thing, Don Fleming had cut taxes; in his first budget, John Crosbie raised them. Admittedly, he did not have much leeway. We were trailing by a large margin in the Gallup poll and, unlike the first Diefenbaker minority government, had passed no popular measures. Joe Clark was determined to govern as if he had a majority. In many ways this was understandable, given the economic times and the tough decisions with which we were faced. The Créditistes could not be counted on. The NDP always yelled and screamed, but when the chips were down, they had a propensity for sliding into bed with the Grits. For Clark, compromising on economic measures to suit the NDP was out of the question.

Cabinet documents are normally supplied to ministers before meetings of the full Cabinet or its committees, so that they can assess the political implications of decisions that may be taken in the full Cabinet. The only Minister who escapes from these procedural require-ments is the Finance Minister. He, his deputy and the Prime Minister, and sometimes the Clerk of the Privy Council, are really the only people who are fully briefed on the import of the budget before its final form is put before the House. This is a tradition that has exacted an unnecessary political toll and will continue to do so until the whole question of the budget's preparation is reformed. Budgets usually have grave political implications. The fact that they are formulated with no proper political vetting seems incredible. No amount of prior consul-tation with interested parties can begin to replace parliamentary control over budget making. No Canadian minister of finance con-sulted more broadly than Mike Wilson. This did not prevent him from plunging into trouble with his first budget.

John Crosbie's budget of December 11, 1979, might seem quite a statesmanlike document in retrospect, but for a minority government just getting underway, it was Russian roulette and bravado, heavily sprinkled with a good dose of subliminal Tory masochism. The pro-posed changes would affect the capital gains tax and help farmers and small businessmen, but nobody on the opposition benches noticed them or talked about them. An immediate excise tax on gasoline was what did it; it's all I heard about in every corner of my riding during the ensuing election. The fact that the Liberals subsequently compounded the felony does not seem to matter. The Conservatives were about to lose power. When finally we went down on prime-time television before the eyes of an incredulous nation, I made no apologies for losing my cool in public during an interview on French-speaking television in the lobby of the Commons, after the vote.

In a recent conversation, Trudeau told me he believed Clark felt the Tories could win the ensuing election. After the vote defeating the Clark government, Trudeau remained in his seat in a state of disbelief and shock. Like myself, he never believed what had happened.

He just sat, staring ahead for quite a while before leaving his seat in the Commons. The night after the vote, all during the night the telephone rang off the hook in Clark's office. Party supporters from all over the country pleaded with him to change the order of business in the House the next day, to turn the clock back, as Pearson once did when his government was defeated on a financial matter, and cancel the vote. They pleaded with him not to go to the people under the prevailing circumstances. Clark had not consulted his Cabinet on dissolving Parliament. He had taken advice, mostly from unelected officials in his office. He was bound to go to the polls and he would pay the supreme penalty.

Originally, many said the Grits would be blamed for plunging us into the election. I knew better. As the election got underway, it is true, the Grits were criticized for bringing us down. Then the pendulum swung and the Tories were blamed for their stupidity in letting the vote take place. Eighteen cents at the pump was the issue. The rest is history. The fact that the Grits reinstated the tax makes no difference.

Within weeks after regaining power, Trudeau was faced with an historic referendum in my province. The separatist forces of René Lévesque's Parti Québécois were pitted against Trudeau and his federalist Liberals, together with Claude Ryan and his provincial Liberal Party in opposition. For my part, the worst had come to pass. The Progressive Conservative Party had been totally marginalized in Quebec. A major question of national unity had been polarized in the extreme between two opposing political parties. I knew that, whatever the result of the referendum, the political polarization of this question meant long-term trouble.

At the beginning of the referendum campaign, the president of the Liberal association in my riding telephoned and asked me to take part in the "No" forces campaign in the upcoming election. While I had severe reservations about the campaign being run out of the headquarters of a single party, I resolved the conflict in favour of accepting. As I stumped my old riding, it seemed strange for me to be in such close contact with Liberal Party headquarters and Liberal organizers working out of the very rooms where they recently gathered to fight me during the elections earlier that winter. I had no choice. My party had virtually vacated the field and eliminated itself from the constitutional debate by a series of disastrous policies and unbelievable stupidity. Eventually Brian Mulroney would bring a gang of Separatists to Ottawa and destroy his party.

In Bromont, Quebec, I campaigned one night with Robert Bourassa who didn't seem to be enjoying his political exile. In speaking for the "No" forces, he claimed to envisage a sort of future European Common Market arrangement for Canada. His views were quite unclear to me. They become even less clear when he was Premier.

On the eve of the referendum vote, I attended the rally for the "No" forces at the Paul Sauvé Arena in Montreal's northeast end. Jean Chrétien had done a magnificent job at the grassroots level for a number of weeks. He went from town to town preaching the virtues of Canada in simple and meaningful terms, thus gaining the eternal enmity of the Quebec elite, the same elites who detested Trudeau. I had been invited to sit on the platform not far from where Pierre Trudeau delivered his historic speech for the "No" forces. At the end of the rally he greeted me warmly. While he had many other things on his mind, I think he realized the lonely road I had been plodding over the years in Quebec and, perhaps how isolated I must have felt during the referendum campaign.

Trudeau had promised constitutional reform to Quebecers in this Montreal speech. This resulted in the historic constitutional conference and the so-called exclusion of Quebec and René Lévesque after the "night of the long knives." I was on hand on Parliament Hill with other Privy Councillors, when the Queen came to sign the repatriation bill in the spring of 1981. The rain fell on the open air ceremonies and I, with others, got soaked. As I sat in the great hall of the West Block at the banquet when Her Majesty the Queen delivered her address, I turned to Tommy Douglas, who was sitting beside me, and asked him if he felt the rain was an omen of things to come. He merely smiled—perhaps he didn't want to rain on the parade. After the election of Brian Mulroney as our party Leader in 1983, little time was left before another federal vote would be held. In the early eighties, a right-wing storm seemed to be blowing over much of the western world. Ronald Reagan was installed in the White House, Margaret Thatcher at Westminster and now Brian Mulroney appeared on the scene in Canada.

Trudeau, a former socialist, was now a left-of-centre Liberal, and he must have appreciated his views were out of step with the times— times I am sure, like myself, he wanted no part of, and furthermore, felt incapable of influencing and participating in. Realistically, he must have wondered about whether or not he could win, but I firmly believe that the temper of the times surely influenced his decision to call it a day. It was no surprise to me when he announced his decision to step down as Liberal Leader and Prime Minister after a long walk in the snow near 24 Sussex Drive.

Since his retirement from active politics, I have seen more of Pierre Trudeau than I did during his active years as Prime Minister. While he no longer practices judo, he keeps fit with skiing and swimming, especially at his pool in his new home. He still has the "wanderlust" in him and at the drop of a hat is off before you know it to some far corner of the world. He seems happiest when paddling a canoe in the wilderness in some corner of Canada's north.

In one way, he reminds me of Hugh MacLennan. Hugh never appreciated being interrupted at meals by admirers seeking autographs. On the other hand, I detected that he liked recognition. Whenever we ate in public, his eyes scanned the room, I think sometimes to see if anyone there recognized the elder statesman of Canadian literature. Trudeau remains a very private man. That does not stop him from walking to his downtown office on René Lévesque Blvd. from his home on Pine Avenue. On his walks between his office and home, he is a happy "boulevardier," often exchanging greetings along the way. One day, I was walking along Sherbrooke Street and ran into him not far from his office. He greeted me with a broad smile. After a brief conversation, I turned to leave him. There was a small queue of people waiting to shake hands.

One of the more interesting conversations I ever had with him came at the end of one of our summer luncheons in the open air. I posed the question of Canada's evolving nationalism in a world where traditional borders are breaking down because of modern communications, global trading blocks and multinational corporations. He gave the question a lot of thought. He agreed with me that this state of affairs rendered traditional notions about nationalism obsolete. While his ideas in response to my observation were more than interesting, we reached few conclusions on the subject. This conversation prompted me to wish that he would write more often on public affairs in the style of his *Cité Libre* days or in the style of his excellent thesis opposing the Charlottetown Accord.

In the spring of 1986, when Hugh MacLennan celebrated his eightieth birthday, Pierre accepted my invitation to attend the reception that I organized with Lorne Webster. MacLennan and Trudeau formed a mutual admiration society. During the FLQ crisis, at the time of the War Measures Act, Trudeau and MacLennan ran into each other on Sherbrooke Street in Montreal. Trudeau didn't recognize MacLennan at first. Only after Hugh had congratulated and praised him for what he felt was his daring and courage during the crisis did Pierre suddenly realize he was talking to the author of *Two Solitudes*. At the birthday celebration, Trudeau obviously recognized and enjoyed talking with many of Hugh's friends from the academic and literary worlds. It was a good and happy occasion.

Pierre Trudeau, since his retirement from public life, now works with the Montreal law firm of Heenan, Blaikie. From the view of his modest, glassed-in office atop the IBM Building in the centre of the city, he has a panoramic view of Montreal looking south over the river toward the Eastern Townships. Much of his work is on the international level. When I saw him late in November 1994, he had just returned from Mexico the night before, looking tanned and fit and wearing a dark blue beret sitting at a slight angle on his head. We had lunch in my home at the Tropic Nord at Cité du Havre in the Port of Montreal. We ate outside on the balcony facing the glassed-in tropical atrium. The other guests were David Culver, former CEO of Alcan, and my very dear friend, Jean Wadds, who had been appointed High Commissioner to the United Kingdom by Joe Clark in 1979. Trudeau kept her on for four years after he took over as Prime Minister. On a visit to London, Jean Chrétien informed Wadds that the Liberal caucus wanted her out, but Trudeau insisted on her staying. In many ways it

Pierre Trudeau walking home from his downtown
Montreal law offices, accompanied by his old Ottawa
assistant, Tom Axworthy, 1995.
Photo: Robert Galbraith

was a wise move on his part. Like myself, he must have realized that Wadds was very able and it made good sense to have a Conservative in the post of High Commissioner at the time when Margaret Thatcher and her Tories were reigning at Westminster. I always found that, when I was a Tory, the British Tories greeted me as a member of the club whenever I visited them at Westminster. Jean helped Trudeau and his Liberal government pilot the constitutional repatriation act through a series of potential hurdles and difficulties in London. She did a superb job. Trudeau often said to me, "Heward, things went well in London for us in the constitutional negotiations because of three ladies, Her Majesty the Queen, Margaret Thatcher and last, but not least, Jean Wadds."

Before the meal, Trudeau and I and the other guests discussed the recent U.S. midterm elections. While he said he had not followed the campaign all that closely, Trudeau, like myself, felt Clinton was attempting to get some pretty non-radical measures through Congress and he believed the President's unpopularity was not deserved. Trudeau, describing himself as a left-of-centre Liberal, felt the health care legislation proposed by Clinton was relatively mild compared to initiatives taken in the same field in Canada many years ago. He said, "It's hard to understand what's happening south of the border." I observed that we should never underestimate the power of special interest groups in the United States. I also ventured the opinion that, in a day and age where people tend to abhor too much direct government intervention and regulation, Clinton could have used different methods to achieve the same goals.

The repatriation of our Constitution was an act of obvious importance for Trudeau, a milestone as he approached the end of his active political career. That Lévesque and his PQ government did not sign on is to be regretted. Trudeau understood the political dynamics at play and felt that no premier leading a Parti Québécois government would ever sign on. He claimed he had no other option but to proceed without Lévesque unless he wanted to give away the store. Trudeau wasn't about to give away the store. That option was left open to Brian Mulroney, who exploited it to the nth degree with disastrous results for his party and Canada.

It wasn't Trudeau's first major confrontation in the constitutional field. In 1968, he had squared off with Daniel Johnson in Ottawa. Later on it was with Robert Bourassa at Victoria, when agreements seemed to be reached only to collapse after Bourassa's Health Minister, Claude Castonguay, got his ear. Bourassa reversed his decision to agree and scuttled the proceedings. Trudeau was no novice at such goings on.

On the September weekend in 1989 when Jean Chrétien was chosen Liberal Leader, the Meech Lake Accord was being negotiated in Ottawa. Everyone I spoke with said passage of the accord was a must, and that it was a last chance for Canada. I disagreed entirely. For me, the passage of the Meech Lake Accord would have encouraged an unhealthy regionalism, a regionalism that would have meant a central authority that was next to meaningless. The rhetoric that claimed that Meech was our last chance was just that—rhetoric. The proponents of such nonsense did not know Canada's strength, for they chose to ignore our history. Mulroney, acting like a negotiator during a strike, neglected to define and defend the federal authority, something every prime minister has done since Confederation. Of course most of the premiers were for it. Mulroney had given the store away. I never expected Meech Lake to wash and was not at all surprised when it ultimately went down.

During the proceedings that lead to the Meech Lake failure, I never conferred or spoke with Pierre Trudeau. Such was not the case with the Charlottetown Accord and the subsequent referendum. It came as no surprise to me when Trudeau spoke out emphatically against the Charlottetown Accord. I had spoken with him and compared notes on a few occasions before his much-publicized speech at a Chinese restaurant in Montreal. Before the speech, he had a hard-hitting article filled with devastating logic published in *Maclean's* and the Francophone publication, *L'Actualité*. After reading the article, rejecting the terms of the Charlottetown Accord, it wasn't hard to know where he stood and how he would vote in the referendum. I had an article published in the *Montreal Gazette* before Trudeau's appeared. Some weeks before the referendum vote, Trudeau expressed fears that the accord would pass. I told him I was more optimistic for the "No" side and felt quite confident that once the general population understood its implications, they would turn thumbs down on it.

In conversation, Trudeau was very modest about the effect he felt his public stand would have on the referendum vote. I felt otherwise. While not everyone always agreed with his constitutional stand, his views were always respected and listened to. I strongly believe Pierre Trudeau influenced the outcome of the vote. Canadians, even while differing strongly with him, generally respected his integrity and were, more often than not, proud of him when he went abroad as a spokesman for Canada.

During the last week of the referendum vote, I was reminded of many federal campaigns in Brome-Mississquoi. As election day approached, the elites wrote me off as a loser. Invariably, I bounced back to win. On the eve of the referendum vote, most of the media, the premiers and all the federal parties in the House of Commons supported the accord. Many asked: "With such an army of establishment support, how could the accord go down?" They underestimated the intelligence and the grassroots concern of individual voters. They also underestimated the distaste for Mulroney's manoeuvring and panic, and the deep sense of pride in Canada in every part of the land, including Quebec. Simultaneously, they under-estimated the population's desire to leave the federal authority intact. Many blame the defeat of the Meech Lake and Charlottetown Accords for our current dilemma. In my view, the passage of either of these accords would have put us on the fast track to eventual breakup. As it is now, while time is running out, we shall surely save and preserve the union. I am more than confident that we shall, but it will take, among other things, hard work, imagination and a profound sense of artistry.

I have stated on more occasions than I can remember beginning in the early 1960s when John Lesage opted out of joint federal programs, that we must get to work to draft a modern constitution for modern times. Although Lesage's initiatives were much on my mind, I felt that such a modern constitution was a requisite for all the other parts of Canada.

Nothing more clearly symbolizes the breakdown of the federal authority and "politics as usual" than the rise of the Reform Party in the West—and the Bloc Québécois in Quebec. Among other things, renewed federal leadership must marry Quebec nationalism with the valid aspirations of western Canada. This will go a long way towards uniting Canada and giving us a new constitution.

Britain had its constitution, largely unwritten, and every schoolchild in the United States knows something about theirs. A constitution is the very foundation of a country, its government, and the basic framework from which most laws emanate. This should also be true for Canada, but unfortunately, our constitutional history symbolized our national uncertainty and division. Constitutions are political documents in the truest and broadest sense of the word. Constitutions and the political will they are founded upon are meant to reflect national stability. Judging by these criteria, we must see that Canada is currently in terrible shape. So much of what is wrong with our practices at all levels of government stems from constitutional confusion and instability. We can and should do better, but those who speak out for constitutional change and reform will have to be more precise in what they mean. For well over thirty years, the constitutional debate has gone on between politicians and bureaucrats. The people have been left out of the discussions. They have been left confused by slogans put together behind closed doors. Who knows what they mean—"Two Nations," "Special Communities," "Maîtres chez nous," "Sovereignty Association," "Separation," "Equality or Independence," "Notwithstanding Clause," "Parallel Agreement," "Opting Out," "Distinct Society." The so-called constitutional experts have had a field day, and the list seems never-ending. Just recently I was at a symposium on national unity at McGill University. For the first time I heard the expression, "asymmetrical federalism." It was based on the notion that sovereignty association could be the result of some new kind of federalism. Since nobody at the symposium knew what sovereignty association meant, it is not hard to imagine that my request for a clarification of the concept of "asymmetrical federalism" was met with prolonged and stony silence among the academic and resident constitutional experts. Lack of precision in constitutional debate leaves the door open for political demagogues.

In order to effect meaningful constitutional change, attitudes must change. In spite of our individual persuasions, we must stamp out intolerance, bigotry, the rise of racism and politicians who pit English against French for votes.

I do not believe Trudeau shares my views about the need for a modern constitution for modern times. While I have already said that he understands the politics of Quebec's separatist movement, I sense that he feels his repatriation initiative of the early eighties was and is good enough to maintain a viable constitutional status quo. Like Chrétien, he steadfastly maintains that Canadians have had a belly full of constitutional wrangling and that political leaders who open up constitutional negotiations in the near future would do so at their peril.

This attitude reminds me of the college undergraduate student who has flunked a mandatory course three times saying, "Further study and action on this course is useless. I'll have to shove the problem under the table and muddle through and graduate anyway." This attitude does not get the student a degree. When it comes to constitutional affairs, the same head-in-the-sand attitude will not serve the Canadian union. Trudeau's and Chrétien's attitudes are under-standable, yet I believe they are talking about the present shopworn constitution in relation to a nation state and nationalism which has no relevance to present times.

As we move into a new century, Canadians from coast-to-coast, including Quebecers, have a golden opportunity to give Canada a modern constitution for modern times. I am not talking about renewed federalism based on the British and North America Act, which has served its purpose long ago. I believe the Fathers of Confederation would be the first to agree with this assertion. They would be the first to wish us well as we embark together in drafting our new Constitution. I am talking about a new unifying constitution that would take us into the twenty-first century.

A few years ago, I went to a garage to have my car repaired. The mechanic said: "Your car is finished; it's no use repairing it. It has served you well, but I'd be dishonest if I did anything to put it back on the road. Turn it in, Heward, and get a new car." The same is true with our present Constitution. We have fiddled with it long enough, especially over the last thirty years. While it has often served us well in the past, we must trade it in for a new one. While Pierre Trudeau hangs on to his old Mercedes-Benz which is now well over thirty years old, he is going to have to reconcile himself to the fact that he cannot do the same with our present Constitution. It must be traded in for a new one.

CHAPTER TEN

Hugh MacLennan

In the preface to my book, *Lessons from the Past*, Hugh describes how he first remembers meeting me. He wrote:

> A long time ago, though sometimes it seems only yesterday, I encountered a little tiny boy, sitting among some eleven other little tiny boys, at a long table in the dining hall of Lower Canada College in Montreal. The little tiny boy was Heward Grafftey—unforgettable then as he is today. It was lunch time and I, as master there, had to serve the boys before I ate anything myself, and sometimes the lunch was over before I had enough time to eat anything.
>
> Lower Canada College today is a splendid school, run by Canadians, and has many more students than it had in my time. It also has fine libraries for the boys, and its teachers, so far as I know, are better-trained than most of the ones in my day.
>
> The dining hall where I first encountered Heward must have been unique in Canada, indeed in the world. It was, as is, a very large room with panelled walls. But the windows are, or were, close to the ceiling, because the hall was part of the basement. It was created by the man who built the school and apparently designed it, Doctor Fosbery. This unique personality had retired a few years before Heward arrived and had returned to England where he was born.
>
> That dining room was enormous, and just below the ceiling it was decorated with the stuffed heads of what once had been

wild animals—moose heads, deer heads, wolf heads, bear heads, and fox heads encircled the room, all mounted so high that they couldn't be touched unless you got on a step ladder. Occasionally dead insects dropped out of them. Beneath the heads of the beasts were small portraits of British admirals who had served during the eighteenth century, admirals of the Red and admirals of the Blue. Surrounded by these apparitions, though below them, the boys and masters ate at tables and were served by cockney and Ulster waitresses from the kitchen.

The gallery of dead animals' heads turned the corners on the west end of the hall and were divided by a large portrait of Dr. Fosbery himself, in academic robes. This extraordinary personality had come out of Canada before the First World War and had, as the saying went in those forgotten days, "made good in the colonies." He was very tall, very lean, and his arms seemed constantly to be waving. His portrait had been commissioned by some old boys who reverenced him and it had been painted by Lilias Torrance Newton just after McGill had given him an honorary degree, the only academic degree he ever had, so far as I know. Mrs. Newton was a remarkable portrait-painter—years later she was commissioned by the Canadian government to paint a portrait of the young Queen Elizabeth II. In some mysterious way, she captured the essence of Dr. Fosbery and he seemed to belong exactly where his picture was hung, the centrepiece in this extraordinary collection of stuffed wild animals' heads.

It was in this setting that I first encountered Heward Grafftey. He was new to the school, he was bubbling with delight in his new surroundings, and was mimicking with remarkable accuracy the eccentricities of some of his teachers. He compared one of them to a mashed potato he was waving on the end of his fork, but at a look from me he restrained himself from throwing it.

Time passed, Heward rapidly matured. He worked hard at his Latin and became very good at it, but he never lost that wonderful eagerness he had possessed as a child. Nor was his life easy. One day, I shall never forget it, I was on duty in the corridors at recess and he came out of the headmaster's office. Some years after the retirement of Dr. Fosbery, Stephen Penton had become headmaster and set about putting the school into some kind of order. In time, he succeeded magnificently. But on this morning, Heward was in distress. Mr. Penton had just told him that his mother had died, and Heward sobbed in my arms.

Now I will venture a comparison that may startle Heward. In one area of his life— or rather, his attitude to it— resembles Winston Churchill. Winston's father, Lord Randolph Churchill, was no easy man in his dealings with his son, and in some respects his mother was even more formidable. Yet Winston reverenced and honoured them both. Heward's mother was far from being the flamboyant creature Lady Randolph Churchill became, but she was certainly a powerful personality. Nor was Heward's father as ruthless as Lord Randolph. He was, however, a very formidable man, a war hero of the highest order when he returned from the terrible battles in France with a flawless record and high decorations for valour. He could not have been an easy parent for a hyper-sensitive boy. Yet Heward avoided the Oedipal trap. Instead of revolting, he was determined to make his father proud of him, but on his own terms.

After Lower Canada College, he wisely decided to avoid McGill University and go instead to Mount Allison. Here there is no big city like Montreal in which a university in McGill's location must struggle for existence amid the pressure of urban traffic and high-rise office buildings. Sackville, New Brunswick, is a very small town and its surroundings are not only beautiful, they are tremendously dramatic, for the town is at the end of the vast Fundy tides at the Tantramar Marsh, about which Charles G.D. Roberts wrote his finest poems. Heward was not only happy there. He absorbed the reality of an harmonious environment in which farm people all know one another and understand the basic human condition without having to describe it.

After graduating from Mount Allison, Heward studied law at McGill and then decided to go into public life in order to be of service to his country. To him this meant being of personal service to his constituents.

Apart from a speech he wrote and would give at Princeton University, Hugh's preface to my book, to the best of my knowledge, was the very last piece he wrote in his lifetime.

In 1895, Samuel MacLennan started his practice as a colliery doctor in Glace Bay, Nova Scotia. Five years later, in 1901, he married Katherine (Katie) MacQuerrie. Their first child was a girl, Frances. John Hugh MacLennan was born on March 20, 1907, five years after the birth of his sister.

Sam was a stern and disciplined Presbyterian. In contrast, Katie was warm and outgoing, with a marked artistic temperament. Frances and Hugh would be strongly influenced by the contrasting examples of their parents. From Sam came a sense of melancholy and many exhortations to "work hard" and "get a good education." For Sam, a good education meant, among other things, being steeped in the classics. From their mother came the artistic side, warmth and affection, the love of music and much story telling. To her two children, she would read Robert Louis Stevenson's *A Child's Garden of Verses* and Tennyson's *The Princess*, together with many other poems. Later on, Hugh would read *Kidnapped* and *Treasure Island* and *Ivanhoe* and Swift's *Gulliver's Travels*. These early experiences would greatly influence Hugh's future writing career.

In 1913, Katie and the children joined Dr. Sam in London, where he was furthering his studies in the specialty of ears, nose and throat. Upon their return to Nova Scotia, the family settled in Sydney. Not long thereafter, in 1915, they moved to Halifax. In Halifax, Hugh attended the Tower Road School. It was in his youth that he witnessed the results of an event that inspired his first published novel, *Barometer Rising*. At 9:06 a.m. on December 6, 1917, the Imo and Mont Blanc collided in the Halifax Harbour—causing, with devastating results and loss of life and injury, the greatest man-made explosion in history to that date.

In 1928, he went off to Oxford with his coveted Rhodes Scholarship. In June 1932, Hugh boarded the S.S. Pennland at Southampton to return home for the summer. Little did he know that his future wife was on board. Dorothy Duncan wrote:

> That night and the next and the next we talked, walking the quiet decks after we tired of the lounge. How the inmates of the cabins below must have hated us, when the hours after midnight seemed to us even better for walking than the hours before. They were the most effortless conversations I have ever taken part in, perfectly adapted to the mood of an uncommunicative young woman; for one question or remark on my part would elicit a half-hour's reply, and while it was being expanded I had ample opportunity to observe and listen to the fullness of things not spoken ... What could Nova Scotia be like, that its people gave this name to themselves with such pride in their voices that one felt they were convinced of a superiority palpable to the rest of the world?

> The falling stars had made him think of some lines of poetry; and as he repeated them without the self-consciousness an American would have shown, I found myself wondering if they were all as filled and running over with vitality and joy and intensity as this one. His voice rounded the cadences of classical verse as easily as it broke later into a popular New York dance tune which he had lately heard played in the Savoy. It was obvious that all the time he was loving it, tasting it, drinking deeply of it, and learning its ways he was managing to see life whole ... His shyness was as real as his charming manners and his ability on the tennis court, and yet ... too much of him at a stretch was apt to be exhausting, like trying to master a new skill without allowing for the psychological pauses necessary when the human mind adapts itself to something unfamiliar.

After Oxford, Hugh went on to Princeton for his Ph.D. He truly disliked the Germanic tradition used to teach the classics at Princeton. He did not perform well there and had difficulty getting his doctorate. In 1935, he was obliged to rewrite and revise his thesis, *Roman History and Today*.

A good part of the time, while at Princeton, he lived with Dorothy who encouraged him in his fiction writing. In June 1936, they were married in Wilmette, Illinois. Dorothy had a serious heart condition which greatly affected her health before and during their marriage.

Looking back at Hugh's early life, there was a remarkable and striking similarity between his and Wilder Penfield's backgrounds. Both came from Presbyterian homes; both were encouraged in scholarship, Wilder by his mother and Hugh mostly by his father. Wilder's mother and Hugh's father each steered their son towards a Rhodes scholarship and, in Hugh's case, it was his father. Both went to Oxford and Princeton. Each, in turn, was greatly influenced by work and travels in Europe. At Princeton, Wilder focussed on his future career in medicine; at Princeton, Hugh clearly saw his future in writing fiction. Both married during their student years and both joined with wives who would influence and encourage them in their life's work.

The year 1935 was not a good one for finding teaching jobs. The Depression ground on and Hugh's finances hit rock bottom. He was twenty-eight years old and much to his horror and humiliation, he was forced to seek further assistance from his father. Teaching jobs at universities, such as Dalhousie, were very difficult for a Canadian such as Hugh. Even with his honours degree from Oxford and his Ph.D. from Princeton, the job Hugh wished to have at Dalhousie went to an American. He registered his name with every teacher's agency in Canada and a few in the United States. Finally, he was offered a post at a private boys' school, Lower Canada College in Montreal teaching history and the classics at twenty-five dollars a week. In his novel, *The Watch That Ends the Night*, Hugh's satire of Waterloo School and its headmaster, Lionel Bigsbee, pointedly indicates the distaste he had for his job at LCC.

In 1937, two years after Hugh's arrival at LCC, I was enrolled, at the age of nine years, in grade three at the school. I would have to wait for my high school years before I actually had Hugh as a teacher. It was on the school bus I first remember meeting him. He sat up front in a single jumpseat near the driver facing across the aisle. He sat silently, and if he talked at all, it was to the driver when he stopped to pick up students. Hugh had a hole in his left eardrum which eventually was responsible for keeping him out of World War II. He always had cotton wool stuffed into his left ear.

I did not see that much of Hugh until I was fourteen and became one of his students. He remembered me at the meal table, and I remembered him. He was a great conversationalist and he never talked down to the younger boys. He talked enthusiastically about current events. I remember, too, how much he liked to talk about tennis. His accent confused me. It was a mixture of his good Cape Breton background and his stay in Oxford where he acquired the accent so easily assumed by many of our foreign service officers at the time. Our table in the dining room was situated near a wooden loudspeaker in the corner. During the meals, good music, mostly classical, was piped over the loudspeaker. The boys were meant to remain silent. Hugh delighted in the music. One day we heard Prokofief's *Peter and the Wolf*. Hugh listened with glee, his head moving from side to side in time to the music.

In February 1939, Dr. Sam died, leaving Hugh in a state of great depression. Hugh felt he was, in many ways, an extension of his father. After his death, Hugh continued to write letters to him. They would start, "Dear Dadden." This was not considered peculiar behaviour in that day and age. Seances with the departed were held in salons all over the country.

Before the time I actually had Hugh as a teacher in 1942, my recollections of him are few and far between. Some, nevertheless, are clear. After classes finished in the afternoon, he would often kick a soccer ball with the students on the large playing field in front of the school. I remember him in sports coat and grey flannels with a blue and white stripped scarf tied around his neck, the ends hanging well below his waist. He normally dressed informally in sports clothes, which included flannel shirts and handwoven ties.

The walls between the classrooms were not thick. Often I would hear him bellow, "There is noise—there is noise in the back of the room." The classroom for the graduating year in 1941 was situated beside mine. In mid-afternoon, for some reason or another, the graduating students decided to give their mathematics teacher, Peewee White, a raucous send-off. Peewee, an Englishman, stood little over five feet tall. The students erected a large notice outside the classroom door, "Little man, we've had a busy day." When Peewee entered the classroom, all hell broke loose. We could hear furniture flying. Fire-works were set off outside the windows. All of a sudden, Hugh entered the room. His bellowing and admonitions could be heard all over. I can hear him now, "Order, order, for God's sake, order!" The next day, there was a special assembly for all students in the dining hall. The headmaster announced punishments for the graduating class which included the sacking of all school prefects.

In his early years at LCC, he would work typing out his fiction in a small room by the infirmary on the top floor of the school. I often heard the click-clacking of his typewriter. On many occasions, when I passed by the teachers' common room on the way to the school library, I would see him in animated conversation, sometimes standing with a cup of coffee or tea in his hand. His special friend was our French teacher, Pit Péron. Hugh never mastered the French language, but, early on, he had grown to love Montreal. A walk down Sherbrooke Street West, between Guy and University Streets, was, for Hugh, pure joy. Little did I know it at the time, but Pit Péron was helping Hugh immensely with his insights into Quebec and French-speaking Canada. In many ways, Pit was indispensable in Hugh's writing of *Two Solitudes*.

I myself was once on the receiving end of Hugh's short temper. A few other students and I were practicing the lines for a school play, *Box and Cox*, in a room adjacent to the teachers' common room. Little did we know that Hugh was attempting to have a little shut-eye in a near-by room and that our thespian efforts were interrupting his rest. Hugh stormed into the rooms, arms waving, cascading abuse.

The Anglican Church of St. Columba was a couple of blocks away from our school. Occasionally, we would attend the church for school services of one kind or another. One day, I remember accompanying Hugh to one of these school services and sat beside him in the pew.

When the prayers were read out, I dutifully got down on my knees, while Hugh merely bent over and slumped. Walking back to the school after the service, I inquired as to why he slumped while I knelt. "Good God, Heward," he replied, "I'm a Presbyterian." From then on, I always referred to Hugh as a slumping Presbyterian.

By 1940, Dorothy convinced Hugh that he should write a novel with a distinctive Canadian flavour and that he should be proud to do so. Hugh dedicated *Barometer Rising*, "To the Memory of my Father." On October 2, 1941, Duell Sloan and Pearce published *Barometer Rising*. On the cover were the *Imo* and the *Mont Blanc*, together with the fiery horror resulting from their collision in Halifax Harbour. Each Monday morning at LCC, students would assemble in the dining hall for prayers, announcements and, sometimes, a little exhortation from a visiting "sky pilot." On the Monday morning after the publication of *Barometer Rising*, the headmaster announced the news. The other masters were lined up behind him and when the announcement ended, Hugh stepped forward, bowed his head and blushed to the screaming approval and clapping of the boys.

It is true that many boys felt Hugh's teaching was directed to the better students in his classes. In many ways, he literally gave up on the dullards. How often I heard him yell at the top of his voice, "I'm sick and tired of casting pearls before swine." In a class of 27 boys, four or five at the most could be considered good students. Knowingly or not, Hugh's teaching was directed to those four or five. The rest invariably created chaos and Hugh couldn't keep order. In many ways it could be said he wasn't cut out to be a school teacher. But for those of us who appreciated his stress on excellence and communicated with his artistic side, it was a privilege to have him as a teacher.

In 1942 I started my Latin classes with him and he was a superb teacher. For him, Rome and its poets lived in the present, and he communicated this sense of timelessness to some of his students. His love of the classics motivated me and a few others. In my third year of high school, at the age of sixteen, Hugh taught me European history and, once more, he was inspiring. He lectured from extensively prepared notes and, often, he would dictate them to us. For Hugh, history was truly a living subject. Again and again he would relate historical events to contemporary realities and conditions, as he had done in his Princeton doctoral thesis and with his studies at Oxford.

Hugh was outspoken and wasn't always easy to get along with. Many of the old boys were of the conservative establishment and were suspicious of him and his views. In old age, Hugh told me of his annoyance at D. S. Penton, the headmaster at LCC. Hugh had been awarded a Guggenheim Fellowship at Princeton. Penton balked at giving him a short leave of absence and Hugh was enraged.

On January 17, 1945, *Two Solitudes* was published. It was instantly acclaimed, the reviews were mostly excellent and sales boomed. *Two Solitudes* placed Hugh solidly on the map as a Canadian writer, writing for a positive Canadian identity as opposed to regional self-destruction. The theme that was central to Hugh's groundbreaking novel was contained in Rilke's famous statement, "Love consists in this—that two solitudes protect and touch and greet each other." *Two Solitudes* received the Governor General's Award for Fiction.

In 1945 Hugh left LCC to teach at McGill. The war was over, both in Europe and Japan. It was my final year, and for me he couldn't have chosen a worse time. Never again, at school or at university, would history or Latin classes be the same. During this last year, Hugh taught until around Thanksgiving and then he was off. I was sad. My subsequent teachers in Latin and history only served to increase my sense of sadness and frustration at Hugh's departure.

Between the LCC years and Hugh's semi-retirement in the mid-1970s, I only saw him now and again, although we did correspond. That didn't seem to matter, as our friendship had long ago taken root. In my freshman year at Mount Allison, we exchanged correspondence. He was happy that I had chosen Mount Allison and wrote most enthusiastically about my choice.

In 1952, Hugh and Dorothy moved to 1535 Summerhill at the end of the street, a cul-de-sac just above Sherbrooke off Côte-des-Neiges Road. The new apartment, where Hugh would spend the rest of his days, was located in an attractive red brick building with a large, black entrance door with white wood trimmings. His apartment was lined with books. If you looked carefully, you could find all seven of his novels, but they were not placed side by side.

While teaching at McGill, Hugh played a lot of tennis at the Montreal Indoor Tennis Club and swam regularly at the Montreal Amateur Athletic Association. Not far from where he lived was a small cafeteria situated in the Medical Arts Pharmacy where Hugh would often breakfast or take a light lunch and read his papers. Another one of his favourite haunts was Ben's Delicatessen situated near McGill and he would often be seen in animated conversation with his students.

The Tennis Club posed problems for Hugh. His world was the world of ideas, of serious conversation, often relating to contemporary events and their relation to the past. Perhaps he can rightfully be accused of being insensitive when he imposed his comments on others in the locker room of the tennis club after completing a set. On the other hand, I can truly sympathize with him. One day at my own club, a well-known Montreal lawyer admonished me in the locker room for wanting to discuss constitutional issues and questions of national unity. He roared, "Shut up, Grafftey. We've come here to relax." Like Hugh, I was painfully bored. Tennis club members pointedly avoided him after the games. He would sit alone while stockbrokers, lawyers and other professionals would discuss their latest salmon fishing trip, golf scores or purchases of such items as dishwashers and stoves. This conversational fare wasn't for Hugh. I was often told how he was shunned. Although he would never admit it, I believe the resulting isolation hurt him immensely.

Hugh told me of one incident at the tennis club that was partially responsible for putting an end to his playing days. His doubles partner had a booming first serve. Hugh was at the net while his partner was serving, and the ball smashed into the back of his neck. Hugh's knees buckled and he collapsed to the court. I frequently saw him in a neck brace during his later years.

I would run into Hugh on Sherbrooke Street. Even if we chatted only briefly, he always left me with something to think about. One example of his perceptions, more often than not amusing, was "Mackenzie King had the same effect on Canada as Queen Victoria had on England."

Maybe because of his strong feelings about Canada, Hugh felt he could easily be a target for the terrorists. He and Tota, his second

wife, left North Hatley early in the fall of 1970. Perhaps he was being paranoid, but he insisted on telling me that he and Tota were being
followed en route to Montreal, where he erected an iron grill over
the window and across the wall of his apartment living room. It remained there until his death.

Like Wilder Penfield, Hugh was delighted when I was first elected
to Parliament in 1958. He would often write me. Sometimes I would
forward his letters to the Prime Minister. The following extract is
from a letter written to me after Diefenbaker's death:

> Diefenbaker, whom I met several times, was surely the most
> contradictory figure we ever had on the public scene. I think
> you understood him very well. We all know that it was not so
> much his failure in Quebec which ruined him and nearly ruined
> his party. It was his absurd notion that Quebec is "a province
> like any other." I myself heard him intone that he was dedicated
> to "unhyphenated Canadianism," that there will be no longer
> "French Canadians, English, Scotch—" he went down the
> whole ethnic list.
>
> I was sorry for Bob Stanfield. In 1967, I had to propose him
> for an honorary degree at McGill and it was assumed that I
> was proposing the next P.M. Then Trudeau entered and that
> was it. In Trudeau's early years Bob could not seriously oppose
> him because he agreed with him in broad terms, and of course,
> in the mood of 1968-1971, no Anglophone, especially one
> who struggled manfully to learn French, and without success,
> would have satisfied Quebec.

Hugh told me how he and Blair Fraser met with Diefenbaker at
24 Sussex Drive. They were preparing an article for *Maclean's Magazine*.
Diefenbaker was on the defensive with them. He had labelled Fraser
as a Grit and felt Hugh was, at best, a closet Grit. Hugh asked Diefenbaker about Quebec and French-speaking Canadians, referring to them
as unique and different on the national scene and then went on to ask
the Prime Minister how he intended to deal with the situation.
Diefenbaker became enraged and went into full flight. "There are no

French Canadians, English Canadians, Ukrainian Canadians, Polish Canadians," roared the Chief. "Only Canadians." The French-speaking/English-speaking subtlety had entirely escaped Dief's attention and appreciation. Hugh was bemused and saddened. Later on, in his last years, he often recounted this story to me. I would listen to it again and again, without interruption, as if I were hearing it for the very first time.

In later years, Hugh never ceased to praise my efforts in Parliament. He appreciated the fact that I was the first English-speaking Canadian to be elected seven times in a largely French-speaking riding. Whenever I spoke or wrote positively about French-English relations in my riding of Brome-Missisquoi, I could count on a word of encouragement from Hugh. I felt it was my role to represent in Ottawa the spirit of my riding where French and English lived and worked side-by-side in a genuine atmosphere of unity.

In 1967, Hugh won the Royal Bank Award which included a good amount of hard cash. I wrote him, "Welcome to the Capitalist Club!"

Sometimes we would meet in the country. In the summer of 1968, after the federal election, I drove over to North Hatley. Hugh's first wife, Dorothy, had encouraged him to garden, and the gardens around his modest country home were very beautiful. In the fall of the year, he loved to chop wood. During this visit, we ate lunch together at the Hovey Manor. Later on, after my re-election in 1972, he drove over to Magog in his four-door black Buick and we ate at a restaurant on the shore of the lake. At this meeting, he brought me a signed copy of *The Watch that Ends the Night*. I gave him a signed copy of my latest book, *The Senseless Sacrifice: A Black Paper on Medicine*. On both of these occasions, our luncheon conversation went well into mid-afternoon.

In the years before his death, Hugh would tell me that while *Two Solitudes* gained much publicity, he felt that *The Watch that Ends the Night* was his best novel. "After all," he said, "it was translated into many languages."

Hugh's teaching years at McGill left nobody indifferent. The reaction to him reminded me very much of the public reaction to Pierre Trudeau. His students either liked him very much or they found him boring and overbearing. The reviews on his teaching at

McGill were mixed.

The Precipice was Hugh's first novel to appear after he started his teaching career at McGill. In comparison to *Barometer Rising* and *Two Solitudes*, it was not received with enthusiasm by the reviewers or by the reading public. Its non-Canadian theme was a diversion for Hugh and forced him to re-evaluate his position in Canadian letters. From now on, whether he liked it or not, he would revert to form. While Hugh always strove to touch upon themes of universal significance, future novels would be distinctly Canadian in flavour and character.

On April 22, 1957, Hugh lost his beloved Dorothy. A final embolism had taken her life. Added to Hugh's great depression from this loss was another factor—Hugh was literally broke. He and Dorothy lived simply, and his writing brought in little in the way of financial rewards. Dorothy had been ill for some time, and in pre-Medicare days, the hospital bills piled up. Hugh had to borrow to pay them off.

The Watch that Ends the Night was published soon after Dorothy's death. He dedicated it to her: "To you wherever you are and whatever you may be, my thanks and this book." On May 15, 1959, three months after the publication of *The Watch that Ends the Night*, he married Frances Aline Walker in a small ceremony at the home of a friend in Montreal. Everybody called her "Tota." He and Dorothy had known and admired her for over ten years in North Hatley and Montreal.

Before I began to see a lot of Hugh and Tota in their final years, Hugh managed to hit the press and media for reasons other than literary. In his last years at McGill, the English department was staffed, to a great extent, by American faculty, and American teachers who, according to Hugh, were relatively unaware of his role on the Canadian scene and couldn't care less. Hugh, in semi-retirement, was given his own office space at the university, very much in the same way Wilder Penfield was given office space at the Montreal Neurological Institute during his retirement years. Because of space requirements, Hugh was asked to vacate his office. He left McGill in a huff and moved over to Concordia University where he was received with open arms. At Concordia, the students delighted in having easy access to him.

Another incident involved Hugh's legendary fight with his landlord on Summerhill Avenue. The landlord was determined to convert the

Hugh MacLennan
McGill University Archives

apartment building where Hugh and Tota lived into condominium units. Hugh claimed this initiative violated his lease agreement. The battle with his landlord was given great public exposure. The impression given was one of a ruthless landlord attempting to eject a poor writer from his lodgings onto the street. Local evening television news showed Hugh walking dejectedly along the sidewalk in front of 1535 Summerhill. He was given first-class legal advice and assistance and finally won his case.

It was during the last years of his life that my relationship with Hugh became unique and truly memorable. From 1982 until the time of his death in 1990, I would see Hugh and Tota at least once a week, normally for an evening meal. They continually said to me, "Heward, you are so kind." That was not the case. Being with them gave me a lot of pleasure. Hugh's affection for me grew into a great and loving friendship. Tota, while she became more and more feeble, mentally and physically, was always a sweet and gentle person.

For me, there is another side to the matter. I like to think I have friends in all age groups—from toddlers to one or two people nearly 100 years old. I cannot begin to understand why North American society tends to segregate the old and ageing. We put them on the junk heap in their old age and forget about them. We are the losers. Hugh and Tota were terribly isolated in their old age. I hardly ever remember anyone making an effort to see them or help them out in their final years. Hugh wasn't always easy. He could, at times, be irascible, but his great conversation and creative genius were always there. They were truly lonely and, with God's help, I like to think I alleviated their solitude and made life a bit more pleasant and happy for them both. If the last two years of Glenn Gould's life were virtually a "private hell" for him, Hugh's final days weren't much better, except, I believe, for our God-given friendship.

The period from 1980 to November 1990, when Hugh died, was not easy for Hugh and Tota in general, and for Hugh in particular. How often he repeated, "Getting old is no fun." Yet, there was more to it than that. After the completion of his last novel, *Voices in Time*, he would publish no more. Tota was losing her hold on reality. There was never any question in Hugh's mind that she should go into a home or institution. The subject never came up for discussion. Hugh was a caring and loving husband and his devotion to Tota was complete. This meant around-the-clock care. It is fair to say that this fact, combined with a certain fatigue, made it impossible for him to do what he loved most—write. In Hugh's last ten years, there was no faculty club where he could argue with the professors; no more garden to work in at North Hatley; no regular swimming at the Montreal Amateur Athletic Association and no tennis club at which to play tennis. He had no immediate family, and was cut off from his associates and friends. Books became his sole companions. One alleviating factor was his finances. In comparison with the decades of the 1940s and early 1950s, they were in relatively good shape. To the general public, it might be fair to say that his latent eccentricities were larger in old age. His paranoia after the FLQ crisis in the early 1970s was strange. He looked unkempt in his old clothes and, like many elderly people not confined to a home, it could be said that semi-malnutrition plagued his last days. His conversational style and intellectual interests isolated him from most people. The lives of artists, in general, are often sad and totally depressing. Hobbies, bridge, golf, cocktail parties, and light reading may sustain many in retirement. This fare does not suffice for the artist, who never really retires in the formal sense. When he or she can no longer compose, paint or write as they would wish, life can become something of a hell on earth. This was the case for Hugh during his last days, as it was for my Aunt Prudence, who would write to A.Y. Jackson just before she died, "If I cannot paint, I do not want to live." The last days of Glenn Gould, Schuman, Beethoven, Mozart and Hemingway, to name just a few, were not really better than Hugh's. My love for Hugh as a friend and his everlasting ability to think and converse on an amazing level mitigated the negative effects of his behaviour in old age—behaviour that was not always comprehensible to many observers. I confess that in looking at Hugh's last years, I cannot count myself as an impartial observer.

In the early 1980s, I moved into a large studio apartment in Montreal where I stayed when I drove in from Ottawa, which was still my principal residence. It was right across the street from Hugh on Summerhill Avenue. After forty years of being his neighbour at the other end of the street, we were together again. Often I would look out my window and see Hugh slowly shuffling along the opposite sidewalk, sometimes at mid-day to get food at a convenience store around the corner. They had a housekeeper, Francesca, who came once a week. She would put a few supplies in their refrigerator, but they only lasted a short time. The rest of the time, I think Hugh merely improvised. They hardly ever ate breakfast, and Hugh would put together a light lunch. The evening meal was their forté. Around 7:30 p.m., I would see Hugh and Tota slowly, ever so slowly, moving along the sidewalk. Hugh would shuffle ahead with his right hand extended behind his back gripping Tota's arm. Sometimes he would leave her standing while he went to the corner to hail a cab. On countless occasions, when not eating with them, I would run to the garage where my car was parked and, over their fervent protestations, drive them to their destination, which was usually Ben's Delicatessen or the MAAA. "At Ben's," Tota said, "I like to watch the people." At the MAAA, they would often eat alone in the main dining room, which wasn't used much at night.

When I ate with them as their guest, it was either at Ben's or the MAAA. The food and drink at Ben's was mediocre at the very best. It was not at all like the old student days in the fifties. Hugh must have recognized this but, while there, he imagined the past with ease. When we ate at the MAAA, we were invariably the last diners to leave. I could sense the staff waiting for us to depart as Hugh and Tota nursed their drinks—rye was his drink and Tota loved her gin and water.

Hugh couldn't leave Tota for long, but sometimes I would prepare a light lunch for him in my appartment. How he loved these occasions. We would talk and I would play his favourite classical music. During his youth, his mother sang Beethoven's *Missa Solemnis* in Halifax. I didn't know that at the time, but the *Missa Solemnis* was still Hugh's favourite classical work. He told me that, sometimes, he would write while listening to Bach. When they were my guests, I would take them to a restaurant, make a meal at my place or go to the Montreal Badminton and Squash Club in winter, or the Hillside Tennis Club in summer. At the Badminton Club there was a small upright piano in the lounge bar and I would often play for them, and how they loved it. Hugh and Tota especially liked to hear the aria from Bach's *Goldberg Variations* which I vowed to learn after being so moved by it at Glenn Gould's memorial service in Toronto. He and Tota appreciated it so much, and I loved to play it for them.

The Hillside Tennis Club, on Côte-des-Neiges across from the University of Montreal, is a beautiful oasis nestled in the side of the mountain. Hugh loved to wade in the shallow end of the pool; he wouldn't swim, but merely stood and bobbed up and down. On the veranda of the clubhouse, he would often hold court. Most everyone recognized him. Some would sit down and engage him in conversation, and he enjoyed it.

Picking up Hugh and Tota was a full-scale operation. Getting Tota into and out of my car was quite a task; she was becoming less and less mobile, and in the winter, the sidewalk in front of their apartment was invariably slippery. I would have to get my car as close to the front door as possible, up the garage ramp beside the building.

During the last decade of his life, Hugh was supposedly writing his memoirs or autobiography. When I asked him how things were going, he would become quite testy but assured me his work was progressing. His editor, Doug Gibson, would inquire, from time to time, if I knew how things were with Hugh's autobiography. My answers were always vague. Sometimes I would prod Hugh. "When shall we have your next novel, Hugh?" I would ask. The reply was nearly always the same. "Good God, Heward, never! I'm an old man now. *Voices in Time* was my last, and writing it nearly killed me." In a way, I was not being fair to him. Life for Hugh wasn't easy. His love for Tota never diminished—he cared for her ceaselesly. His ancient Underwood stood idle amid the paper chaos in his office at the end of the hall. But this did not stop him from encouraging others.

Creative writing can be a lonely business. My guess is that few creative artists, including the very famous, maintain close contact with their friends while writing, composing or painting. At the risk of generalizing, I firmly believe that the solitude the creative artist requires results in him or her being alone most of the time. I think of Mozart, Brahms and Beethoven. When they were not actively composing, they were thinking creatively *alone*. There is one compensatory factor—the artist lives with his or her work. Even in my own non-fiction writing as I lost contact with my friends, the book in progress became a constant friend and companion. It takes on a life of its own. When finally the publisher accepts your manuscript and you hand it over, invariably the loss is great and a real feeling of loneliness sets in. So it was with Hugh. With *Voices in Time*, Hugh had handed in his last manuscript and his loneliness was complete. On the other hand, it is my impression that the artistic mind tolerates loneliness somewhat more easily than others. The artist always has the companionship of a lively and creative imagination, and Hugh had such an imagination in abundance. He would call his old friend from Halifax, Charles Ritchie, usually on Sunday evenings, but I was frankly appalled that he never saw much of anyone in his later years, even if the situation was understandable. Charles Ritchie had a distinguished career at External Affairs and Hugh felt his subsequent writing was superb. He would say, "Charles' book, *Diplomatic Passport*, is a masterpiece. He'll be read a hundred years from now." Doug Gibson was also Ritchie's editor at Macmillan. It is interesting to note that Lucy Maud Montgomery of *Anne of Green Gables* fame, Hugh and Charles lived a stone's throw from each other during their youth in Halifax.

Conversation with Hugh was demanding. Small talk was rarely the order of the day. He was not a creative listener and one had to fight hard for equal time. His clothes became more and more worn with the passing of time. I don't think he bought any more clothes after the early 1950s. He normally wore a sports jacket and slacks, but had one medium grey coloured striped suit. He had trouble with his neck and often wore a brace.

One night as I was about to leave his apartment, he put his hand on my shoulder. I was surprised, for Hugh was reticent about expressing his emotions. Writing about human emotions was never a strong point in his novels. Before I left, he told me quietly of his love and friendship for me and added a little sadly: "Maybe you are the son I'll never have."

Hugh had to go beyond the novel to survive. He wrote for countless magazines and his *Rivers of Canada*, beautifully illustrated, speaks for itself. Apart from that, he wrote over 400 essays.

Two subjects that came up from time to time tested Hugh to the extreme. Maybe it was because of his Presbyterian background, but he showed little or no tolerance for the homosexual lifestyle. It may be fair to say that he never understood it. It is hard for many heterosexuals to understand the gay lifestyle, just as it is hard for the tone-deaf to appreciate Bach or the colour-blind to understand Picasso.

You could count on another subject to send Hugh into complete orbit. Because of his love of Canada, he detested Mulroney. Long before the ex-Prime Minister plummeted in the polls, Hugh held him in total contempt. Like others, he referred to him as "Muldoon" and recognized that Mulroney never stood up for Canada by defining and defending the federal cause. The author of *Two Solitudes* detested the appeaser who brought Quebec separatists to Ottawa and validated the separatist movement. When Hugh would rail against Mulroney in a loud voice, Tota would often interrupt. "Oh, Hugh, you can't say that. If anything happens to him, you will be suspect." Like myself, from the very beginning, he felt Mulroney was a national disgrace. Even though Hugh's vituperative attacks were so great, I could only sit and smile.

Sometimes Hugh would embarrass me in the extreme. Without notice, he would say in a loud voice and inform all within hearing distance, "Do you know who this man is? Do you know what he did for Canada and his people in Brome-Missisquoi? If you don't, you should. Heward is a remarkable man. He represented a largely French-speaking riding. What do you think of that?" Those he confronted in this way listened in silence and rarely commented. I sat embarrassed with my head down praying for a quick end to his enthusiastic and complimentary outbursts. Another evening, when I was entertaining Hugh and Tota at the Ritz Carlton Hotel was a little more embarrassing for me. When we were drinking our coffee, the late Maurice Sauvé came over and sat with us. As the conversation came to an end, Sauvé said: "You know I'm the husband of the Governor General?" Hugh demonstrated his indifference to our uninvited guest by conveying a "who cares" attitude. I knew Sauvé from the days we sat in Parliament together, and as he got up to leave, I couldn't help feeling sorry for him.

When Tota, Hugh and I went out for dinner together, someone invariably recognized Hugh and came over to our table. At other times, people would approach me because of my years in public life. Let me be frank. I always appreciated, and still do, when people come up to me to shake hands and say: "Thank you for what you did for Canada." I rather think Hugh enjoyed the recognition, too, but sometimes pretended otherwise. People would approach our table and usually the comment was the same: "I'm sorry to interrupt you, Mr. MacLennan, but my husband and I loved reading *Two Solitudes*." If Hugh was in an irascible mood, he would reply rather abruptly: "I've written other novels, too, you know." After which the visitor would smile and beat a hasty retreat.

Had she lived, July 8, 1988 would have been my mother's ninetieth birthday. Before dinner, I drove Hugh and Tota to my church of St. John the Evangelist. The door was locked. Luckily the sexton heard my banging and let us in. The organist was practicing some Bach and played magnificently as we sat silently beside the memorial plaque to my mother on the wall—a carving of the Madonna's head that had been done by a cousin in England. Later they accompanied me as I lit a candle in memory of my mother. Standing beside the candles, as I touched the wick with a match, I couldn't help asking myself how this Anglo-Catholic ritual affected Hugh's Presbyterian sensibilities.

Tota continued to decline and Hugh consequently suffered. He told me she had been struck by lightening in North Hatley in the seventies and had not been the same since. In describing the incident, he was very vague.

In the spring of 1987, two of the happiest events took place with Hugh and Tota. The first involved his eightieth birthday on March 20. Lorne Webster and I organized a party and celebration for him. Lorne is a member of the historic Racquet Club, and he arranged to have the dinner held there. The dinner turned out to be a virtual banquet with about a hundred guests. The food and wine were superb. Frances, Hugh's older sister, flew in from Halifax. Doug Gibson, his editor, flew in from Toronto. Representatives from the Canada Council came, too, as did a host of others, including his dear friends, the John Howlett's. Pierre Trudeau turned up for the reception, but had another engagement later on. The Racquet Club building is surely one of the oldest in Montreal, and the dining room could not have been a better place for the occasion. The room was lit only by candles at each table. Maureen Forrester, as head of the Canada Council, was invited, but she had accepted a previous engagement and couldn't attend. Nevertheless, even in her absence, she provided one of the true high-lights of the evening. She taped a song for Hugh and the tape was played to the entranced guests while coffee was being served. She also provided a decorated song sheet for the guests.

> I once loved a boy
>   And a bold country boy,
> Who would come and would go
>   At my request;
>
> And this bold country boy
>   Was my pride and joy,
> And I built him
>   A bower in my breast.
>
> But this girl who has taken
>   My bonny bonny boy,
> Let her make of him
>   All that she can;
>
> And whether he love me,
>   Or love me not
> I will walk with my love
>   Now and then.

At the conclusion of the song Hugh had tears in his eyes. When I drove Hugh, Tota and Frances home, Hugh was almost speechless.

The second happy event took place later on in May during the launching of my book, *Lessons from the Past,* at the McGill Faculty Club, a familiar haunt for Hugh. There was an excellent turnout of friends and others interested in the book. Hugh spoke and succeeded once

more in completely embarrassing me. He didn't talk about the book—
he talked about me and our friendship.

One evening I arrived home to see an ambulance in front of 1535.
Tota had fallen and broken her leg and she was hospitalized for about
three weeks. To make matters worse, while she was in the hospital,
Hugh was summoned to Halifax because Frances was terribly ill. Soon
after his arrival she died of cancer.

One of Hugh's very last trips was to Princeton, his alma mater,
where he received official honours and delivered a speech. On his
return, he handed me the text of his speech and said: "Hang on to
this." I don't know how his address was received in the States—it
compared the contemporary American scene to the rise and fall of
the Roman Empire. I had heard him express the central theme of this
speech on many occasions.

Hugh and Tota seemed very tired at this time. Tota was becoming
somewhat incoherent in conversation. Hugh didn't like getting old
and an air of sadness crept into his conversation. I attempted to arrange
meals with two or four friends but, frankly, they were not really
successful. On another occasion, I attended a panel on national unity
in Montreal. Many distinguished speakers addressed the gathering.
Hugh was one of them. He spoke in a low and rambling fashion and
was totally exhausted. I was worried.

On Monday, November 5, 1990, I invited Hugh and Tota for dinner
at the Montreal Badminton and Squash Club. After parking my car
near the club, I went ahead of Hugh with Tota on my arm. Upon arriving at the club, Tota sat down on a bench in the entrance hall. Hugh
didn't show up, so I went back out onto the street to investigate.
There was Hugh, bent over a car near mine. He had his hands on the
roof of the car. He was groaning and was obviously in some pain. He
sat beside Tota and I went into the men's locker room to see if I could
find a doctor. I was lucky. The doctor examined Hugh and told me his
pulse was weak, that he was very cold, and that I should get him to
hospital right away. Hugh became livid and would not hear of going
to the hospital. The doctor shrugged his shoulders and left. Despite
my entreaties Hugh absolutely refused to go to the hospital. "You've

invited me for dinner and that's that. If you don't want to dine, just take me home."

We went to a small cafeteria beside the bar and lounge area since the main dining room was closed. Hugh ate a huge meal that included a good helping of ice cream, wine and three drinks of rye. During the meal, he talked animatedly. Food and drink seemed to restore his health. We recited poetry to each other. After we left the cafeteria, we moved slowly across the lounge area. He spotted the upright piano at the end of the room and, as we approached it, asked me to play. He listened with his head down. Tota moved her head from side to side in time with the music and conducted with her right hand. The very last work I played was from Bach's *Goldberg Variations* and I ended, once more with the great aria. When I looked around, Hugh lifted his head and there were tears in his eyes. I drove them home and told them I would be away for a few days since I had to go to Toronto and Hamilton on business. I said I would call immediately upon my return. He smiled and put his hand on my shoulder. "Please do," he replied in a low voice before shutting the door.

On Wednesday I left for Toronto and registered at my hotel. I'm an early riser, and around 5:30 Thursday morning I opened my bedroom door to pick up the *Globe and Mail*. As I bent over to pick up the newspaper, I could see the words "Hugh MacLennan" in large print on page one. I didn't need to read any further. Hugh had died at home on Wednesday from a heart attack. Although I knew he was failing, my shock and sadness were great. Later in the morning, I contacted Tota. It seemed she was not entirely aware of what had happened, but she gave me the approximate dates for Hugh's private funeral, to be followed by a public memorial service. That night, I had to travel to Hamilton. I was one of the speakers at a roast for my dear friend, Bob Morrow, the Mayor of the city. My heart was heavy.

Upon my return to Montreal, I rushed over to be with Tota. She gave me the same greeting I always got from her when I phoned. Hugh was rarely the first one to pick up the receiver and Tota's opening words were usually, "Oh, Heward, it's so nice to hear your voice." In this sad instance, her greeting was, "Oh Heward, it's so nice to see you once more." I realized Tota was not fully aware of what had happened. She just repeated, "Isn't it awful, he's not around anymore." The next few days are hazy in my mind. People from the distant past turned up. Hugh's accountant appeared on the scene and seemed to have a good handle on his affairs. At Doug Gibson's request, I reviewed all the papers in Hugh's office to see what, if any, progress had been made on his autobiography. My search only served to fulfil my expectations. He had not even begun the project—"I've got it all in my head, Heward." That's where it remained to the very end.

The private service at a funeral home not far from Summerhill Avenue would have amused Hugh. No more than about twenty-five relatives and very close friends attended. He would have smiled to see Tota and me sailing along his beloved Sherbrooke Street in a black Cadillac limousine. It was apparent, in his last years at least, that Hugh's church attendance was minimal at best. The funeral director had to engage a minister to conduct the service. The only problem was that the minister didn't show up on time. We all waited silently and nervously in our pews. Finally, Tota suggested I take the service. Others concurred in this request. I approached Hugh's casket with my prayer book in my hand, ready to read out some appropriate prayers and verses. Just as I was about to begin, the minister rushed into the chapel, hastily adjusting his ministerial garb. I was quickly relieved of my role which, in many ways, would not have been appropriate.

On Thursday, November 15, 1990, a memorial service was held at McGill's Birks Hall. My telephone rang off the hook as everyone and their cousin wanted to speak at the service. I made sure Doug Gibson was one of the speakers. David Johnston, the principal of McGill acted as sort of a master of ceremonies. Once more, Tota and I travelled along Sherbrooke Street in a black limousine. Tota had a sense of humour and she felt the whole procedure was slightly ludicrous. A small string ensemble played in the hall. Most of the speakers had not been in touch with Hugh for some years and their efforts reflected this reality. In tribute to my beloved friend, I worked hard on my brief remarks. I mentioned that the last music Hugh heard was from Bach's *Goldberg Variations*. I also mentioned that on the same Monday evening I played for him I recited the *Sermon on the Mount* with its beautiful ending: *Let your light so shine before men ....*

Hugh let his light shine before us all, and how we benefitted.

After the service, there was a reception for the guests at McGill's Royal Victoria College. Elspeth Cameron, Hugh's biographer, was so sad to see Tota, who seemed lost and bewildered. I left the hall with Doug Gibson. As we walked together along Sherbrooke Street, I couldn't help but think how much Hugh would have loved to be with us on the street that meant so much to him.

A few days later, Tota moved into a home for old people on Montreal's South Shore. Tota's room was furnished with some belongings from Summerhill Avenue. A picture of Hugh in his younger days stood on her dresser, but her memory of him was confused. For the next three years or so, I would visit her each week. We would eat together in the main dining room. Once or twice we drove into the city where we ate at Ben's. One Sunday evening, an organist came to play at the home. Tota loved to dance and I could see many of the elderly people sitting in their chairs, waving their hands in tune to the music. Tota and I danced together and, somewhat to the consternation of the authorities at the lodge, I organized a sort of conga line of old people, some leaning on their walkers

Tota was in her ninetieth year. One day when I arrived at the home she was not waiting for me in the lobby as usual. I found her fully clothed lying on her bed feeling under the weather and not wanting to eat. I was saddened when Tota passed on. Each day I remember Hugh and Tota in my prayers—someday we shall meet again. In the meantime, I am inspired by Hugh's example and his love for me. He said: "With hard work and with time, Heward, I'll make a writer out of you." My time with my teacher was relatively brief. It is for the reader to judge whether or not his shortlived efforts have borne some fruit.